The American Enterprise Institute for Public Policy Research
A Conference on Philosophy, Religion, and Public Policy

Capitalism and Socialism

Capitalism and Socialism
A Theological Inquiry

Edited by Michael Novak

Politics begins in mysticism, and mysticism always ends in politics.
CHARLES PEGUY

AMERICAN ENTERPRISE INSTITUTE FOR PUBLIC POLICY RESEARCH
Washington, D.C.

Cover illustration by Karen Laub-Novak.

Library of Congress Cataloging in Publication Data

Main entry under title:

Capitalism and socialism.

    Bibliography: p. 187
    1. Socialism—Congresses. 2. Capitalism—Congresses.
3. Theology—Congresses. I. Novak, Michael.
HX13.C36   1978   261.8'5   79-14220
ISBN 0-8447-2153-0
ISBN 0-8447-2154-9 pbk.

AEI Symposia 79D

Printed in the United States of America

CONTENTS

FOREWORD

This volume marks one of the first manifestations of still another phase in the growth of AEI. The Institute has proceeded in its historical evolution from inquiries grounded primarily in economic matters step by step into other significant areas of public policy study.

A distinctive characteristic of AEI's approach has been the attempt to foster interaction among the various disciplines associated with public policy—economics, law, government, diplomacy, and the social sciences generally—in the belief that such interaction will lead to new insights and better modes of thought in the development of public policy.

With the publication of *Capitalism and Socialism: A Theological Inquiry*, AEI reaffirms its interest in the importance of religion and spiritual values to the formation of public policy. The conference from which this volume stems was held at Airlie House, in Warrenton, Virginia, from July 9 to 16, 1978. Some thirty fellowships were provided to participants at the week-long conference, most to professors or advanced students in the field of religion. By contrast, most of the speakers were chosen because of their mastery in the social sciences and economics.

The conference was cosponsored by AEI and the Department of Religion at Syracuse University. Special thanks are due to Dr. Ronald Cavanagh, chairman of the department, and Michael Novak, resident scholar at AEI, for the leading roles they played in organizing, shaping, and directing the conference.

WILLIAM J. BAROODY, JR.

PREFACE

When people are turned loose in seminars, the logic of the seminar seldom follows the logic of the advanced preparation, and that is as it should be. There is a design in these proceedings, however, which should unfold with a kind of internal logic through the papers and discussions.

Participants in this conference have been asked to read a symposium on "Capitalism, Socialism and Democracy" in the April 1978 issue of *Commentary*; sections of *Failure of a Dream?*, edited by Seymour Martin Lipset and John H. Laslett; and Sidney Hook's *Manifesto for Democratic Socialism*. These readings provide the initial background for our investigation of some theological concepts basic to both socialism and capitalism. Such concepts as utopianism, the future, liberty, discipline, fellowship, justice, and a whole host of others have a strong theological base and are explicit in the literature.

The title *Failure of a Dream?* suggests another theme for the conference: the tacit and less explicit practices, habits, and institutions of any social order. Neither socialism nor capitalism is in practice the way it is portrayed in books. It is worth trying to put into words some of the unformulated experience that arises from systems that call themselves socialist or capitalist. Such a comparison was not possible before the emergence of many socialist systems after World War II.

We begin this argument quite differently from the way our forebears in theology of thirty years ago did, when the last major ideological debate on this question took place. Much experience has been accumulated in the intervening years. Theories have been tested. Experiments have occurred.

The seminar will also consider who sets the terms of the debate. Who formulates the issues and promulgates the understandings that become the conventional wisdom? That is to say, What interests and powers are served, by which theories? What is the nature of that new class which plays so large a role in symbolic formulation today, not only in this country, but around the world?

Also under consideration will be Third World development,

multinational corporations, the environment, and many other issues related to capitalism and socialism.

We are fortunate in having a contribution by Muhammad Abdul-Rauf. His reflections will provide a perspective on Islam, capitalism, and socialism that differs from our own more familiar ways of addressing these questions.

Finally, we hope to counter the conventional wisdom. We wish to examine all those things we "know" about socialism and capitalism that are not, in fact, true; all those things we say and imagine because everybody else does. On reflection we may discover that our existing theories are not good enough; that reality has exceeded theory. In the end, we hope to be in a position—wherever we now stand on the issue of socialism and capitalism—to be considerably more sophisticated in rejecting certain arguments, in making distinctions, in recognizing bodies of fact we had not taken cognizance of before, and in developing some new concepts and some new formulations that help us to think more clearly.

A word about the organization of the conference: The five major speakers delivered two lectures each, one in the evening, followed by discussion, the other the next morning, followed by discussion. Each day, smaller seminars explored further issues. In addition, conferees requested a formal afternoon seminar from Eugen Loebl, whose book *The Responsible Society* (with Stephen Roman) has just been published, and a lecture each by Penn Kemble and the editor. The tests of the latter two lectures are presented below. Dr. Loebl's remarks, in a seminar, were not transcribed, but readers are enthusiastically recommended to inspect his book, a fascinating effort to go beyond the presuppositions of socialism and capitalism.

The Religion Department of Syracuse University joined with the American Enterprise Institute is sponsoring this five-day seminar at Airlie House in Virginia. Dr. Ronald Cavanagh, chairman of the Religion Department, was the moderator. It is hoped that the summer seminar will become an annual institution.

MICHAEL NOVAK

EDITOR'S NOTE

Most of the texts that follow are based upon an oral delivery and derived from an edited transcript. In their published form, they have retained the flavor of their original immediacy, in a form quite different from that of essays written out in advance in the privacy of one's study.

The Spiritual Roots of Capitalism and Socialism

Irving Kristol

I want to say first what a privilege it is to have the opportunity to deliver a sermon to theologians, aspiring theologians, and theologians *manqués*. This is not the first time I have performed that function. I can think of three occasions in the past five years when I have spoken to large bodies of "concerned clergy" in various American cities. I always say the same thing. I tell them to stop being so interested in politics, and I ask them why they don't take an interest in religion instead. And they always reply that I am "a black-hearted, uncompassionate reactionary." Our dialogue has not shown much progress since. But perhaps, on this occasion, we can go a little beyond that.

I have been called a neoconservative—never mind precisely what that means, the term does suggest the general ideological posture from which I speak. I should make it clear that I also speak as a neoorthodox Jew, in belief at least. That is, I am nonpracticing—or nonobservant as we say—but, in principle, very sympathetic to the spirit of orthodoxy.

Christianity and Judaism in the United States today face many of the same problems, though they do not share all the same problems. When I talk about religion, I talk as an insider, but when I talk about Christianity, I think it will be very clear that I talk as an outsider. When I say I am not a Christian, I do not say it polemically, of course. But whether one is Jewish or Christian does, it seems to me, affect one's attitude toward capitalism.

Orthodox Jews never have despised business; Christians have. The act of commerce, the existence of a commercial society, has always been a problem for Christians. Commerce has never been much of a problem for Jews. I have never met an Orthodox Jew who despised business—though I have met some Reformed Jews who are businessmen and despise business.

Getting rich has never been regarded as being in any way sinful, degrading, or morally dubious within the Jewish religion, so long as such wealth is acquired legally and used responsibly. I was raised in a

1

fairly Orthodox Jewish home, and everyone I knew was in business, including most of the rabbis. No one could make a living in those days as a rabbi, so rabbis ran shops, or their wives ran shops for them. It was generally assumed that the spirit of commerce is perfectly compatible with full religious faith and full religious practice. I think this is true in Islam as well, but it is not true in Christianity. The difference is that both Islam and Judaism are religions of the Law, and Christianity is a religion that has repealed the Law. This difference gives Christianity certain immense advantages over both Judaism and Islam in terms of spiritual energy; but in its application to the practical world, it creates enormous problems.

The Two Poles: Orthodoxy and Gnosticism

A year or so ago, I was chatting with a prominent rabbi, an old friend who heads a major institution of Jewish learning. He had just returned, sweating and angry, from a meeting with some of the faculty at Union Theological Seminary. He said he could not understand why they would talk about nothing but "prophetic Judaism" and "prophetic Christianity." At the end of the meeting, he told them that he was a rabbi, and asked why they would not talk about rabbinic Judaism, or rabbinic Christianity—to coin a phrase. They did not understand what he meant, or were not much interested in what he meant.

Now this dichotomy, this antagonism, I think, is absolutely crucial to an understanding of the relationship between any religion and the real world—the real world of politics, the real world of social life. The terms "prophetic" and "rabbinic," which come, of course, from the Jewish tradition, indicate the two poles within which the Jewish tradition operates. They are not two equal poles: the rabbinic is the stronger pole, always. In an Orthodox Hebrew school, the prophets are read only by those who are far advanced. The rest of the students read the first five books of the Bible, and no more. They learn the Law. The prophets are only for people who are advanced in their learning, and not likely to be misled by prophetic fervor.

These two poles, of whatever different intensities, are present in all religions, so far as I have been able to determine. One may, adapting the concepts of Eric Voegelin, call the one pole orthodoxy and the other pole gnosticism. I think these are quite useful categories. I assume the tension between the prophetic and the rabbinic—or the orthodox and the gnostic—to be eternal.

We are talking about an eternal debate about the nature of reality, about the nature of human authenticity. When are human beings most perfectly human? When are they fulfilling their human potential to the utmost?

These two poles—the orthodox and the gnostic—tend to give different answers. The gnostic pole, in Voegelin's terms, tends to say that the proper and truly authentic human response to a world of multiplicity, division, conflict, suffering, and death is some kind of indignant metaphysical rebellion, a rebellion that will liberate us from this prison.

That thrust, that tendency, exists within Judaism, within Christianity, within Islam. It seems to be a natural human response to reality, because in some respects this world we live in is, in fact, a hell. Little children, as Dostoevski pointed out, suffer hideous pain—innocent little children die of cancer, of ghastly diseases. Is it not proper, then, for us to be indignant at the world and desire either to escape from it or to reconstruct it radically in some way?

This is the gnostic reaction to the existential reality in which we all have to live. The word "prophetic" may be misleading; in traditional Judaism, prophetic is not really the same as gnostic, since the ancient Prophets were law-observers, not law-repealers. But in recent decades the term "prophetic" has come to allude to a similar spiritual impulse.

These gnostic movements tend to be antinomian—that is, they tend to be hostile to all existing laws, and to all existing institutions. They tend to engender a millenarian temper—that is, to insist that this hell in which we live, this "unfair" world, can be radically corrected.

Orthodoxy, on the other hand, has a very different view of how human beings achieve their full human authenticity. The function of orthodoxy in all religions is to sanctify daily life, and to urge us to achieve our fullest human potential through virtuous practice in our daily life, whether it be the fulfillment of the law in Judaism or Islam or *imitatio Christi* in Christianity.

Orthodoxy, in other words, naturally engenders a somewhat stoical temper towards the evils of the world. It says that evils exist, that we don't know why they exist, and that we have to have faith that, in some larger sense, they contribute to the glory of the world. Orthodoxy seriously concerns itself with the spiritual governance of human beings who have to live in this world and whose faith is being tested and tried every day. Orthodoxy has to do its best to give answers to questions that are unanswerable, that is, questions of why we live in a world that is "unfair," to use a term that has recently entered political discourse.

Christianity emerged out of a Jewish rebellion within Judaism. Christianity emerged out of what, I think, can fairly be called a

Jewish gnostic movement. We know very little about it, but it seems evident that in the decades prior to the appearance of Jesus, there were all sorts of gnostic millenarian bubblings within Judaism. There were sects appearing that were resentful of the Law, resentful of the world, promising to—or attempting to—achieve a radical reconstruction of reality, and a redemption of human beings from a condition that they perceived to be inhuman.

The trouble with gnosticism, however, is that it cannot ultimately win, because such radical reconstructions never do occur. Human nature and human reality are never transformed, so whether gnostic movements seem to win or lose, they always lose in a sense. The very different ways in which they lose, however, are terribly important. They can lose destructively, or they can lose constructively. A gnostic movement can mature into an orthodoxy, which from the gnostic point of view is a loss. From the world's point of view, however, a new orthodoxy is a good thing, if it is a genuine orthodoxy, one that people freely consent to. A gnostic rebellion can also spend itself, of course, in futile dissent, in revolution and blood baths, or whatnot.

For the first two centuries of the Christian era, the church fathers had to cope with precisely this problem. Namely, how to take the gnostic temper of Christianity—so evident in the New Testament, as contrasted with the Old—and convert it into an orthodoxy. They had to convert it into a doctrine for the daily living of people, into something by which an institution could spiritually govern the people. I find it interesting to note that one of the ways the church fathers did this—and they did it in many ways—was by incorporating into Christian scripture the Old Testament.

I remember reading many, many years ago about the Marcionite heresy, the fearful dispute over whether or not the Old Testament should be included as part of Christian scripture. Marcion, who eventually lost, had a very good argument—why include the Old Testament when the New Testament transcends and repeals it? That seemed reasonable to me. Since the books did not say why the church fathers thought otherwise, why they insisted on including the Old Testament into Christian scripture, I did some desultory reading on the matter. It became clear that the church fathers needed the Old Testament to help convert what was originally a gnostic movement into a new creative orthodoxy, which they did brilliantly. They needed the Old Testament for certain key statements that are not found in the New Testament, or at least are not found there in an emphatic way, such as that when God created the world, he saw that "it was good." That is an

Old Testament doctrine. It became a Christian doctrine, and it is crucial to any orthodoxy, since gnosticism says that no one knows who created the world—a demiurge or whatever—but that the world is certainly bad.

The second key statement needed for a new orthodoxy was, of course, the injunction to be fruitful and multiply, which is an Old Testament injunction, not a New Testament injunction. Again, this is crucial to any orthodoxy, any institutionalized religion that spiritually governs human beings and helps them cope with their inevitable and irresolvable existential problems. It affirms the goodness of life, in addition to the goodness of Being.

The reason why Christianity and Judaism both take the same controversial view toward homosexuality is not because they are narrow minded, but because legitimization of homosexuality flouts the injunction to be fruitful and multiply. As a matter of fact, a gnostic movement can always be recognized by its reaction to that command- ment. Gnostics are always very interested in sex, since it is such a dominant human passion. Sometimes they become orgiastic; sometimes they become ascetic—the monastic movement was a form of gnostic asceticism that was co-opted by the church. It simply told the monks they could be ascetic so long as they did not go around teaching that everyone should be ascetic. But whether orgiastic or ascetic, gnostic sexuality rejects the injunction "be fruitful and multiply." In gnostic sexuality it is obscene for a woman to become pregnant in an orgy. Homosexuality does contradict that principle too, as does abortion at will.

Judaism and Christianity have common attitudes towards these matters because they are of ultimate theological significance. They determine whether an orthodoxy is viable or not. A viable orthodoxy must insist on the legitimacy of the commandment to be fruitful and multiply. It is the key test, because it determines whether we are to have a positive or negative attitude toward the human condition.

The modern secular world, as it emerged after the Renaissance and the Reformation, is shot through with gnostic elements. Since the dissolution of the great Roman Catholic orthodoxy of medieval Europe, the modern world has oriented itself toward beliefs that premodern theologians, Christian or Jewish, would have quickly identified as heresy. In fact, the Catholic church, almost until yesterday, did regard them as heresy. I used to require my graduate class to read Pius IX's *Syllabus of Errors*, a wonderful statement of the credo of modernity. Pope Pius IX issued it in 1870 as a list of what it is anathema to believe, and he included just about everything that every one of my graduate students believes. They believe it all implicitly, as if it were natural and unarguable.

The Catholic church probably would not say quite the same things today. The *Syllabus* represents the premodern view. The modern view, to which the church increasingly leans, is much more gnostic in its lack of calm acceptance of the world. And, in its political versions, gnosticism takes the form of utopianism.

Two Characteristics of Modern Thought

Modern thought has two characteristics not to be found in classical Christian thought or in classical Jewish thought.

One is the absence of the idea, in any version, of original sin. This is crucial because a belief in progress, in the sense in which modernity believes in progress, is incompatible with a belief in original sin. (One must remember that a belief in the advancement of certain fine arts or technical arts is not quite the same as a secular faith in progress.) The modern way of thinking did not emerge fully until the doctrine of original sin—or whatever its counterpart would be in Judaism (and there is a counterpart)—had been abolished in favor of a doctrine of original innocence. The doctrine of original innocence meant that the potential for human transformation here on this earth was infinite, which is, of course, the basic gnostic hope.

The second element that made the modern secular world so gnostic-utopian by classical standards was the rise of science and technology, with the promise it gave of man's potential mastery over nature, and over human nature through something called the social sciences. And the modern world, in its modes of thinking, has become so utopian that we do not even know when we are utopian or to what degree we are utopian. We utter utopian cliches in politics as if they really were cliches—for example, "a world without war." What would happen if a president of the United States said to us tomorrow: "I understand that previous presidents have told you that one of the aims of our foreign policy is to create a world without war. Well, let's face it, there will never be a world without war. Human beings have fought ever since the beginning of time, and human beings as we know them will not cease fighting. I will give you a world in which we will try to avoid war; if we get into war, we will try to limit the war; and if we get deeply into war, we will try to win the war. But I can not promise you a world without war."

Can you imagine a president of the United States saying such a thing on television? Yet, everything that is said in that imaginary speech is true. Not only is it true, it is the only truth to be said about war in this world. The very notion of a world without war is fantastic. The lion shall lie down with the lamb, but not until the Second Coming.

An example of just how utopian modern thought is is found in a very good book, *Political Messianism*, by J. L. Talmon, the intellectual historian. And the opening sentence of that book is: "The present inquiry is concerned with the expectations of universal regeneration which animates men and movements in the first half of the nineteenth century." After I first looked at that, I asked the author whether his allusion to "expectations of universal regeneration," in a book about politics, was meant to be ironic. He responded that this was a fair description of what political thought was like in the first half of the nineteenth century. And he was right.

Political thought in the first half of the nineteenth century was gnostic to the point of insanity. Saint-Simon was insane. Comte was insane. Fourier was insane. Marx was insane. Prior to the eighteenth century, anyone enunciating the notion that politics is concerned with the expectation of a universal regeneration of humanity, of the world, would have qualified for the looney bin. Regardless of political views, no one ever thought that politics could offer any such ambitious promise. It is only in our era that this conception begins to prevail. We even teach the Utopian Socialists in our history courses as if they were political philosophers, instead of religious fanatics of peculiarly modern kind.

The Appeal of Socialism

The major form which the expectation of universal regeneration takes is, of course, socialism. Modern political messianism or utopianism eventuates in the socialist beliefs and the socialist movements of the last century and a half. These socialist movements have been increasingly attractive to Christians and to Jews. The Jews who have played a prominent role in socialist movements are, on the whole, those who believe in what they call "prophetic" Judaism; not those who believe in rabbinic Judaism. These are Jews who rebel against rabbinic Judaism as something stale and decadent. They feel they have a historic mission to fulfill and then proceed to engage in the cardinal sin known to both Judaism and Christianity as "the hastening of the end," that is, the ushering in of the Messianic Age or the Second Coming through magic, or politics, or some other human contrivance.

Still, socialism does have a natural attraction to both Jews and

Christians because of its emphasis on community, as distinct from a liberal society's emphasis on individualism. I think socialism has an attraction to everyone in the modern world because of this emphasis on community. In an individualistic society, voluntary communities can be created and sustained only with great difficulty. Indeed, an individualistic society is constantly subverting the voluntary communities the individuals themselves establish. This has been our own past experience in the last hundred years with voluntary institutions, including churches. Individual initiative, simply on its own and without official support, cannot support communities or ways of living together that satisfy the natural desire for community among human beings. This happens to be one of the crucial weaknesses of capitalism. By capitalism, I mean the individualistic liberal society characteristic of the modern era. In this individualistic society, it is extremely difficult for human beings to fulfill their natural impulse toward community.

I think the attraction of socialism also has something to do with the decline of certain "primitive" aspects of both Christianity and Judaism. Above all, there has been a decline in the belief in an afterlife, in whatever form—the belief that, somehow or other, the "unfairness" of this life in this world is somewhere remedied and that accounts are made even. As more and more people cease to believe any such thing, they demand that the injustice and unfairness of life be coped with here and now. Inevitably this must be done by the government, since no one else can claim a comparable power.

Capitalism and modern secular society encourage a rationalist way of looking at the world that renders incredible any notion of an afterlife, of eternity, or of a supernatural redress of experienced injustice. To the degree that capitalism does this, it generates an avalanche of ever greater expectations directed to the temporal power—demands which no socioeconomic or political system can in fact meet. The consequence is that even a victorious socialist politics, arising out of these urgent demands, can only survive by repressing them.

These seemingly inherent weaknesses of liberal capitalism unquestionably encourage people to turn toward socialism. But there is a way in which socialism is peculiarly attractive on its own merits to Christians, or people who have what are thought to be Christian impulses.

Socialist economics is more appealing to people with a Christian impulse than is capitalist economics. The root of all socialist economics is the separation of the distribution of wealth from the production of wealth. Socialist economics assumes that there is no problem of production, only a problem of distribution. This appeals to Christians, or to people of Christian impulses, because Christianity, as a religion, fares much better in a static society and in a static economy than in a dynamic one. Moreover, socialist redistribution bears some resemblance to Christian charity.

Now, it is true that, if there is no economic growth, and if distribution can be separated from production, then the question of distribution becomes an overwhelming moral issue. In my opinion, it is a trivial moral issue in our world because economic growth solves the problem— the problem of poverty—toward which redistribution aims. But Christianity has never much liked a commercial society that produces economic growth, a dynamic society in which everyone improves his condition. It prefers a static society in which Christian virtues are practiced, and the merits of that are not to be sneezed at. They have been eloquently expressed by T. S. Eliot in his *Idea of a Christian Society*. That kind of society can be very fine, for Christians anyway.

The trouble, however, is that socialism offers redistribution that only looks like Christian charity, and that socialist societies, when they come into being, are but grotesque parodies of a Christian community. One major reason why this is so is that the socialist promise is not truly a Christian promise. It offers redistribution *and* abundance—and on this promise it simply cannot deliver.

Attitudes toward the Poor

There is another reason why people who are experiencing a Christian impulse, an impulse toward the *imitatio Christi*, would lean naturally toward socialism, and that is the attitude of Christianity toward the poor. And here, again, I have to speak as a Jew. Traditional Judaism does not have Christianity's attitude toward the poor.

I know of no sacred Jewish writing that says it is particularly difficult for a rich man to get into heaven; it is just not in our tradition. But Christianity does begin, as I said, as a gnostic movement, with the attitude that there is something especially good about poor people, that they are holy in a sense. They are God's children, in some special sense, even though their poverty is not voluntary (one could understand voluntary poverty being regarded as such).

The result is interesting to watch today in our political attitudes toward poor people and toward movements that either speak in the name of the poor or, for that matter, may actually be representative of the poor. Let us imagine there is a revolution in Mexico in the name of poor people, one that may even be genuinely supported by them. I am giving myself the hardest possible case. Poor people, in fact, never make revolutions. They are made by professors and students and intellectuals in the name of the poor. But let us assume a case where it is really the poor people who are making the revolution. And we know, as students of political theory and history, that this revolution will only end in tyranny, in the destruction of the economy and of the society, and in a situation in which the poor themselves will be worse off than before, with the destruction of whatever liberties may have been provided by tradition, if not by liberal legislation.

If we know that, would we call this an unjust revolution? How many of us would really put ourselves flatly in opposition to a revolution of poor people, even if we had good reason to think that this revolution would lead to disastrous results? Not many, I think. And I believe the Christian attitude about the presumed special quality of poor people is part of the reason. One feels, somehow, that if the poor act this way, they must be doing it for good reason. I assume they may be doing it out of desperation, but desperation is not a good reason.

One of the difficulties of American foreign policy today in coping with so-called socialist and communist countries is the claim of those countries to represent the poor, and the claim of revolutionary movements in the so-called Third World to represent the poor. The claim is usually false, but it might in some instances be true. In my view, it would not matter whether it were true or false. But I suspect it would matter very much to most people, who would be most uncomfortable to find themselves opposing a majority composed of poor people. In terms of political philosophy, however, there is no reason why one should feel uncomfortable opposing a majority of poor people. There is no reason to think that poor people are wiser or nicer than any other people, or that they have an inherent sense of justice which other people do not have.

In the churches today, there is an attitude toward poor people that derives from Christianity, though it is in its profoundest sense anti-Christian. In Dostoevski's novel *The Brothers Karamazov*, the Grand Inquisitor says that when the Antichrist comes, his message will be first to feed the people of the world, and then to ask of them virtue. But is that not the message that most Christian churches today preach?

Again, Judaism differs in this respect from Christianity. Judaism gives no exceptional status to the poor. Charity is a primary virtue, to be sure—Judaism is certainly not neglectful of the poor. But no one can claim any exemption from any of the Jewish laws because he is poor. In contrast, the conventional Christian wisdom of today is that the poor—what we call underprivileged people—need not be expected to behave virtuously until their material situation has been remedied.

The Socialist Quest for Perfection

Socialism being an inherently gnostic movement—that is, trying to achieve the impossible in this world—always fails. The world remains unredeemed under socialism, as much as it was unredeemed under capitalism.

As a matter of fact, one can even see why and how the failure is inevitable. Socialism, like all gnostic movements, has a morphological structure. There is a group at the top, the "perfect" is the gnostic way of describing them. According to Marxist-Leninist dogma, this group would be the Party. Then there are also the believers, and finally the masses. All gnostic movements have this structure, and anyone with political experience would know that this structure could only lead to a government of the perfect over the believers and the masses. And, since the believers and masses are not perfect, the perfect will have to coerce them, in order to make them perfect. Our experience with human nature throughout history shows they will fail to make them perfect and that the coercion will, therefore, be permanent.

Even granting all conceivable good intentions to the communist movements of the Soviet Union, Eastern Europe, and China, that is precisely what has happened. A movement has to be led by a small group of people because they are the only ones who have *gnosis*, the arcane knowledge of how to reorganize the world, so as to make it a perfect place. And those high ideals then sanction the most Machiavellian means.

All of modern socialism is a movement that says it will create a good society, which will then create good people. I can think of no political doctrine more contemptuous of both the Jewish and Christian traditions, which say that there cannot be a good society unless there are good people.

It is true that a good government can improve the people somewhat, with difficulty. But the notion that a handful of true believers can, by manipulating the mass of the people, create a good society inhabited by good people is pernicious nonsense. All such movements end the same way, coercing people "for their own good" until, at a certain point, the people who are doing the coercing forget why they are doing it and come to regard the coercion, in and of itself, as legitimate.

The Sterility of Socialism

Socialism today is for me a very boring subject. What can one say about socialism today? It does not work anywhere. No one believes in

11

it, except in some capitalist countries. In the so-called socialist countries, the rulers do not believe in it, the people do not believe in it.

Socialism is a gnostic movement that has been unable to transform itself into an orthodoxy. It could not create a new orthodoxy, as Christianity did in its day through the creative brilliance of the church fathers, who added a new dimension to man's religious experience. Although I am a Jew, I am perfectly willing to recognize that Christianity certainly did enlarge man's spiritual vision. Socialism evidently cannot do anything like that.

What interesting socialist book has come out of the Soviet Union in sixty years? There has not even been a decent biography of Karl Marx. There is no hagiography coming out of the Soviet Union, because no one wants to write it or read it. To discuss Marxism, go to Berlin, or to Paris, or to Rome, or to Berkeley, but not to Moscow, where no one is interested in discussing Marxism. The doctrines of socialism are dead within the socialist world, as the Russian dissidents are showing us.

There are no church fathers in modern socialist thought. There were some who tried to be, but they all ended up being denounced as heretics and driven from the fold.

In the area where it promised so much, namely economics, socialism has been a calamitous failure. That failure is due to its basic conception that production can be separated from distribution, that is, that production can be organized according to the dictates of whoever is running the state, and that distribution is a separate process also at the command of the state.

But it turns out that there is a link between production and distribution, the link called human incentives. In order to distribute, there must be something to distribute. Production is not autonomous, and distribution is not autonomous. Human incentives are what create wealth, and to create affluence, as socialism promises, an economy must be respectful of human incentives.

Socialism says that we do not need that human incentive we call self-interest, that we can rely on altruism, on the pure spirit of fraternity. The experience of the world says, no—not in large societies. In the Israeli kibbutz, a self-selected elite may work altruistically for the common good for a generation or two. But this is not possible in a large heterogeneous society. It is not only impossible; it is inherently absurd.

To increase wealth, production must be increased through the use of materialistic incentives. Without those materialistic incentives, there will be less and less to distribute, and any redistribution will become less effective in bettering the material condition of human beings than was the capitalist system it replaced. Again, I think this is quite evident in the economies of all the socialist nations.

The Surrender of the Churches

It is most ironic to watch the churches, including large sections of my own religion, surrendering to the spirit of modernity at the very moment when modernity itself is undergoing a kind of spiritual collapse. If I may speak bluntly about the Catholic church, for which I have enormous respect, it is traumatic for someone who wishes that church well to see it modernize itself at this moment. I have felt I ought to fly to Rome and tell them to go the other way. Young people do not want to hear that the church is becoming modern. Go tell the young people that the message of the church is to wear sackcloth and ashes and to walk on nails to Rome, and millions would do it. The church turned the wrong way. It went to modernity at the very moment when modernity was being challenged, when the secular gnostic impulse was already in the process of dissolution. Young people, especially, are looking for religion so desperately that they are inventing new ones. They should not have to invent new ones; the old religions are pretty good. New ones are being invented because the churches capitulated to modernity at the very moment when the rebellious, gnostic, self-confident spirit of modernity was entering a major crisis and was moving towards its own discreditation.

It is interesting to look at where the spiritual impulse has gone today. If I were asked where the spiritual impulse could be found in modern society, I would say, not in the churches and not in religion, but in the arts. That is where the spirit is at work. To have a spiritual experience, read a book rather than go to church. That, in fact, is what young people do. That is the reason the arts offer such a powerful experience for young people today. That is where the true spiritual energy has gone.

If I have been too contemptuous and too dismissive of some things that people here feel strongly about, I do apologize and I will blame it on my own life history. I began as a socialist. As a young man in the depression, I was a Trotskyist, but then I evolved and evolved and evolved. My life has been a learning curve, and I don't know where it will stop, that learning curve going rightward. But I just find it too tedious to argue with young socialists today. I went through it, arguing on that side, and then learning the superior arguments against that side. Perhaps I cannot take it as seriously as I ought to.

Similarly, I know the question of equality is something that many religious people are quite obsessed with. Here, I will simply plead my Jewishness and say, equality has never been a Jewish thing. Rich men are fine, poor men are fine, so long as they are decent human beings. I do not like equality. I do not like it in sports, in the arts, or in economics. I just don't like it in the world.

A world of equality for me would be a very dreary place, and I do not even know how to argue the issue of equality. Apparently, many of my professor friends feel very keenly on the issue of equality, and I have lived long enough to know that people's feelings must be respected, even if one cannot make sense of them. If I am deficient in the respect I pay to their arguments, I will simply plead that my background and experience lead me to be rather bored with a great many subjects that exercise the passions of my fellow intellectuals.

Editor's note: Unfortunately, the lively discussion that followed Irving Kristol's talk the opening night was not properly transcribed because of an unobserved malfunction of technology—a not unfamiliar experience at public events, alas. Later discussions are presented, in edited form, following the other papers.

The Disaffection from Capitalism

Irving Kristol

One cannot discuss capitalism, per se, as a political philosophy because capitalism is a byproduct of that political philosophy we call liberalism. There is such a thing as the liberal view of man and the liberal view of society. There is no corresponding or unique "capitalist" view. Historically, liberalism has roots, however tenuous, in the millenarian speculations of various dissenting medieval sects, speculations involving the progressive liberation of man from traditional authoritarian constraints. Now, this intellectual history is very tangled, and I do not intend to unravel it. The Enlightenment of the eighteenth century is the period within which modern liberalism takes shape, though its roots go back further.

The defining character of liberalism is the claim that we do not need the spiritual governance by any religious institution because (a) man is not in any way radically evil, and (b) the history of the human race can be defined in terms of progress toward rational self-governance by human beings. In the light of these two theses, institutional religion no longer need play the role of spiritual governance which all previous thinkers and all previous societies thought to be so crucial—a governance that enabled ordinary men and women, or even extraordinary men and women, to cope with their existential experience of the world. Liberalism says, in effect, that if we read its books and understand its ideas, we can do it on our own, though there is nothing to stop us from joining a voluntary association, which we may call a church, and which may be good for the children.

In that sense, liberalism does emerge out of a gnostic impulse, that is, an impulse which challenges the prevailing orthodoxy, Christianity. It challenges the entire Christian church—not just the Catholic church but the established Protestant churches as well—and it expresses itself within the churches as well as outside them. It expresses itself in new ideas of church government, new ideas of religious tolerance, new ideas of prayer, new ideas of communication with the Divine, always tending to become more individualistic and discarding the need for the church as an intermediary in order to achieve one's religious aspirations.

But something happens to liberalism in the course of the eighteenth century, in the course of that period we call the Enlightenment, and I am focusing on this because of its pertinence to the issue of capitalism.

Liberalism gives rise generally to the notion that a society does not need spiritual governance. The idea that the truth will make us free is the central idea of liberalism. No church has ever believed that the truth will make us free in a simple sense. All churches believe that the truth *properly interpreted by the church* will make us free. But liberalism sees no need for such authoritative interpretation. It believes that humanity is on the march, that knowledge is on the march, that man is liberating himself from traditional fetters, and that humanity can and eventually will control its own destiny in a rather Promethean way.

This liberal impulse itself gives rise to both capitalism and socialism. While socialism is a reaction to liberalism in one sense, it can also claim to be the fulfillment of liberalism. It offers humanity things that liberalism does not offer, like community, but it offers them in order to fulfill the liberal promise, namely, of a humanity self-perfected, self-governed.

But there really are two enlightenments, one which we study and one which we, on the whole, overlook in our college education. There is the French Enlightenment, a very complicated phenomenon out of which emerge many things, including socialism. And then there is the Anglo-Scottish enlightenment, out of which emerges capitalism, by which I mean more than widespread commercial activity.

One of the problems with our discussion of capitalism is that we confuse it simply with commerce, with business. But we have had commerce and businessmen since the beginning of recorded history. In the ancient Near East there were merchants, and there is no evidence that they were any different from merchants today.

The difference between capitalism as a system and the existence of mere commercial activity—what Robert Nozick so nicely calls commercial transactions between consenting adults—is that capitalism says this activity should be the dynamic force which defines and shapes the civilization. Free commercial transactions not merely should take place, but should be permitted to shape the civilization as a whole. No previous society or civilization—and certainly no church, not even Judaism, which was very sympathetic to commercial transactions—had ever said that commercial transactions should shape the society. They believed rather that society should regulate and shape commercial transactions.

The French and the Anglo-Scottish Enlightenments

In France, the Enlightenment takes a form in which the premises of the ideas of progress and of human perfectability are radicalized. It is not unfair to see Saint-Simon, Comte, Fourier, the utopian socialists, and eventually Marx, whom they fathered, as the heirs to the French Enlightenment tradition. I am simplifying, of course. The French Enlightenment was more complicated than that, but those thinkers certainly claimed to be the heirs of that tradition, and I think that claim is more legitimate than not.

This tradition was radical in the sense that it was quite millenarian. The French Enlightenment writers without question expected a radical improvement in the human condition to result from a radical restructuring of the social order and, above all, of the religious order. The influence of organized religion would give way to the dominance—if not legal, then actual—of enlightened philosophers, who would teach the public how to live. The *philosophes* of the Enlightenment understood quite clearly that they were replacing the clergy as a source of spiritual authority.

That was their goal, and they said so. They felt that their philosophy could replace all religions, and certainly for educated people would replace all religions. They, as *philosophes*, would become the heirs of the clergy as the spiritual authorities to whom humanity should look for instruction.

This attitude helps promote the socialist impulse, as a small group of people who see themselves as having been "enlightened," or having the gnosis, then go out and instruct the masses, raising their consciousness, creating a "movement" toward an ideal society. This elite seeks to raise consciousness and to transform society and the human condition.

Bourgeois capitalism emerges as a theory, as a way of life, and as an orthodoxy in the Anglo-Scottish tradition, which is also "enlightened." But because England was England and Scotland was Scotland, those two countries somehow gave rise to an enlightenment that was not antireligious. It was not proreligious in any philosophical sense, but it was not antireligious in any practical sense. This is the key difference between the French and the Anglo-Scottish enlightenments.

In the French Enlightenment, the cry was *écrasez l'infâme*, and *l'infâme* referred to the Catholic church and to the "organized superstition" of all churches. There was no such slogan in the Anglo-Scottish enlightenment. I know of no open attack on institutional religion by any leading thinker of the Anglo-Scottish enlightenment—not Hume, not Locke, not Adam Smith, even though one knows from reading their philosophy that they were not particularly religious men. They may have been deists—and it is not even clear that they were—but they do not challenge the institutional authority of the churches and the clergy as guardians of morality. There may have been a hope, as there was in the French Enlightenment, that humanity would evolve beyond the need for churches, but there was no challenge to the actual role of the churches as teachers of moral doctrine from the new class of writers, thinkers, philosophers, and publicists in England and Scotland.

They believed that institutional religion, if not good, was necessary —indispensable—to spiritual governance. That is why Adam Smith and Edmund Burke, for instance, were very good friends and admired each other's writings, even though Smith was the father of modern individualism and Burke was the father of modern conservatism. Adam Smith's individualism was of a peculiar kind. It was an individualism that did not challenge, at least not explicitly, the spiritual authority of organized religion as the moral educators of the mass of men and women.

The Anglo-Scottish enlightenment did with Christianity what the church fathers had done with the Old Testament: they co-opted the moral code of the Judeo-Christian tradition and made it part of the liberal capitalist tradition. The major thinkers of the French Enlightenment, on the other hand, made the repudiation of the entire Judeo-Christian tradition a precondition of being "enlightened."

The Anglo-Scottish thinkers, as liberals, absorbed the Judeo-Christian tradition and reinterpreted it in all sorts of ways that might make theologians unhappy, but they certainly did not challenge its moral teachings. In effect, the Judeo-Christian tradition became the Old Testament for bourgeois capitalism as it emerged in the thinking of the Anglo-Scottish philosophers—Locke, Hume, Ferguson, Adam Smith, and most of the founding fathers of the United States. They needed the Judeo-Christian tradition, whereas the gnostic impulse of the French Enlightenment was radical and self-sustained and felt no need for an Old Testament. Philosophers of the French Enlightenment said that they had a new evangel, represented by themselves. They were the apostles of the new evangel and they did not need Christianity or Judaism to teach morals or good behavior, or to talk about the meaning of life.

On the other hand, in England and Scotland—and I have to

keep mentioning the Scots because, for some reason I do not quite understand, they played an extraordinary role in this intellectual history —the Judeo-Christian tradition, and especially its moral aspects, was added to the new liberalism as an integral part of those liberal social and political arrangements in which people, as individuals, contracted to live together.

Now, why did the Anglo-Scottish enlightenment feel the need for the Judeo-Christian tradition, whereas the French *philosophes* did not? Here, I think, we are dealing with different degrees of intellectual presumption and different philosophical heritages.

The French did not feel the need for the Judeo-Christian tradition because they thought that the *philosophes* could supply everything that this tradition had supplied, and do it better. They thought they could teach morality, provide the consolations traditionally associated with religion, and give meaning to people's lives.

The Anglo-Scottish tradition, though certainly a skeptical tradition in many ways, was not a tradition that denied the need for organized religion. It did invent philosophies in some ways comparable to the French. Adam Ferguson's writings might make us wonder why we have to be a Christian, but Adam Ferguson did not expect everyone to read Adam Ferguson. He expected ordinary people to need the guidance of their churches. Similarly, Hume did not expect everyone to be converted to Hume's philosophy, and probably would have been horrified at the prospect.

The consequence was that in England and in the United States, where the same traditions prevailed, the gnostic liberal impulse for 100 or 150 years creatively absorbed the Judeo-Christian tradition, so that no inherent conflict between the Judeo-Christian tradition and the liberal social and economic order was perceived. In France and on the Continent, on the other hand, there was a repudiation of this tradition.

Rationalism and Spiritual Governance

Attitude toward religion is the key factor in the history of eighteenth and nineteenth century intellectual life. It is no accident that the young Hegelians, from whom Marx descended, became a controversial sect on the issue not of economics but of religion—on the issue of whether Jesus was a man or a God. It was David Strauss's book on Jesus that created a scandal in Germany before Marx added British political economy and French utopian-socialism to this radical impulse. That explains the difference between the political history of the United Kingdom and the United States on the one hand, and that of the

19

Continent on the other. The political turbulence on the Continent has contrasted notably with the political stability achieved by the liberal societies of England and the United States. On the Continent, the past, for the most part, had not been absorbed as part of modern secular liberalism. In England and the United States, the Judeo-Christian tradition was absorbed as an essential part of the liberal social, political, and economic order. In that sense, England, until recently, and the United States have always been more religious than Europe, even though Europe has had a much more intense religiosity.

The instability in Europe derives from the fact that its version of modern liberalism, which is an extreme form of rationalism, says that human reason can explain the world, comprehensively and finally, to our satisfaction. We need no spiritual governance aside from the unaided efforts of our collective reason. Today, this enterprise of radical-rationalist liberalism to repudiate the Judeo-Christian tradition and to establish a new "secular religion" is evidently failing. In retrospect one can see that it was bound to fail. We can now better appreciate the wisdom of the Anglo-Scottish tradition, which was never so presumptuous as to assert that man's reason can, unaided, answer all the ultimate questions of life in such a way as to serve as a guide to the perplexities of ordinary men and women.

Since long before the Enlightenment it has been known that reason can ask all the important questions but, unfortunately, cannot give all the important answers. Reason and philosophy are involved in the quest for truth, the quest for knowledge, but unless man becomes God he can never achieve a certain knowledge of anything. Yet human beings in their conduct of life need certain knowledge. No hypothesis can tell anyone whether to be honest or to become a thief. No hypothesis can determine whether or not to honor one's father and mother. No hypothesis can assess our obligation to give charity to the poor.

The hypothetical mode of reasoning, which is characteristic of rationalism, inherent in it, and necessary to it, becomes absurd when it attempts to deal with the existential problems that confront people.

A morality cannot be derived from reason. I think that is quite clear. Philosophy has been working very hard to derive a morality from reason for over 250 years without success.

Harvard University Press recently published a book on lying by Sissela Bok. I would not denigrate it in any way, but I doubt that anyone who has read that book will say flatly that it is not good to lie. What we learn when we study the philosophy of these issues is that sometimes it is not bad to lie; but that is not the way we can raise children. We have to tell our children that it is bad to lie. Then, when they grow older, they will learn that it is a little more complicated than that. They will learn on their own that all of the commandments need adjustment. If they do not learn it on their own, the church is there for spiritual governance, to make the necessary adjustments of the absolute commands. The absolute is necessary, however, to train children, to form good character.

Children cannot be raised without a system of comprehensive moral assertions that can be supplied only by religion. We know of no other source of morality. A study of history or of contemporary affairs reveals no other source of morality.

It is interesting to read the Marxist writings on morality. They are an absolute tangle of contradiction. In the end, they can only say that what is moral is what the Party says is moral. That is what Georg Lukacs and Bertolt Brecht and the most sophisticated of modern Marxist thinkers say in the end. The Party is the authority that defines what is moral and what is not. There we have a rationalism that evolves into the most dogmatic and hideous kind of authoritarianism.

The Anglo-Scottish tradition—never challenging religion as the ultimate authority in the area that counts most, namely, morality—was able to create an orthodoxy which has shown astonishing survival power, an orthodoxy which we call the bourgeois way of life. Even on the Continent, the intellectuals may have been disaffected from this bourgeois way of life, but ordinary people found it indispensable. Religious traditions and respect for religious traditions are essential to this way of life. It may be rationalist in many ways, as Max Weber pointed out, since it does encourage people to calculate, to reckon. It does encourage a kind of rationalist attitude toward reality and toward social institutions, and this can be very destructive. Crucial to the bourgeois way of life, however, was the notion that religion is absolutely indispensable to permit people to live harmoniously and morally together.

Further, one of the functions of a liberal government was to see that religious institutions prospered. That is a very important point. Regardless of what the Constitution says about separating church and state, it does not separate state and religion. The Founding Fathers—with the possible exception of Jefferson—had no intention of separating state and religion. The state in Anglo-Saxon liberal thought had a positive responsibility to encourage established religions, because those established religions supplied what a liberal philosophy could not of itself supply, namely, a sense of moral responsibility.

Religion gives answers to unanswerable questions, such as: Why should I be honest? Rationalism cannot answer that question. Utili-

21

tarianism tried for over a hundred years to answer that question and failed. Utilitarianism could prove that the world would be better if everyone were honest, but each individual could see that the world would be still nicer if everyone would be honest except himself, in which case he would do extremely well. Utilitarianism cannot tell us why we as individuals should be honest. To be honest, we need an absolute injunction that this is the right way to be, that generations of experience assure us that this is the right way to be, and that there is a spiritual authority to sanction that assurance.

This bourgeois orthodoxy is something we are all familiar with, since most of us were raised in its shadow. It is an orthodoxy for a society in which civilization is indeed shaped to an extraordinary degree by commercial transactions, in which commerce is liberated from the control of an aristocracy or of a clergy. But it is also a society in which commerce is not liberated in all respects. The fundamental moral creeds inherited from the Judeo-Christian traditions are maintained, and no one is liberated from them. Indeed, it is the job of government to preserve them. This is why there were laws against blasphemy and pornography in practically every state almost until yesterday. It was thought to be a proper function of government to preserve this Judeo-Christian tradition, without which a liberal civilization is all sail and no anchor.

The Great Inversions

One of the crucial things that has happened in the past twenty years—and one of these days we will see it in its true historical perspective—is what I would call the great inversion. Until twenty or twenty-five years ago, it was thought to be natural for liberal governments to interfere in matters pertaining to individual morality, and it was thought to be wrong for such governments to interfere too much in economic matters.

We have turned those two propositions around. We now think it right for government to intervene in economic matters and wrong for government to intervene in matters of individual morality. This inversion is the great disaster of our age. Government can be productive in interfering with morality but it is likely to be counterproductive when it interferes with economic affairs.

We have the situation today—and some day this will be inscribed as the epitaph of our civilization, if and when it dies—in which it is legal for a young woman of nineteen to engage in public fornication in a blue movie, but it is illegal if she does so for less than the minimum wage. Government now has an obligation to see that she is adequately paid, but not to stop her from public fornication. Fifty years ago we assumed that government had the authority to ban blue movies. Now, we feel that such authority is unnecessary, but that government does have the responsibility to make sure that the minimum wage prevails, thereby, of course, raising the general wage level for people who work in blue movies.

Our bourgeois civilization used to be defined by commercial trans- actions in all respects except the fundamental ones, namely, matters of belief about good conduct. In our own lifetime, liberalism has become self-destructive by dissociating itself from the Judeo-Christian tradition which was the source of these beliefs. This evolution is something that we have all observed, though many have not seen it in quite that light. In my view, it will inevitably lead to the destruction of liberal civiliza- tion itself.

The Capitalist Social Order

The bourgeois-capitalist social and economic order is not necessarily the most attractive civilization the world has ever seen. That has to be understood. It represents a very prosaic society, and it is no accident that the typical art product of this society is the novel written in prose, not poetry—and certainly not in epic poetry, dealing with grand events in artificial but beautiful language.

It is a mundane society. The society itself proposes no transcen- dental goals to its citizenry. It assumes that those goals are defined by the churches of the Judeo-Christian tradition. Society does not do it; government does not do it. In our society, the responsibility of gov- ernment, aside from maintaining public morals, is to permit everyone to better his condition, in a quite material sense, through economic growth. One of the major functions of this society is to permit people to become less poor, to live more comfortably. In this goal it is enor- mously successful, precisely because it is the first society which officially vindicates self-interest as a legitimate, human motive. And it is self- interest that produces economic growth.

Socialists believe in obtaining economic growth by having every individual place the common good before his own interest. Indeed, if there were such a society, it would be nice, but my reading of human nature indicates that there cannot be such a society. Capitalism, in con- trast, is not at all utopian about human motivation. It recognizes that people will better their condition only if they have an interest in bettering their condition. Under capitalism, economic growth is natural because self-interest is a natural, human motive.

Previous societies also considered self-interest a natural, human motive—but one that must be repressed. Capitalism considered it something not to be repressed, but restricted—restricted to the area of economics. It saw self-interest as a natural human motive which, if permitted to operate within the market—as Adam Smith indicated—would make everyone better off. But self-interest had to be restricted by the moral codes established by the Judeo-Christian tradition. Not everything can be marketable. Human beings cannot be marketable. There was a big fight about that in the nineteenth century, in which the bourgeois ethos—the source of the antislavery impulse—was victorious.

Capitalism does not deny the possibility that human beings can perfect themselves, but it leaves that to churches and to the individuals themselves. It has no official prescription for human perfection, unlike all previous societies, which had an aristocracy, a theocracy, or an established church with an official prescription for human perfection.

The Egalitarianism and Humanitarianism of Capitalism

In many ways capitalism produces an egalitarian society. In fact, by historical standards, capitalism has unquestionably produced the most egalitarian society that ever existed. Look at the distribution of income under the Renaissance aristocracy. Look at the distribution of income in the Middle Ages or in classical antiquity. A history of France from the courts of the Middle Ages through the modern era shows conclusively that the more people are involved in commercial economic activity, the more nearly equal is the distribution of income.

Though capitalism does not promise economic equality—and sees no reason to promise it—the net effect of economic growth is to reduce the difference between extremes of wealth and poverty. We lack the historical perspective to see that. We fail to understand the degree to which American society is, in fact, egalitarian as against any traditional society. We have a horde of economists and sociologists who study inequalities in all their aspects. But if an economist is necessary in order to measure inequality, then inequality is not a serious issue in a society. In traditional societies, inequalities were so obvious that it would have been pointless to measure them. Similarly, if we need a sociologist to tell us whether or not we have a class system, we have no class system. When there is a class system, it is no secret—everyone knows it. In England twenty-five years ago, there was a class system.

In Latin America today, there is a class system. No sociologist is needed to tell us whether there is one.

When a sociologist solemnly studies the American community and divides it into three classes, and another sociologist says, no, that's wrong, there are four classes, and still another says there are actually five classes, then we know it is all nonsense. The concept of "classes" is being misapplied to this kind of social order.

If we go to a Holiday Inn and look at the people—their clothes, the food they are eating, their cars—it is impossible to determine their social status, or their income, or what jobs they have. By historical standards that represents a unique kind of egalitarian society. In all other societies, one could tell a person's class from the way he spoke or dressed, from his possessions, or sometimes from his very name.

In addition to being quite egalitarian, capitalism is also a very sentimental society, and this, of course, is not often perceived because of its emphasis on self-interest. But what is the purpose of self-interest once it has succeeded in its object of acquiring money? What is there to do with the money in a bourgeois order, an order that still has powerful links with the Judeo-Christian tradition? On this matter, Adam Smith and eighteenth century Anglo-Scottish philosophers were very clear.

What does a rich man do with his money? He can only eat so much. He can dissipate it if he wants to, but in the end it is stupid to drink oneself to death or to gamble oneself to penury. The one thing he can and should do with his money, and will do, said Adam Smith and Adam Ferguson, is try to gain the good repute of his fellow citizens through philanthrophy and through public service. In fact, this is precisely what has happened within the bourgeois capitalist civilization. Our wealthy families become philanthropists, enter politics, become civic leaders. All of the great humanitarian movements of the modern era—prison reform, antislavery, the feminist movement, the pacifist movement—have been funded and led by wealthy bourgeois.

The Bourgeois Ethos

The "bourgeois" is the link between Judeo-Christianity and capitalism. If society in recent decades has become less bourgeois and more capitalist, it is as much the fault of the apologists of capitalism as of its critics. Apologists for capitalism have helped to destroy this system by defining it as a system of greed, which it never was; a system based merely on the satisfaction of human appetites, which it never was. They also have called it a system in which the law of the jungle prevails and the fittest survive, a Darwinian system—but such "social Darwinianism" is utterly inconsistent with the bourgeois capitalist view of life, just as it is utterly inconsistent with the Judeo-Christian view of life.

Bourgeois capitalist society does lower the sights of the whole social order. All previous civilizations had higher official goals than does a liberal bourgeois capitalist society. The literature of the Greek tragedians, of Homer, of Racine and Corneille, and of Shakespeare, celebrates those aspects of human nature that are the most noble, and, therefore, available to the fewest. Bourgeois capitalism lowers the sights—but, on the other hand, the prosaic virtues it celebrates are achievable by everyone. It says that everyone can try to be as perfect as he wants but if we try too hard to go beyond the level of the prosaic virtues, we shall probably get into trouble, which is why bourgeois mothers do not encourage their sons and daughters to become saints. Bourgeois society doesn't know what to do with saints. It prefers that everyone be a good bourgeois citizen—a good parent, a good husband or wife, a good citizen, earning a living and keeping a family together, obeying the laws.

The bourgeois virtues, which are the Judeo-Christian virtues assimilated into capitalist society, are available to everyone. In that special sense, they are egalitarian. The bourgeois capitalist society is the most egalitarian the world has ever seen, in terms of values that are open to everyone. It is much more egalitarian, in this respect, than any Communist society, which again reestablishes an elite that has the gnosis and incarnates the system's values. One wonders: Is it really an accident that our present-day egalitarians set so much store by equality of income or wealth, while being so blithely indifferent to other, more important inequalities?

The cultural historian or the social historian can trace the ways in which capitalism slowly empties itself of its bourgeois content and becomes a merely hedonistic society. I will not go into them except to point to the obvious fact that this change has been happening over the past fifty or seventy-five years, slowly at first, then gathering momentum, and encompassing more and more of our culture. There was a time when the bourgeois ethos was denounced in novels but was safe in the movies. A movie that attacked the family could not be produced. Then the bourgeois ethos crumbled in Hollywood and was replaced by a new ethos, which is antibourgeois. The bourgeois ethos still survives on television, but it is now under attack there, too.

We are now witnessing a kind of gnostic rebellion against bourgeois liberal orthodoxy, to be found mainly in the arts, in the cultural life, but also to some degree in the politics of people who are dissatisfied with this mundane, prosaic society. Capitalism survives today as more than a hollow shell because it has very profound roots. It does meet the aspirations of ordinary men and women, but not of the men and women who have been educated by our culture out of any commitment to the Judeo-Christian tradition.

In classical political thought, democracy is considered a very dangerous system, because the masses in a democracy will tend to expropriate the more affluent minority and destroy the institutions of the society in a vain effort to create a new egalitarian society, which results in tyranny. Classical political teaching on the dangers of democracy, however, is premised on the notion of no economic growth. But that economic growth can be continually achieved is fundamental to modern liberal democratic capitalism. The possibility of continual economic growth is the one thing it officially offers—and delivers. This has made modern liberal democracies the most stable of regimes, by any reasonable historical standard. The masses need not expropriate the affluent in a vain effort to escape from poverty.

Because we live in a world where continual economic growth has, in fact, been a reality, we have a very odd situation. The radical egalitarians now are not the ordinary men and women but the college educated and, above all, the college professors. At Harvard there are many egalitarians who think the family is an unfair institution, one which gives some children an advantage over children from bad families. Ordinary people do not think that—we have to go to Harvard to learn that. At major universities egalitarianism is a respectable point of view, but in a factory it is not.

The ordinary people have a loyalty to this society. The upper middle class, particularly the educated middle class, has been educated out of the bourgeois conception of capitalism. It detests the capitalism it has come to perceive as simply an aggregate of raw, individualistic appetites. It is in this class that we find the dissidence, the rebelliousness, and the gnostic impulse to restructure the world in a fundamental way.

The Survival of Capitalism

Capitalism survives because it still satisfies the basic, simple impulses of ordinary men and women. It will not continue to satisfy them, however, without the bedrock provided by the Judeo-Christian tradition that ordinary men and women need—that we all need. It gives certain answers to ultimate questions that modern philosophy or modern thought, of whatever kind, cannot provide. All that modern philosophy

27

can do is to show that the last thinker who asked the question gave the wrong answer—no more than that.

This spiritual condition is the true crisis of capitalism. There is no economic crisis of capitalism. If people would let capitalism work, it would work reasonably well. It still works reasonably well. Everyone disparages economic growth of only 2 percent per year, but if the world had had 2 percent growth a year in GNP, beginning in the year one, our wealth would be unimaginable.

If, however, we make unreasonable demands on any society, that society will collapse in trying to satisfy them. It was the function of the bourgeois aspect of capitalism to make people reasonable, reminding them not to make utopian demands upon our economic, social, or political systems. Those demands were satisfied by religion. Expectations of happiness, of contentment, of solace, of spiritual comfort, were satisfied the way great expectations have always been satisfied—by organized religion.

To the degree that organized religion has decayed and the attachment to the Judeo-Christian tradition has become weaker, to that degree capitalism has become uglier and less justifiable. In the end, it will become less productive because it will be wrecked by those who prefer other things to economic growth and to the satisfaction of the demands of ordinary men and women.

I am convinced that, when the history of these decades is written 150 years from now, there will be a chapter called "The Aristocratic Impulse," because what we are seeing in the United States today is an emerging aristocratic impulse. The environmentalist movement as well as all movements for economic planning embody an aristocratic impulse, an impulse to tell this society what shape it should take. The environmentalists and the economic planners do not want ordinary men and women to participate in such decisions. They know; they are the experts, the spiritual authorities on what is good for humanity and what is not. This is an aristocratic impulse. Maybe it will become a good aristocratic impulse in the end. Maybe it will end in the creation of a new orthodoxy, though I find that very hard to believe.

What young people want today is really quite different from what they say they want. Young people keep saying they want participation when they actually want leadership, as is quite evident. When they are given the opportunity to participate in anything—whether it be in universities or elsewhere—they never participate. When they are given the opportunity to follow a leader, they follow a leader. They claim that the Harvard curriculum is too constraining, but they go to Cuba and chop sugar cane under the supervision of Castro's police, and they think that's great.

There is a psychic disaffection from this society, which no longer has its spiritual roots and no longer can explain itself to itself. We have what Lionel Trilling has so aptly called the adversary culture, constantly subverting itself, constantly raising questions it finds unanswerable, and constantly attacking religious and traditional institutions. I think it is fair to say that we have a gnostic culture. Twentieth century literature is gnostic in every sense, including the most literal. Hans Jonas's book *The Gnostic Religion* shows us that Kafka's description of reality could have come from the second century A.D.

Capitalism today is facing, not an economic crisis in any real sense of the term, but a crisis of belief. Demands are being generated by groups and individuals that will wreck this society. There is a culture that despises this society, because it despises the Judeo-Christian tradition and because the society itself has lost its loyalty to that tradition.

Discussion

QUESTION: Karl Marx would seem to agree with you that a "bird dog society" is always necessarily one in which leadership along new paths is provided by those with a sense for it.

PROFESSOR KRISTOL: Of course, he would. But where would Marx say the true consciousness lies? With Marxism, right? Marx, in that sense, is an heir to the European *philosophes* who wanted to replace religion with a truer religion. "False consciousness" is the accusation made by true consciousness, and there's no question that Marxism sees itself as the true consciousness, the gnosis. Marxism is a gnosis in that it is a perception into reality available more or less to everyone, but only comprehensively to a few, the leaders, who then guide the followers by elevating their consciousness gradually into the kingdom of perfection.

QUESTION: You've contrasted orthodoxy with gnosis. Is it not more accurate to speak of the contrast between the priestly (or orthodox) and the prophetic?

PROFESSOR KRISTOL: No, I think that for the modern world, gnosis and orthodoxy are better. Marxism is not just a call for the reform and rectification of bourgeois orthodoxy. It is a movement whose structure is gnostic. Marxism will not say it is natural for every individual to be a Marxist. In fact, the Marxists understand that it is impossible for everyone to be a Marxist, to have a comprehensive understanding of Marxism. A hierarchical movement is indispensable to Marxism. And this movement itself is engaged in a kind of metaphysical rebellion. There is no question that Marx himself saw it as a form of metaphysical rebellion. His first writing was, after all, on religion. Religion is the very issue that defined the young Hegelians and then the Marxist movement. It was not until he felt he had disposed of religion that he went on to study economics, and there is no question that, in effect, he was proposing a new religion for the world, based on his teachings. I mean by "religion" a set of teachings that would be embodied in an authoritative institution that would govern society. That is what Marx had in mind, and that is what Marxists have in mind.

QUESTION: I would be happier if you would talk about the gnostic as one who is more individualistic, who sees the world as evil, who sees redemption as escape from the world, so that the purpose of gnosticism is not to change the world, but to make a reactionary escape from it. How can you call Marxism "gnostic"?

PROFESSOR KRISTOL: I really don't want to make an issue of the term "gnosticism," but I find it useful. It is interesting that, in Jonas's very fine book *The Gnostic Religion*, whom does he discuss? Heidegger. One doubts that Heidegger ever studied gnosticism, but he reinvented gnosticism down to the very imagery. Now, it's true, gnosticism is an impulse to escape from a hideous, wicked, distorted world. On the other hand, I would say it is intimately related to millenarianism; in the end, the impulse to escape from the world ends up in the impulse radically to transform the world, and I think that's a natural, psychological progression. Everything that I have said is discussed by Camus in *The Rebel* as "metaphysical rebellion" rather than gnosticism, and, as far as I am concerned, it's just as good a term.

QUESTION: Is the Judeo-Christian morality with its growing fundamentalism eventually going to save us, or will the gnostic impulse eventually begin to undermine it?

PROFESSOR KRISTOL: You asked me to make a prediction. I'll make it. I think gnosticism will win, fundamentalism will lose. I have no real faith in the fundamentalist movement that is now taking place. I think it is a passing reaction to the experiences of the past twenty years. We still don't have a serious fundamentalist theologian, do we? What fundamentalist book can be given to a young man or a young woman to read? One by Billy Graham? On that rock, no one can build a church, not one that will last.

QUESTION: Isn't it one of the common features of the Anglo-Scottish philosophy to take morality out of the context of dogmatism?

PROFESSOR KRISTOL: Yes. What they did was take Christian morality, divorce it from theology, and try to locate it in human psychology as in some sense "natural." The French philosophers believed that one can have all the Christian virtues without believing in the Christian God. In Anglo-Scottish philosophy, this possibility was left open to the learned, but not to everyone. They did not believe the virtues would continue on a large scale if ordinary people gave up their religion.

QUESTION: What is the relationship of business ethics to religious roots, specifically the Christian tradition?

PROFESSOR KRISTOL: I think business ethics cannot be discussed seriously apart from a serious discussion of ethics and morality in general. It annoys me that the world seems to be full of people who don't give a damn about ethics and morality in general, but care very much about business ethics.

QUESTION: I want to be realistic. I see that I have a self-interest and I have been under the impression that my interest and my neighbor's interest have a point of convergence, that there is a need for some cooperation and for community. I find a lot of support for that in the Biblical tradition. But in the society in which I live, I see competition shutting out compassion and concern for cooperation in communities.

PROFESSOR KRISTOL: In regard to compassion, compassionate individuals are all one could ask for. Compassionate bureaucracy is, in my opinion, a contradiction in terms, and no more can be asked of a businessman than that, as an individual, he be a man of compassion, which is a virtue. On the question of cooperation, Adam Smith believed that the market is a form of cooperation—that competition is for mutual benefit. The commercial transaction is supposed to be an activity out of which both parties gain. No one will engage in commercial transactions if it is to his disadvantage, so the market was seen as a kind of cooperative effort through competition. At the same time, Adam Smith certainly believed in community. His conception of community derives from the Judeo-Christian tradition.

QUESTION: Isn't there more tension between the Judeo-Christian tradition and the ethic of self-interest which you attribute to capitalism?

PROFESSOR KRISTOL: The tension is absolutely real, there's no question about it. I would simply say that the tension was accommodated rather well for a fairly long period of time. The tension between self-interest and what might be called the common good or self-sacrifice—the instinct to render compassionate service—is also real. Although no institutions emerged to cope with it, ways of living did emerge to cope with it.

There was no denunciation of self-interest in the Jewish tradition; here is a difference between Judaism and Christianity. Jews have done so well under capitalism not simply because they had a long, mercantile tradition, but because self-interest has never been a source of great tension in Judaism. Judaism, like Islam, is a religion of the law, and the limits of self-interest can therefore be—and have been—specifically and objectively circumscribed. Christianity is not a religion of the law. In Christianity all these circumscriptions and limitations of self-interest have to be internalized. That requires a great deal of spiritual instruction and internal spiritual effort. Nevertheless, I would say that the tension between self-interest and the common good was held within bounds that permitted western civilization to flourish.

QUESTION: It seems clear that Adam Smith's system no longer exists today, so how would you define capitalism? It would seem to me that one could say capitalism doesn't exist, just as some have said that socialism doesn't exist.

PROFESSOR KRISTOL: Something recognizably capitalist as a system still exists, namely, a system where the civilization within certain limits—limits set by religion—is shaped by commercial transactions between consenting adults. Now, if someone says capitalism today isn't what it was a hundred years ago, I can only answer, what is? If someone says that the institutions of modern capitalism such as the large corporation or the large trade union may, in the end, pose a fatal threat to the system, that may well be right. But the United States still is a capitalist country. It is still a society shaped to a significant degree by commercial transactions, though it is also true that it is now more and more being shaped by governmental, bureaucratic, or political decisions.

American Exceptionalism

Seymour Martin Lipset

I would like to discuss in general and analytical terms a phenomenon that once was described under the peculiar label of American exceptionalism. That term—referring to the fact that America is different from other nations—was debated for a while in the Communist International, or Comintern, in the 1920s. The issue was whether or not America was different—whether or not the tactics and analytical schemes that Marxists applied to all other capitalist countries applied to America. A faction in the American Communist Party, led by Jay Lovestone, the secretary of the party, who was later expelled and became the international director of the AFL-CIO, argued that America was exceptional. That is, the Lovestonites contended that America was different and that the tactics the communist movement had to use in America should therefore be different.

Stalin violently disagreed with this position and threw Lovestone out of the party. If it were acknowledged that countries were different and that different kinds of tactics and analysis should be applied to them, that would undercut the logic of having a communist move-

These remarks have drawn upon various of my scholarly writings on American politics and religion. For further elaboration, as well as documentation of the themes discussed here, see: "Religion and American Values," in Lipset, *The First New Nation* (New York: Basic Books, 1963), pp. 140–169; "Religion and Politics in the American Past and Present," in Lipset, *Revolution and Counter-revolution* (New York: Basic Books, 1968), pp. 246–303; "Trade Unions and American Value Systems," in *The First New Nation*, pp. 170–204; (with John H. M. Laslett), "Social Scientists View the Problem," in Laslett and Lipset, eds., *Failure of a Dream? Essays in the History of American Socialism* (Garden City, N.J.: Doubleday-Anchor, 1974), pp. 25–82; "Why Is There No Socialism in the United States?" in S. Bialer and S. Sluzar, eds., *Sources of Contemporary Radicalism* (Boulder, Colo.: Westview Press, 1977), pp. 31–149, 346–363. "Coalition Politics—Causes and Consequences," in Lipset, ed., *Emerging Coalitions in American Politics* (San Francisco: Institute for Contemporary Studies, 1978), pp. 437–463; (with Earl Raab), *The Politics of Unreason: Right-Wing Extremism in the United States, 1790–1977* (Chicago: University of Chicago Press, 1978); and (with Irving L. Horowitz), "Polity," in Horowitz and Lipset, *Dialogues on American Politics* (New York: Oxford University Press, 1978), pp. 1–54.

ment centrally controlled from Moscow, with a common line everywhere. For power reasons, if no other, Stalin, therefore, could not agree with the theory of American exceptionalism.

The Weakness of Socialism in U.S. History

What defined American exceptionalism was the fact that the socialist and communist movements were very weak in America. This weakness has, of course, continued down to the 1976 elections. Parties and candidates calling themselves socialist received something like one-quarter of 1 percent of the vote. This poor showing did not result from the absence of socialist parties on the ballot. There were, in fact, at least six: the Socialist Labor Party, which is the oldest socialist party in America, dating from 1876; a group calling itself the Socialist Party, a minuscule splinter of what once had been a larger party using that name; the Peoples Party, who called themselves democratic socialists; the Socialist Workers Party, who are Trotskyites; the Communist Party; and a group called the U.S. Labor Party, an offshoot of a faction of the Students for a Democratic Society, though there is some debate whether or not they are socialists and whether they are left or right.

None of these parties polled as much as 100,000 votes nationally out of a total of almost 80 million. That sorry record of electoral support for socialism represents one of the lowest points in a century-long series of efforts to build a Socialist Party in the United States.

Socialists did have more success in the past. The Socialist Party, the party led by Eugene Victor Debs, received 6 percent of the vote for president in 1912, when Debs, himself, was running. It elected over a thousand public officials, mainly on a local level—mayors, members of legislatures, and the like—but also including two congressmen. It played an important role in the labor movement before World War I.

The party declined after World War I, partly because of government attacks on it for opposing the war, but mainly because of its split with the communists. The communists drew away many left wing members to form a party affiliated with the Third International. Both the communists and socialists were generally weakened by the competition for support within the labor movement.

The Great Depression of the 1930s, which presumably validated assumptions about the anticipated collapse of capitalism among socialists, communists, and Marxists, did not lead to the building of a socialist movement here. The Socialist party regained some strength, compared with what it had in the 1920s. Norman Thomas received 2 percent of the vote for president in 1932. It was much less than Debs had received in 1912, but it was the high point for both Thomas and the Socialist party from the 1920s to the present. The communists were weaker than the socialists most of the time when they both ran candidates.

Since World War II, there have been various efforts to build left wing third parties. In terms of electoral strength, the most noteworthy was the Progressive Party, which was largely controlled by the communists. The Progressive presidential candidate, Henry Wallace, received 2 percent of the vote, but the party disappeared shortly after the 1948 election.

The weakness of the socialist parties in this country has been a major embarrassment to Marxist and socialist theory, though many Marxists and radicals are no longer embarrassed by it. Until the Russian Revolution in 1917, however, an assumption basic to Marxist theory was that socialism would come to power in the most advanced industrial societies, that socialism would be a social and economic system of a post-industrial society, though in a different sense of the term from the current one. In the context of advanced industrialization, the workers, who would be the majority of the population, would come to political consciousness and would form and support a revolutionary socialist party. That party would ultimately come to power as a result of the crises inherent in capitalism.

As Marx himself put it in the preface to *Das Kapital*, the country that is most developed industrially shows to less developed nations the image of their own future. A basic assumption of Marxism was, and is, that the dynamic, the causal, variable, in the development of socialism is the economic and technological structure of a society and the class relations that derive from it. Therefore, a more economically developed society would be assumed to have the most progressive and the most advanced political and social institutions, values, ideologies, and the like. Since such things were thought to be a consequence, a dependent variable, of the economic system, it followed from this theory that the first socialist country would be the United States, the most advanced capitalist country.

During the late nineteenth and early twentieth centuries, most Marxists believed that the United States would be the first socialist country. On at least two occasions, for example, August Babel, a leader of the Social Democrats in Germany before World War I, recommended that his fellow socialists pay close attention to the United States, to see what socialism would become. Because Babel was a good Marxist, he expected to imitate the United States, to learn about socialism from the American experience, even though his party was, in fact, the largest and most powerful party in the Socialist International. In 1912 it won 112 seats in the German Reichstag, about a third of the total, at the time when the American Socialist Party had one member of Congress. Nevertheless, Babel still believed that America would become the first socialist nation because Marxism required it.

Marx and Engels paid a great deal of attention to the United States in their letters, correspondence, and private discussions because they also believed this. They were concerned with what was holding up the American revolution, what was holding up American socialism.

It is ironic that Marx derived his belief that the workers would come to class consciousness, form their own party, and take power in the world from his reading or misreading of an American experience. The first political party in the world to call itself a labor or a workingmen's party was an American party. The Workingmen's Party was formed in the late 1820s and 1830s in New York, Philadelphia, and Boston. This party received a considerable vote, at least by later labor and socialist party standards. In a number of places, it won 10 or 20 percent of the total and elected members both to the city councils and to the legislatures. It set a precedent which was followed by various left wing groups in the future, merging with the Jacksonian Democrats in the middle 1830s. Marx read about the Workingmen's Party in a book by an English conservative, Thomas Hamilton, who had visited the United States when the Workingmen's Party was at its height. When people later raised the issue of the lack of socialism in America, Marx would point to the fact that the United States had what he called its social democratic school from the 1820s on, and that it had set the model for the rest of the world. Hence, he and Engels wrote a great deal about American events and tried to explain the weakness of socialism in an ad hoc way. They were constantly looking for signs that socialism would develop, and therefore they would often have an exaggerated impression of what it meant when some party was started or some strikes took place or something else happened. That is, they exaggerated what would follow with regard to the strength of socialism and left wing tendencies.

The belief that the United States would be the first socialist country came to an end, of course, with the Russian Revolution in 1917. From then on, there was little discussion of the idea and little memory of the anticipation caused by the logic of Marx. Ironically, the governments that claim to be Marxist have come to power in countries which, by all of Marx's logic, should not have a communist party and should not be socialist—namely, the less developed, pre-industrial societies.

Though we obviously have Communist parties in various industrial nations, communism is essentially a movement of pre-industrial society, not of industrial society. The countries in which communists came to power in their own right rather than on the bayonets of the Red Army were all preindustrial; they were agrarian societies that had not even experienced capitalism. That fact occasioned a great debate in Russia itself before and immediately after the communists took power in those countries.

In terms of the logic of Marxism, these countries were sociological monstrosities; that is, structures that did not follow from the nature of the system, but were forced on it. Trotsky, who remained a good Marxist, quoted Marx on the subject—if socialism were introduced in societies lacking advanced industrialization and other social conditions necessary for socialism, then a sociological monstrosity would be created. In Marx's language, "the old crap"—meaning a sharply stratified exploiting society—would return or would develop.

Sociological Factors in American Exceptionalism

One could spend more time than we have on analyses of what it is about the United States or any other country that has led to the strength or weakness of socialist or communist movements. But I would like to list various factors that have been suggested as causal variables in the absence of socialism in America. Unfortunately, there are many of them, and they are not mutually exclusive. If studied in detail, each one almost becomes a sufficient cause. Three sets of factors have been adduced for the weakness of socialism in America. The first set is societal or sociological factors, that is, aspects about American society that weaken the potential for socialism. The second set of factors is aspects of the American political system that make it difficult to build third parties. The third set of factors deals with the behavior of the actors, things people did—particularly what the socialists, themselves, did—that made socialism either more or less possible. Some of the literature on socialism in America blames the inappropriate tactics of the socialists for the weakness of socialism. In the judgment of some of the writers, mostly socialists but also some others, if the socialists had done the right thing and followed the tactics advocated ex post facto by the writer, they might have built a socialist movement.

I would like to go through the different variables in these three sets of factors—the societal, the political, and the action factors.

The first factor can be put in the category of America as a new society. The literature on the subject is most identified with Louis Hartz, an eminent political theorist, but H. G. Wells and others have advanced similar theses. America was a different kind of society because it was a new society, and not just a transplanted form of European society. Particularly, it was a society which lacked the feudal tradition of stable hereditary class relations.

According to this argument, European society, coming out of feudalism, had very social class lines. People were defined in explicit ways in terms of their class position. Constructing class oriented politics in Europe was relatively simple because Europeans thought in class terms. People were perceived, defined, and addressed in class terms. America, however, never had feudalism and, hence, never had social class relations comparable to those of Europe.

There is an egalitarianism in America, in terms not of economic position but of social relationships, the kinds of things stressed by Tocqueville in *Democracy in America*. This egalitarianism has made it much more difficult to create class politics—and socialism is a version of class politics.

A second social explanation focuses on the political tradition of America. Louis Hartz emphasized the liberal tradition, the antistatist tradition, a tradition supposedly stemming from Locke and from the American Revolution, as the predominant national tradition. According to this view, America is a child of the liberal forces of the late eighteenth century, which were antistatist and egalitarian, and that liberal tradition became the dominant American ideology, so that we never had a conservative statist and aristocratic tradition in America in the European sense.

Leon Sampson, a socialist writing in the 1930s, presents Americanism as surrogate socialism; the values he sees encompassed in the concept of Americanism—the American ideology or the American definition of the nation—are similar to those socialists expect from the socialist revolution.

Both the first and second approaches suggest that Americans see their society as egalitarian and democratic—in a way as a leftist society—and have found no need for drastic changes to attain already existing objectives. Sampson argued in his book, *Towards a United Front*, published in 1933, that the socialists promised to bring to America what Americans thought they already had, and that, consequently, they saw no need to support socialism.

Third, there is an emphasis in the American value system on individualism, on the antistatist tendencies that supposedly derive from our Protestant sectarian past and the revolutionary values deriving from the American Revolution. This factor implies support for decentralized political systems and, if one wants to be radical, for a decentralized radicalism, rather than a strong collectivity-oriented state. The syndicalist character of the American labor movement, evident in the history of both the American Federation of Labor (AFL) and the revolutionary Industrial Workers of the World, has been related to the American political tradition's antagonism to the state.

A fourth factor has been the higher standards of living, particularly of the working class in this country, as compared with other countries. The United States has been the wealthiest country in the world, at least since the post-Civil War period, and American workers have lived better than workers elsewhere, until very recently, when some Northern European nations caught up to us. The less privileged sectors of the population have received a steady increase in the proportion of the growing per capita gross national product. As a result there has been a continual upgrading of the lower levels of the population through much of American history.

Various consumer goods, particularly education, which is the road to social mobility, have been more widely distributed in America than elsewhere. Increased opportunities for social mobility have accompanied the growth in productivity, the shift to large scale economic organization, the growth of corporate capitalism, and the spread of educational opportunities. People have been able to move up, particularly into the upper reaches of the system, in this country more than elsewhere, and this has contributed to the lack of appeal of socialism in the United States.

Parenthetically, I have always found intriguing a paragraph in Leon Trotsky's autobiography, *My Life*. Trotsky and his family spent two or three months in the United States in late 1916 and early 1917. If the Russian Revolution had not occurred, he probably would have stayed here and become a leader of the American Socialist Party. In 1929, after he had become the commissar of war and the second most important leader of the Russian Revolution, Trotsky still wrote with awe of his apartment in the East Bronx. It was in a low-income apartment district, a workers' neighborhood. His autobiography describes how impressed he and his family were with this apartment, which had a refrigerator, a stove, running water and toilets, and so forth. That does not strike us now and presumably would not have struck us then as anything great, but it was terribly significant to him. Workers in Vienna and the other parts of Europe he knew had nothing like that.

From Trotsky's point of view, the workers in the Bronx were living in the style equal to that of the bourgeoisie in Europe. Twelve years after the Russian Revolution he still remembered that apartment in the Bronx, and wrote a paragraph about it in his autobiography.

The fifth factor deals with the emphasis in some recent studies by historians and social scientists on geographical mobility in this country. They have documented what they call the remarkable volatility of the American working class, the propensity of Americans generally for geographic movement, and the lack of stable community roots here, compared with elsewhere. They have seen this as a factor operating to inhibit the formation of class consciousness. Whether this factor was important is questionable since the Socialist Party had its greatest strength in areas of most rapid population growth.

Finally, the last societal factor I will adduce deals with the consequences of America's being a multiethnic and multiracial immigrant society. One effect is the impact of continued immigration in encouraging upward mobility by native-born whites. Studies of census data have indicated that from the second half of the nineteenth century through at least the 1930s, immigrants tended to fill the lowest status, least skilled, and lowest paying jobs, enabling the children and grandchildren of earlier immigrants to occupy more privileged positions. As immigrants continued to come into our society at the bottom, bringing their muscle power to the system, those already here could advance over them. The worst jobs were taken by the latest immigrants, many of whom found the bottom here better than what they had left.

That pattern stopped with the restrictive immigration legislation of the 1920s, but in more recent years, blacks, Chicanos, Puerto Ricans, and new waves of immigrants have seemingly played the role once played by European immigrants. Hence, in addition to greater productivity, this pattern of immigration or migration within the country gives an advantage to native-born whites.

The second supposed consequence of this immigrant pattern is that ethnic, religious, and racial differentiation has been held to fragment the working class. Members of this class became united in ethnic groups, religious groups, and racial groups, and that phenomenon, supposedly, inhibited class conscious politics in this country. People could not be rallied in class terms, as workers against business and so on.

Thirdly, the large Roman Catholic proportion of the working class in the late nineteenth and early twentieth centuries is assumed to have weakened prospects for socialist strength. There are sharp differences in political orientation between Catholic and non-Catholic industries and unions. The church and church-supported organizations worked actively—particularly in the pre-World War I period when the socialists were growing and had strength—to resist socialist appeals.

Political Factors

The second set of factors, as I mentioned, is the political. One of the most important of these is what Selig Perlman called the gift of suffrage. In the United States, the masses attained the suffrage prior to efforts to organize them into class conscious parties. We had universal manhood suffrage long before the Civil War in most of the states, but much of Europe did not have it until the late nineteenth century or the early twentieth century.

In Europe, for the most part, Socialist parties appealed to the workers for support before the vote was universal. Socialism grew in many European countries in the struggle for electoral democracy. Nobody competed with the Socialists for the allegiance of the working class, because the workers could not vote. In the United States, however, the franchise for the workers and other less-privileged people predated the efforts to create a socialist party. That's what is meant by the "gift of the suffrage," that is, the workers did not have to fight for the suffrage. It was there when they and their organizations appeared on the scene.

The second political factor is the constitutional system, a system that presses towards a two-party coalition system in electing a president. It has been argued by many students of comparative elections and parties that a two-party coalition system is almost mandated by the Constitution, and that efforts at slowly building up third parties have to fail. It is almost as if we had a system that only allows two parties. The subsequent introduction of the primary system of party nomination strengthened the two-party factor.

The logic of this is fairly simple; it follows from the separation of the executive from the parliament. In Europe and many other countries, the parliament chooses the executive. Members of parliament are elected and then come together in coalitions of different parties to form governments.

In the American system, we vote for a president, or a governor, or a mayor. Realizing that only two candidates have a chance of getting elected, we reject the hopeless candidates in favor of the lesser of two major evils, from the two major parties. A third party candidate is terribly disadvantaged in an election in which the effective constituency is the whole country or the whole state.

In a parliamentary system with single member districts, third parties can gather strength in certain ecologically homogeneous areas. The British Labour Party first elected people in coal mining districts, where Labour could get a majority. The fact that the party had only ten, or twenty, or thirty members of Parliament did not matter. People were not voting for the prime minister directly but just for those people running in their own district. An appeal to farmers or an ethnic or religious group concentrated in a district can win an election, even though a given party has no chance of winning a majority nationally. Hence, in a parliamentary system, third and fourth and fifth parties can elect candidates.

When various of these parliamentary countries adopted proportional representation systems, this facilitated even more the introduction of third, fourth, and fifth parties. But the American system, with its focus of electing one president or one governor who in turn picks a cabinet, pushes towards a two-party or two-candidate system.

The impact of this system was demonstrated in the 1977 election for mayor in New York City, when there were Republican, Conservative, Liberal, and Democratic candidates for mayor. It became evident after the primaries that the two leading candidates were Koch, the Democrat, and Cuomo, a Democrat who was running on the Liberal party ticket, a small third party. The Republican candidate then faded from the scene and received only 4 percent of the vote, because most Republicans voted for Koch, who won, or Cuomo since they were the only two who could be elected.

That logic operates in most of our elections. The polls show that third-party candidates invariably lose much of their support between the announcement of their candidacy and the election.

Occasionally, of course, some third-party candidates—like George Wallace in 1968, Robert LaFollette in 1924, or Teddy Roosevelt in 1912—receive significant votes, but such elections seem invariably to involve a situation in which some major portion of the population has felt excluded from the coalition process and has temporarily gone outside the system. Basically, however, our constitutional electoral system prevents third parties of any kind—from the left or the right.

The nature of our system means, of course, that the two parties are not parties in the European sense, that is, groups with a consistent ideology. American parties are coalitions of highly disparate forces. In Europe, the different tendencies form independent parties. In the United States, they constitute loose factional parts of a major party, often highly varied ones with sharply different interests and values.

Since 1934, the Democratic Party has managed to encompass the most virulent white racists in the country and the blacks. In 1976,

43

Jimmy Carter received overwhelming support not only from the blacks but also from George Wallace and his followers. Both groups managed to operate within the same political party.

Conversely, the Republican Party has become less flexible and less of a coalition party. That is one reason why it is much weaker than it once was. Traditionally, the Republican Party also had highly varied groups, including what was the most successful socialist faction operating in American politics. A group calling itself the Non-Partisan League was formed by a socialist, A. C. Townley, in North Dakota in 1915. They captured the state as Republicans. They established a state-owned bank, which still exists, a state-owned flour mill, producing Dakota Maid Flour, a state-owned insurance company, and so forth. They spread to other parts of the Midwest, operating largely within the Republican Party.

A story is told about William Langer, a Non-Partisan Leaguer, who was governor of North Dakota in the 1930s and subsequently served as a U.S. senator, as a Republican, for many years. In 1952, when Adlai Stevenson was running for president against Dwight Eisenhower, Langer told Stevenson that he was the first Democrat Langer had ever supported for president. Previously Langer had always voted for Norman Thomas.

All of his life, William Langer was a Republican, and that was an indication of the flexibility of the Republican Party, which included socialist, agrarian, and progressive wings. The two-party coalition system in America has been extraordinarily flexible in its ability to respond to or co-opt any manifest evidence of pervasive discontent, the sort of discontent that can take the form of mass protest movements or third parties.

Parenthetically it is interesting to note the two words used to describe the behavior of American political parties vis-à-vis protest movements. One is that they co-opt them, or pull them in, and that, of course, is an invidious term. The other is that they are responsive, which is a positive term. What happens when they co-opt or they respond, however, is exactly the same phenomenon. If one likes it, it is responsive, and if not, it is co-optation. But, essentially, this is what happens whenever there is striking evidence of protest within the system, either in the form of mass movements or third parties. Whenever there is evidence that significant groups in the population feel unhappy with the system in one way or another or feel excluded, the standard way of eliminating them has been to co-opt or respond to them.

Because of this flexibility, the third parties sometimes charge that the major party steals all their thunder by adopting the policies they have long advocated. The socialists in America complained that their thunder was stolen by the New Deal, that Roosevelt took over policies that they had long advocated. This was certainly Norman Thomas's argument.

In the 1960s, we had various forms of protest, identified by some with the New Left. The New Left was really only a small part of the anti-war movement, which became allied to black protests, women's protests, and so on. That movement in part collapsed when the Vietnam war ended.

Many radicals who became leaders of that movement thought they would finally succeed in building out of the protests of the 1960s a radical movement in America—a socialist movement, a third party. Of course, they did not.

And one reason the protest of the 1960s did not end up as a radical movement outside the political system is that the Democratic Party responded to it. The radical movement in the 1960s was destroyed by three people, Eugene McCarthy, George McGovern, and Bobby Kennedy.

People within the establishment—U.S. senators—offered themselves as leaders of the most important aspect of the movement, opposition to the war, as well as some others. For most people in the movement, there was no need to become radical or to form a third party. All they had to do was to operate within the primaries of the Democratic Party.

The same thing occurs on the conservative side. Many people advocate creating a conservative party outside of the Republican Party, a new party on the right. Some of them wanted to do it in 1976, but the candidacy of Ronald Reagan undercut them. How could they go outside the party if Reagan was available inside?

There is the political process of constantly undercutting the left and right because the parties are sufficiently flexible to incorporate different groups. The primary system enables the different factions, whether or not they are organized as an explicit faction, to operate within either one of the parties and to nominate their candidates.

Movements, rather than parties, have been the American response to social crises, to the failures of the two parties. The history of the United States since the early nineteenth century has indicated a propensity for short-lived, often single-issue, moralistic movements, rather than for institutionalized third parties.

The parties invariably respond to the movements, thereby reducing the potential base for institutionalized radical parties. Whenever the radicals become involved in one of these movements, they say with glee that they at last have a set of issues, of demands, the system cannot give, cannot grant, cannot respond to, but invariably it does.

Finally, one should note a factor that some radicals like to mention —repression. They do not emphasize it much, because it has not been that great. The syndicalist, socialist, and communist movements in the United States have, at times, suffered from political repression, which has helped to break up the continuity of radical protest. This was particularly true during World War I and immediately after.

During World War I, many socialists, including Eugene Debs, went to jail for opposition to the war. After the war, there was a great deal of anti-radical hysteria, partly stemming from the Russian Revolution, and there was a crack-down on socialists, communists, and other radicals and labor people. The repression of the early 1920s was far more extensive and far more significant than the phenomenon we know as McCarthyism, of the early 1950s. With all due respect to Senator Joe McCarthy, he was a piker compared with those responsible for what went on in the early 1920s. In neither case, however, can one account for the weakness of radicalism in America by repression. I am not suggesting it had no impact, because it did, but various European and Third World socialist and communist movements suffered much greater repression at different times in their history and were not destroyed by it. Repression could have an effect in America, because the radical base was so weak.

Tactical Factors

Finally, to complete the list of the factors, there are tactics and behavior of individuals. Socialist behavior is adduced as a major causal element of radical failure in critical literature, which is mostly written by socialists.

Socialist criticism takes two forms, which exhaust the possibilities. Some claim that the trouble with American socialists was that they were too opportunistic, too moderate. The Socialist Party allegedly was too prone to emphasize attainable social reforms, such as the eight hour day, trade union rights, and Social Security pensions. Thus, according to this argument, the socialists failed to differentiate themselves from the major parties, who could give into these demands, and, hence, people constantly drifted off from the socialists to support the more left wing elements within the Democratic or Republican parties. If the socialists had only focused more on things that were unattainable except by complete changes in the system, and if they had done so during the strains of early industrialization and subsequent major crises, they could have built a socialist movement that would have survived, that would not have constantly lost support to the other parties.

The other argument is that the socialists failed because they were too sectarian, too dogmatic, too out of touch with the realities of the system, and that they followed policies which undercut the possibility of building a Socialist or Labor Party along the British Labour party lines in the United States. It has been suggested that in the early part of this century, the majority of the AFL wanted and would have supported a labor party. The emphasis on a pure socialist party, which was not stressed by the British socialists, prevented the formation of a labor party.

A more telling criticism along these lines is that the American Socialists did not understand the party system and the electoral system. They did not understand that a socialist party could not be built within the American electoral system, but that a socialist faction could be built within one of the major parties. If the socialists followed the example of the Non-Partisan League in North Dakota and elsewhere, they would have received support in the primaries within the major party system. Efforts to do this had a fair amount of success on a state level in the 1930s.

Upton Sinclair ran for governor of California on the Socialist Party ticket in 1932 and received 50,000 votes. After that, he decided, as Townley had earlier, to move into a major party. He formed a new movement, called EPIC (End Poverty in California), which proposed to end unemployment by taking over all the closed factories and setting up a cooperative economy within the larger society. The unemployed would be put to work servicing each other. Sinclair, running on this EPIC program, captured the Democratic nomination, received over 900,000 votes for governor. A tremendous amount of money was put into the campaign to beat him because of the fear of having a socialist governor of California. Socialist factions under other names at different times controlled the Democratic Party in Oregon, Washington, and other states.

According to this argument, then, the socialists have misunderstood American politics. If they had understood how to operate within the political system, they could have transformed one of the major parties, much more likely the Democrats, in most cases, than the Republicans.

Various socialists today are following this strategy with greater or less success. Tom Hayden, one of the leaders of the Students for a Democratic Society, is trying this tactic out within the Democratic

Party in California right now. He ran for senator and received about a third of the vote in the last election. His organization, the Movement for Economic Democracy, is operating within the Democratic primaries. Various socialists have been elected to office as Democrats in recent years in different parts of the country.

Sam Brown, who is now in charge of the Peace Corps and VISTA in the Carter administration, is a socialist. He was elected state treasurer of Colorado, running within the Democrat primaries. Ronald Dellums, who represents Berkeley in Congress as a Democrat is also a socialist.

There is considerable literature analyzing the behavior of the socialists and attributing to them responsibility for the weakness of socialism. That is, it says they followed the wrong tactics, that if they had only followed the right tactics, there would be a major socialist party. I, personally, do not credit that notion very much. There is not just one factor which killed the efforts to build a party here, but a number of them. Each of these factors was enough to kill it. The absence of feudal tradition does explain the weakness of class conscious and class related politics; the antistatist, individualist tradition also explains the weakness of socialism. We often do not realize in America the extent to which a statist tradition in Europe is not just a socialist or communist tradition but also a conservative tradition, a fact which helped to legitimate the socialist appeal there. The word "conservative" has meant something quite different in Europe from what it means in the United States. All European countries came out of a system of governance in which the alliance of throne and altar predominated—the State church and the monarchy, with leadership of the system being invested in the aristocracy, the hereditary ruling class.

The pre-capitalist, pre-industrial tradition of Catholicism and of the feudal artistocratic state was one that assumed community responsibility. In a society organized on lines of estates, of explicit social classes, the dominant class and the dominant religious institutions were responsible for the people under them. They emphasized a personal relationship stemming from the feudal agrarian value system. Leadership was hereditary but the assumption was that the leaders were responsible for the people under them, for their community, for their followers. When capitalism came into the picture, with the rise of business, it brought with it a liberal ideology, meaning in this sense, antistatism. The liberals were against various policies of the monarchical feudal state which involved responsibility for the whole community, known as mercantilism. They wanted a society in which business was totally free to operate, but this meant also that no one had any responsibility for anybody else. The essence of this value system was competitiveness and individualism.

The leaders of the pre-industrial, pre-capitalist society—that is, the conservatives, the traditional elements—had great contempt for the businessmen and the liberals, who felt no responsibility for poor people, for the people who worked for them. If business conditions grew worse, people were fired; if people grew old, they were fired; if they got sick, no one took responsibility for them. The pre-industrial assumption was that the leaders of society had responsibility for everybody. People were not thrown out because they were old or economically unnecessary or sick.

In a sense, there was a welfare tradition, a communitarian tradition in pre-capitalism, and the movement of liberty, equality, and fraternity of France and elsewhere was not only antistatist but also anticommunitarian, antiwelfare. The conservatives stood for social responsibility, for welfare objectives, and for state involvement in economy and society.

The liberals, who represented the rising business classes, were against this. America developed as a liberal society in this sense. There is some conservative tradition, some tradition of noblesse oblige here, but much less than in other countries.

In Canada, the country of the counter-revolution, where the American Revolution was defeated, conservatives behaved somewhat like European conservatives. For much of their history, they were statist and welfare oriented. But in America, the national tradition is the liberal tradition, as Hartz emphasizes, so that American conservatives are really European liberals—that is, antistatist. We have no American conservatives in the European sense, or almost none. Some have developed since the 1930s, in the traditional European Catholic, almost pre-capitalist, sense, but this is not the dominant tradition.

Given that the national conservative tradition in many other countries was statist, the socialists arose within this value system and were much more legitimate than they could be in America. Since the dominant value system in America can be seen as liberal, as well as egalitarian, radicalism here has often taken an antistatist form; it seeks not to enhance the state, but to enhance the power of the oppressed, as against other groups in the society. As I mentioned earlier, the American Federation of Labor and the IWW were both antistatist. Until the depression of the 1930s and the introduction of welfare objectives under President Roosevelt and the New Deal, the AFL was against

49

minimum wage legislation and old age pensions. The position taken by Gompers and others was, what the state gives, the state can take away; the workers can depend only on themselves and their own institutions, and it must be the unions, not the state, which improve the situation of the lower strata. That was the view of the moderate wing of the labor movement.

The radical wing, the IWW or Wobblies, were anarchosyndicalists. They wanted an anarchist society. They sought to destroy private capitalism and to replace it not by the state but by a kind of cooperative, decentralized system of social and economic control.

Hence, the socialists in America were operating against the fact that there was no legitimate tradition of state intervention, of welfarism. In Europe, there was a legitimate conservative tradition of statism and welfarism. I would suggest that the appropriate American radicalism, therefore, is much more anarchist than socialist.

Today, we find an interesting pattern emerging, as radicals of the left and right come together as antistatists. The radicals of the right have even formed a third party, which happens to be the biggest third party in the country right now, the Libertarian party. They seek to weaken the state; they want no state regulation. They want competitive free capitalism on the level of competitive small business. They ignore, of course, the whole problem of what to do about General Motors and AT&T, and so on. Essentially, they are antistatists and decentralists; small is better, and small is beautiful.

On the left, we see a new kind of anarchism, in part stemming from the 1960s. The leftists do not call themselves anarchists, but they also want decentralization, and they want to weaken the power of the state. They prefer communes, cooperatives, and self-governing institutions.

One of the interesting phenomena of recent years is the extent to which these radicals of the left and right have come to join each other and help each other. A magazine published in San Francisco, *Inquiry*, is financed by the radicals of the right, but it publishes mostly radicals of the left, a curious coalition.

In the late 1960s, an organization opposing taxation had on its board of directors Noam Chomsky and a number of other leading left wing radicals, together with Milton Friedman, Henry Hazlitt, and various other libertarian economists. They called for an ending of the income tax and suggested that welfare should be a matter of private gifts and private charity. The Committee for a Voluntary Army also included on its board Chomsky and Friedman, and others like each of them, because they do not like the state having the power of conscription.

When we talk of the left and right in Europe getting together at their extremes, we mean that the communists and fascists are like each other in that both are statists. In America, the extremes are anti-statist. In this sense, fascists are un-American, and communists and socialists are un-American; our extremists are anarchists or libertarians.

This does not mean we have not moved in the direction of the welfare state—we obviously have. The great dividing point in American history was the 1930s, during the Great Depression, which hit two countries hardest economically—Germany and the United States.

The United States, a much more resilient and legitimate society, was able to get through the Depression in infinitely better shape than the Germans were. Still, the Depression, with its 20 million unemployed and tremendous numbers of bankruptcies and foreclosures of farms and the like, had an enormous impact on the American social system. Its most important effects were to break the belief that every person should be for himself and that the state should not do anything and to establish the notion of a welfare state, of state responsibility, of planning, Keynesianism, and the like, with the New Deal as its spokesman.

That change, while it was dramatic in the context of the American past, still left the United States with less of a commitment to welfare statist objectives and with a much stronger antistatist strain than exists in any other country in the world. We tend to look only at ourselves, however, and therefore we regard the magnitude of the change as dramatic.

We now have a taxpayers' revolt, for example, which is interpreted as being directed against the growth of the state. There is, however, only one other country in the developed industrial world that has a lower tax burden than we do, Japan. This terrible tax burden we suffer from—and I am not suggesting I want to pay more taxes than anybody else wants to pay—is much less than any country in Europe has, by a considerable degree. We are not committed to financing a big state to anywhere near as much as any other country except Japan. It should be noted that a significant part of our tax burden, at least on the federal level, is devoted to military defense expenditures higher than that borne by the Europeans, so that the difference in our comparative tax burden is even greater. The defense part of our budget is much greater than that of the European countries because we are financing their defense in part. We have not made the commitment to a social democratic welfare state that has been made by European countries.

While one may explain in part the failure of Socialist parties in this country by the electoral, political, and constitutional systems, an aspect of the weakness of the left in this country which can be explained only by sociological factors is the comparative weakness of the labor movement. Little more than 20 percent of the employed labor force in the United States now belong to trade unions. This is a decline from the high point, which was around a third in 1960. We not only do not have a socialist party, we have a weak labor movement.

In the Scandinavian countries and Austria, nearly two-thirds of the labor force belong to unions. In Britain and Germany, about half belong. The Latin countries of southern Europe have a lower percentage, but their unions operate in a somewhat different way from ours. They have strong Socialist and Communist party movements, and their unions are much more politically organized. Compared with Europe, we have a terribly weak labor movement.

If American conservatives think they are living in a laboristic, socialistic economy, they should move to Europe for a while. They should pay the taxes that the Europeans pay and see the strength of the social democratic welfare state and trade unions in various European countries. It is the old reference group phenomenon—things will seem better if people see something worse. If they judge by comparison, then they may come back and see that, from their point of view, things are not so far gone in the United States as they had thought.

By a variety of criteria and for a variety of reasons, American exceptionalism still lives. The United States remains different in very significant ways from the rest of the industrial world.

Discussion

QUESTION: It occurs to me that the factors that you have discussed that might account for the failure of the Left in America would also account for the failure of the Right. Incidentally, one of the strange things about both the Right and the Left in America is the peculiar absence of any sense of comedy. Given the inability for the "extremes" to attain power, how could there be any radical change in the structure of the two major parties and how could one replace another? How did the Republicans replace the Whigs? How did the Democratic party come to advocate so many "socialist" reforms?

PROFESSOR LIPSET: These are good questions. The reasons the Republicans replaced the Whigs was that the Whigs disappeared. The Republicans were never a third party. The Republicans were largely the northern Whigs wearing another hat, in essence. The Whig party, which included a lot of Protestant moralists, could not hold together, since moralists could not fudge on the slavery issue.

The Democratic party, which is the oldest political party in the world and dates from Jefferson's day until the present with continuity, has also been the most flexible political party in the world, and, if you will, one of the least moralistic. It has been able to encompass people of diverse strains.

The Federalists, Whigs, and Republicans have all found it much more difficult to do so. The Federalist party collapsed; it simply ran down, in part, because its members took its ideology too seriously. Alexander Hamilton would rather have been right than be elected, so he was not elected and his party disappeared. The Whigs broke up because they could not handle the slavery issue, which did not disintegrate the Democrats. Today the Republicans may be going the way of the Federalists and the Whigs because they also are too moralistic.

I would say that American history shows no examples of a third party succeeding. It reveals examples of one of the two parties disappearing or breaking up, and then being replaced by another.

53

The Democrats have tended to appeal to the less privileged, to the Catholics rather than the Protestants, to the irreligious and the nonpietistic groups, rather than the pietistic groups. And the Federalists, Whigs, and Republicans have tended to have their base in middle-class pietistic Protestants. The economic policies that these two tendencies project have changed dramatically. The Jeffersonian and Jacksonian Democrats were more antistatist than the Federalists and Whigs, who wanted to use the state for development purposes, particularly to build up urban industry. The Democrats were more rural, and they were against using the state. In a sense, the American Left was more antistatist than the American Right for much of the nineteenth century, but in this century they inverted their positions.

As to whether or not socialism has triumphed in America, certainly we have a strong social-democratic strain in American politics today. We have a commitment to a planning state, a welfare state, but this, I would say, is not socialism in the true sense. Michael Harrington insists on the distinction between social democracy and socialism, and I think he is right. Richard Hofstadter made the point that the New Deal introduced social democracy to American politics. The AFL-CIO, in many ways, has become a social-democratic movement. George Meany has described himself as a socialist and as a conservative, and I would argue he is right both times. The political energy of much of the Democratic party has shifted toward a social-democratic movement, but not toward socialism.

QUESTION: What is the status of neoconservatism in American social science?

PROFESSOR LIPSET: The word "neoconservatism" was originally intended as an invidious term, since conservatism is regarded negatively by most American intellectuals. Those described as neoconservatives cover a wide range. Irving Kristol is a Republican, and Daniel Bell describes his politics as socialist; both are described as neoconservatives. In some cases, the label is applied to people who are traditional conservatives, not "neos."

The true neoconservatives have a number of things in common. They are liberals or leftists who are conservatives in their philosophical assumptions about social change and social process in society. Many of these people were disturbed by the events of the 1960s. Although many of them shared the objectives of the movements of the 1960s, they opposed, for the most part, the organizations because of the tactics they used, for example, civil disobedience. The neoconservatives have a sense of the fragility of democratic institutions. They feel that democracy requires adherence to the rules of the game. Civil disobedience is a tactic which should only be used in cases of extreme provocation, not in the exercise of ordinary politics. Neoconservatives are also disturbed by the reactions of the dominant groups in the liberal community to the Soviet Union and to the Communist parties in various other countries. Neoconservatives feel that the Communist menace is real and continuing; they remain hard-line on foreign policy. The most prominent neoconservatives are Scoop Jackson, Pat Moynihan, and George Meany. Most neoconservatives belonged to socialist parties or organizations in their youth. Neoconservatives, even Irving Kristol, criticize corporations, favor using government cautiously to improve the situation of the less privileged, and preach vigilance in the struggle for liberty. Kristol advocates that the Republican Party should have a conservative welfare state program, one which places less emphasis on central state planning. He is very critical of business for not developing a welfare orientation. Neoconservatives are strong supporters of the labor movement. Most of them, I think, supported the recent proposals for labor law reform. They are publicly supportive of the trade union movement as a positive force in American political life. I think it was Michael Novak who suggested he preferred the term "neoliberal."

QUESTION: It seems that various political labels, like religious labels, tend to have a diminishing value after awhile. What are the actual characteristics of the socialist, the conservative, and the neo-whatever.

PROFESSOR LIPSET: I think the place where many of us are is the center, vital or otherwise, to use Arthur Schlesinger's old term. The question remains can the center hold. Maybe it cannot, but a characteristic of the center is that it is a mixture of the Left and Right. The characteristics of a socialist, a conservative, or a centrist are determined by whether he is defined in political or sociological terms. As I noted in my talk, conservatism means different things politically. In Europe and in Canada, "conservatism" until recently has been a statist, welfarist orientation, while "liberalism" has meant an antistatist orientation. From this point of view Social Democrats have had more in common with the conservatives than with liberals.

Back in 1912, when the German Social Democrats won 112 seats in the Reichstag and one-third of the vote, Kaiser Wilhelm II wrote a letter to a friend in which he said that he really welcomed the rise of the socialists because their statist positions were much to be preferred to the liberal bourgeoisie, whose antistatism he did not like. The Kaiser went on to say that, if the socialists would only drop antipatriotism and antimilitarism, he could be one of them. The socialists wanted a strong Prussian-German state which was welfare oriented, and the Kaiser also wanted a strong state. It was the pacifism and the internationalism of the socialists that bothered him, not their socialism.

In the American context, the word "conservative" in recent decades has come to connote an extreme form of liberalism; that is, antistatism. In its purest forms, I think of Robert Nozick philosophically, of Milton Friedman economically, and of Ronald Reagan and Barry Goldwater politically. They believe that the state has no business in the economy; that the less government there is, the better; and that society and economy operate best if people seek to maximize their self-interests. The pure socialist believes that it is necessary to move toward a more equalitarian, democratic society; that the liberty of the rich man and the poor man to compete with each other is not true freedom; and that state economic intervention and state welfare policies should serve to make opportunity more meaningful to more people. Socialists, of course, differ among themselves. There are many who believe in democratic socialism, that we can eliminate capitalism and still preserve all our political and social freedoms. There are some who feel that, ultimately, we will have a totally free society, in which the state can wither away and man can be totally free, but some believe the state must be used coercively in the period of transition. By contrast, the conservatives believe that as the power of the state is expanded, the freedom of the individual is reduced while the potential for dictatorship, for authoritarianism, and for the downfall of democratic rights is increased.

The center—whether that means "neoconservative" or not—has no philosophy. There is no good philosopher of the center today. The center disagrees with both extremes and draws on elements of both for its political positions. Characteristic of many people in the center is a kind of neoconservative socialism. The term "conservatism" here applies to a concern for the fragility of institutions, for the slow pace with which one should attempt social reform because of the concern for the unanticipated consequences of social change, and for the maintenance of particular institutions which should not be undermined in order to gain needed social benefits. The centrists reflect a philosophical conservatism combined with social compassion. Many traditional American conservatives and Republicans seem to lack compassion. They do not seem to be interested in helping less fortunate people.

I think one reason the Democrats have the stronger popular appeal is that they seem to show more compassion than their rivals.

QUESTION: Will the game go to an open-ended conservative who is open for innovation and change, as opposed to a closed-end conservative, who nurses a reactionary nostalgia for a past that never was?

PROFESSOR LIPSET: We have in the American ideological and philosophical tradition some very strong strands. The important elements of the American revolutionary tradition still live, and egalitarianism, which means something different from the socialist usage, has been and remains a strong part of the American scene. Leon Sampson suggested that Americanism is a surrogate socialism. He argued that American conservatives are very different from European conservatives. And he noted that Americanism is a political ideology, in the same way that communism or fascism is, with a set of concepts about the nature of the good society and the nature of man. Sampson, in his book, listed two columns of statements about the good society, one from a number of leading Americans and the other column from a number of leading Marxists—Marx, Lenin, Engels, and Stalin. He sought to show that these American leaders had the same conceptions about society and people as the Marxists. The Americans he quoted were people like Herbert Hoover, Andrew Mellon, John D. Rockefeller, and Andrew Carnegie. They were egalitarians; they talked about an open society, social mobility, and an end of poverty. The good society for them was an egalitarian society in which the only reason anybody is in a higher position is because he has won in a race. Sampson's point was that no European upper-class conservative would ever say the kinds of things the Americans said; the European privileged did not feel that they had to justify themselves and their society in terms of competition and equal opportunity, or that society should abolish poverty.

In America, there is a constant vitalization of the struggle for equality, for equal treatment, for the upgrading of the lower strata, stimulated by the value system of the larger society. Where did the renewed movement of the 1960s for equality across the modern world come from? It came from the United States, from the American movement. The War on Poverty was an American innovation. The term is an old socialist slogan, but now there are wars on poverty in Europe. "Poverty" is now a Russian word, but it was not fifteen years ago—the Russians became concerned with poverty because it became an international concern. Brown versus Kansas, which had a big impact on our educational system, also had an enormous impact on the Swedish system, the British system, and the German system. In much of Europe, there was a two- or three-class educational system. Ninety percent of the youth went to schools that would not lead to university education. Their non-academic schools were designed for the lower-middle and working class, and the socialists never tried to change the situation. The Swedish Social Democrats had been in office since 1933, but continued this stratified education system until the late 1950s. What led them to do something about their educational system was Brown versus Kansas. The Americans began pouring out books and articles about the impact of a stratified social system of segregated education, and so the Swedes finally became concerned about the fact that the proportion of working-class youth going to the university had not increased 1 percent in twenty-five years of Social-Democratic rule.

Americans feel guilty about a lack of equality. This concern for equality keeps pushing us to try something new. The normal operation of stratified social structures keeps refurbishing inequality. It does so here, it does so in Britain, it does so in the Soviet Union, it is doing so in China today. To do something about it requires a constant struggle. The message of Jean-François Revel is that America is the most revolutionary society, not Russia and not China, that the revolution of the 1960s came out of America, because of the continuing vitality of the American Revolution even though the people in the movements were subjectively anti-American.

Neoconservatives are pro-American. The "New Politics" people —I am not speaking of the New Left—think the enemy is us. Far be it for me to argue that we have anything like a utopia in this country; we are far from a good equalitarian society. Every society is, and every society will be. Ideally, every society should be much more democratic, much more egalitarian. To move in these directions there must be a certain dynamic tension within the system. The American tradition involves an unending struggle between what we call the Left and the Right, between the emphasis, on the one hand, on equality and, on the other, on liberty. Some people focus on one and some on the other, and, of course, there are many people, perhaps most, who are simply self-interested.

I was recently talking to an eminent neoconservative, Norman Podhoretz, the editor of *Commentary*, who said he almost never spoke to a Republican businessman without feeling the only thing he cared about was the profit margin, the balance sheet, that he didn't care about communism, he didn't care about liberty, he didn't care about poor people or about rich people—his politics reflected his concern for the balance sheet. Liberal Democrats, from his point of view, were less balance-sheet oriented, more ideology-oriented. I think he was exaggerating; obviously, there is plenty of self-interest, including corrupt self-interest, among Democrats as well as Republicans.

At any rate it is this kind of interactive play between self-interest, liberty, and equality that is involved in the American political scene. People who strive for too much ideological consistency are not dangerous in the American context, but they are often impractical in their politics. Education seems to produce ideologists. Who are the ideological liberals? They are college-educated professionals, those in the knowledge industry, scientists, media people, and the like. Who are the ideological Republicans? They are the college-educated businessmen and executives. The college-educated Republicans tend to be the consistent conservatives, that is, followers of Ronald Reagan. The college-educated Democrats tend to be the more ideological Democrats, that is, McGovern New Politics liberals. Both groups are more activist, more vocal, more able to organize, and therefore, have an influence disproportionate to their numbers.

QUESTION: There are some of us in this educated class, about which you were just talking, who become very frustrated when the two parties or the two candidates are so marginally differentiated that it is hard to distinguish one from the other. Do you think there would be anything to gain, politically speaking, by having a genuine Left and a genuine Right?

PROFESSOR LIPSET: If you want an answer in one word, no. Let me explain why. It is true that, as election day approaches, the two parties often sound very similar. This does not mean they are similar in purpose or action. What it means is that both of them are consciously competing for the same group of voters. They converge towards the center, towards the marginal group with "swing" power. This pattern is characteristic of two-party systems. As the British election comes closer, Margaret Thatcher, leader of the Conservatives, has moved over towards the center. She no longer is talking about dismantling the welfare state, about a free economy, about the values of competitiveness. I'm sure her polls are telling her where the available votes are. The people who agree with her Friedmanite politics will all vote Tory, whereas people who do not have such views are the ones whose support she has to get to win the election. The question is, Is this hypocrisy? No, it's the nature of democratic politics. If she insists on her ideology, she will not be able to carry out any part of the political program that she would like to carry out. She is constrained by what is needed to win a majority. This is the essence of democratic politics.

Would it be better for America if both parties stood for clear-cut ideologies? This simply is not possible in two-party systems. Both parties would then be alienating the voters in the center. Barry Goldwater was nominated in 1964 and what happened? He won 40 percent of the vote. George McGovern was nominated in 1972. Who did better? Goldwater did, I think, by half of one percentage point than McGovern did. Given the American nomination system now, particularly with the increasing number of open primaries, we may have an election in the future between a Barry Goldwater and a George McGovern. Do you think that will be a good thing?

In America we have two coalition parties. The American government is always a coalition government even though one party at a time controls the presidency. By contrast, many European countries have coalition governments of several parties. When three, four, or five parties run for election, each one can be ideological and consistent, because each is not trying to win a majority of the votes. It is running to maximize the vote available for a certain position. During elections, therefore, the parties actually become more different rather than more similar. Parties that have sat together in coalition for four years or ten years suddenly during the election campaign bitterly berate each other. Once the election is over, they come together again. The parties in a multiparty system emphasize the differences among themselves. In a two-party system, they stress their similarities during the election. Once the election is over, we see that they are different.

Religion in American Politics

Seymour Martin Lipset

To interpret both radical and nonradical American politics, as well as American society in general, it is necessary to understand what is unique about the United States in religious terms. In the preceding discussion of "American Exceptionalism" I have stressed the importance of the absence of a feudal tradition in the United States, together with its character as a new society, an immigrant society, which make it a society with a special political tradition. The concept of Americanism as a political doctrine stemmed from the Revolution.

The Only Protestant Country

The United States has another unique aspect—one often forgotten both in the United States and in Europe, its special religious character. From one perspective, the United States is the only Protestant country in the world. By "Protestant" I am referring to Protestant sects as opposed to state churches. The Anglican church in England, the Lutheran in Germany, the Greek Orthodox in Eastern Europe, the Dutch Reformed, all of these denominations were—and many of them still are—state churches, much as the Catholic church was and is a state church in some countries. The majority of Americans, however, practically from the beginning of the Republic down to the present have been members of churches that are not supported by the state and, in turn, do not support the state. These are the Protestant sects. The majority of Americans belong to the Methodist or the Baptist sect, but there are many others.

There is a profound difference between a Protestant sect and a state church. A characteristic of the latter was the alliance of throne and altar, the alliance of the state and religion. As Tocqueville and others have emphasized, these churches received financial support from the state. Often their ministers or priests were technically state civil servants or appointees. The Bishops often had to be confirmed, if not directly appointed, by the government, either by the king, or, later, by cabinets or prime ministers. Receiving this kind of support, they did not have to go out among the people for the contributions a voluntary denomination has to provide.

From Tocqueville down to the present, it has been suggested that one reason for the vitality of American Protestantism, compared with Protestantism and other religious faiths elsewhere, is that these voluntary associations were and still are constantly under pressure to mobilize membership support. In a mundane fashion, they must raise money that simply came from the state budget in other places. In return, the state church was expected to legitimate the state and support its policies. The divine right of kings was the extreme form of that support. Since most of the people of the state belonged to one church—the Anglicans in Britain, the Catholics in France and Italy, the Greek Orthodox in Russia, the Lutherans in Scandinavia—most of the membership in the state church was coterminous with citizenship.

When the society was in trouble and involved in the situation of greatest tension in a society—namely war with other countries—the state church always called upon its parishioners to support the war. The church was an ally of the state.

The sects, however, were different. The term the British have for the sects—the denominations that are the majority in the United States —is an insightful one. They are called "nonconforming," or the "dissenting" sects, since they are nonconforming and dissenting with regard to the Anglican majority.

In the United States, they could not be called nonconformists or dissenters, since there was no majority, except themselves. Still, the nature of these denominations is not to be state-linked, not to be state-supported or supportive. They are the most truly Protestant of all denominations, in the sense that the relationships between the individual and God and between the individual and society are ones which emphasize the conscience of the individual. He or she has to make a personal decision as to what is right, proper and moral. He or she has to relate directly to God, rather than through the intermediary agent of the church, the pastor, the priest, or the bishop.

The actual institutional structure of the Protestant sects is often not very different from that of other churches, except for the emphasis on individualism, on the individual's conscience and his personal relationship to God and other people.

Conscientious Objection to War

This emphasis led to conscientious and moralistic politics. An example is conscientious objection—the refusal to take part in any war, or the refusal to take part in a given unjust war. Conscientious objection obviously could not be condoned by a state church. A state church could not advise its people to object or to refuse to serve in wars. It did just the opposite. It called on its people to serve in the war, to support the war. It often blessed the war as a holy war and put down curses on the enemy. But almost all the sects emphasized individual moral responsibility. That emphasis produced and enhanced the phenomenon of conscientious objection, which is almost totally a phenomenon of the sects. Some of the sects, like the Quakers, took an extreme position.

In Britain, where the sects represented about 20 percent of the population, conscientious objection did appear, but only as a minority phenomenon, since the sects were minority denominations.

In the United States, however, they have been the majority denominations, and although no majority of American people ever conscientiously objected to a war, it is interesting to note how often conscientious objection has been expressed. There was little in World War II, which was initiated by an external military attack by the Japanese at Pearl Harbor, and in the Revolution, but the War of 1812, the Mexican War, the Civil War (both North and South), the Spanish-American War, World War I, and the Korean War all witnessed relatively large scale protest. In some cases, hundreds of thousands of people refused to serve in these wars.

There was considerable public opposition to the War of 1812; New England was basically antiwar. Many abolitionists and northerners opposed the Mexican War because they saw it as an extension of slavery, and they voted against it. Moreover, though it is not exactly hailed in the annals of American military history, thousands of Americans deserted the U.S. army and joined the Mexican army. The Mexican army had battalions of Americans fighting against the United States because they believed Mexico was right and the United States was wrong in that war. People believing that actually went over to the enemy and fought for them.

In the Civil War, many southerners supported the North and either refused to fight or joined the Northern army. And there were northerners who refused to fight in the Northern army and objected to the war. Some of them even fought in the Southern army. The Spanish-American War did not last long enough to produce massive opposition, but there was considerable opposition, before and during that war.

During the Philippine insurrection, which did last for a long time, there was widespread public opposition. In World War I, there were

63

hundreds of thousands of objectors. The socialists, who opposed the war, received the biggest vote in their history during World War I as an antiwar party. They received 20 percent or more of the vote in a number of major cities.

The opposition to the Vietnam War—in terms of its effect on the war and on the society—probably was the most successful antiwar effort, but it did not necessarily have the greatest popular support. It simply accomplished more.

This phenomenon of antiwar activity in the United States is, I would suggest, a Protestant phenomenon. It is a phenomenon rising from the emphasis on individual conscience. One finds it nowhere else in the world, though one can point to antiwar movements of some degree in other countries.

When I say it is a Protestant phenomenon, I am not suggesting that most of the people involved in the antiwar movement—particularly in recent years—were Protestants. To a considerable degree, however, the non-Protestant denominations and churches such as the Catholics and the Jews—have as Americans been Protestantized, because the larger secular culture has taken over elements which come from this Protestant tradition. In contrast to situations in other countries, a Jew or a Catholic growing up in America absorbs, as part of the American way of life, elements that reflect some of this Protestant character.

Protestant Moralism

In the book *The Image of America*, Father R. L. Bruckberger, a French Dominican (in spite of his name), discusses American society from a comparative perspective. He says American Catholicism is unrecognizable to a French Catholic, or an Italian Catholic—or, he suggests, a Mexican Catholic. To him American Catholics look more like Methodists or Baptists than like Catholics. Their attitudes, values, and behavior, their orientation to religion, their concepts (in practice, though not, obviously, in theology) are much more like those of a Protestant than like a Catholic in Europe.

One of his main emphases is on a higher degree of intolerance (or moralism) here—he was here during the ascendancy of Senator Joe McCarthy. Father Bruckberger said that such intolerance is not found among European Catholics because—following what he considered correct Catholic theology as against false Protestant theology—they assume that people are inherently imperfect and sinful. Since one does not expect anything approaching perfection from people, one does not persecute them for their lack of perfection. He felt he found many American Catholics and Protestants doing just that.

He saw Joe McCarthy not as a Catholic figure but as a Protestant figure. Of course, one can raise questions about the Inquisition and other practices of European Catholicism, but he pointed to many elements in American Catholic practice (not theology) reflecting American Protestant behavior. Much has also been written about the extent to which Protestant orientations have affected American Jewry.

To return to the political impact of Protestant moralism. I think it has strengthened both individualism and antistatism, and, along with that, has developed an opposition to welfare. A characteristic of both Catholicism and of Judaism is strong communal orientation toward welfare. Protestantism—particularly in its sectarian, denominational form, with its emphasis on individualism—has been antagonistic to these welfare concerns.

Even contemporary public opinion survey data show that among Americans from the same income levels, the same educational backgrounds, and so forth, Catholics and Jews are much more welfare oriented than are Protestants. It also shows up in political party choice: the welfare-oriented Democratic party has received disproportionately more support from Catholics and Jews.

To a considerable degree, this difference may be explained by status conflicts. Catholics and Jews have been out-groups. They have seen themselves, to one degree or another, as oppressed socially, politically, and economically by the dominant white Anglo-Saxon Protestant group, which, in turn, has been allied to the Whig and Republican parties. That in itself may explain the traditional religious disproportion in voting patterns.

In addition to that, however, the differences between the ideological or social orientations of the two political coalitions correspond, to some degree, to the differences in orientation between Protestants and Catholics and Jews. Voting studies also have differentiated between pietistic and nonpietistic Protestants, with the pietistic much more likely to be found among Republicans than the nonpietistic.

Religious Orientation toward Socialism

One would have expected the Protestant sectarian orientation to be a source of resistance to efforts to build a socialist movement in the United States. And one would have expected Catholics and Jews to be a much more likely source for socialist and labor support than Protestants would be.

In the case of the Jews, this was correct, in large part, because the Jews brought their radicalism and socialism with them. Before they emigrated from eastern Europe and from Tsarist Russia, Jews were severely oppressed economically, and were denied political rights. If they were to be political, they had no option except to be revolutionary, in opposition to the status quo. Many Jews were involved in the socialist and other revolutionary movements in Tsarist Russia and in other parts of Eastern Europe.

But the Catholics—who probably constituted the majority of the working class and of the trade union movement of the United States from the late nineteenth century on—proved to be one of the most severe obstacles to the socialist movement. The reason was not that the Catholics had either an individualistic orientation or a pro-capitalist value system. They did not—certainly not as compared with the Protestants. What bothered the Catholic church and what bothered many Catholic leaders about socialism in America was, to a considerable degree, not the economics of socialism but the attitude toward religion. The American Socialist Party contained large numbers of Marxists, who took their lead from the antireligious European socialist movements. While there was a significant group of Christian socialists within the party—most of them Protestant clergy—there was a much larger group of militant atheists. Efforts to persuade the party to be neutral on religion had some success, but they were generally opposed at party conventions by at least half the party, who regarded neutrality as a betrayal of socialist principles and who wanted the party to be actively hostile to religion.

The Catholic church saw that the potential influence of socialists on Catholic workers could be negative. They might attempt to take them away from their religious beliefs.

In this context, a variety of organizations were formed with the support of the church, working within the AFL against the socialists with considerable success. The organized Catholic groups supported Samuel Gompers, who was Jewish but who strongly resisted the socialists.

The division of socialist–antisocialist strength within the AFL would seem to belie my argument that Protestantism is inherently more individualistic and antisocialist than Catholicism. The Catholic union leaders almost without exception were antisocialist. Socialist strength—which at the time was considerable—came from the unions that were predominantly non-Catholic—Jewish or Protestant. The Catholic opposition to socialism was extremely effective.

But the doctrines of some of the Catholic working-class groups organized to resist socialism were not conservative. They took positions that were almost socialist. They backed trade unions strongly; they supported cooperatives; and they were sharply critical of business, capitalism, the trusts, and the monopolies.

Some of the Catholic leaders who were involved in these movements from before World War I down through the New Deal could easily have been Socialist party leaders—and I think some of them probably felt this way, too—except for the feeling that the socialists could not be trusted on religious terms.

In other parts of the English-speaking world—in Britain, Australia, and New Zealand, and later, in Canada—the Catholics backed the socialists and the Labour parties. In these countries, however, the latter were consciously pro-religion, or not irreligious. In Britain, this link to religion occurred in part because many of the leaders and founders of the Labour party were devout Protestants, who could hardly be irreligious. But the Marxist antireligion influence was extremely weak in the socialist and Labour political movements of the commonwealth.

One can envisage retrospectively a movement like the British Labour party in the United States, with many Catholics taking part. In fact, some people argue that one of the mistakes made by the socialists was to mobilize the Catholics against them. If there had been a different kind of socialist-labor movement in this country, it is argued, that need not have happened.

In any case, Catholic opposition helped prevent the AFL from supporting socialism, while American Protestantism was decisive in forming and perpetuating the emphasis on individualism and anti-statism in the larger American polity, as well as the propensity of Americans for politics in the form of moralistic movements, which runs through our history.

Few Parties, Many Movements

The United States is a country of few parties but many movements, while Europe has had many parties and few movements. These two phenomena are interrelated.

The succession of peace movements goes back to early American history. In the early days particularly, they were closely linked to religion. The Temperance-Prohibition movement was also closely allied to religion. The abolitionist movement was very much linked to Protestant sectarianism.

From the point of view of non-Protestant groups in the United

States, one problem was that Protestant moralism could also be anti-Catholic and, at times, anti-Semitic, and generally xenophobic.

Many of the Protestant movements that we now view favorably had reactionary tendencies in terms of our current notions. Many of the abolitionists, for example, were nativists.

In the 1850s Isaac Wise, a famous rabbi in Cincinnati, warned that once the abolitionists freed the slaves, they would turn on the Jews, because they would need something else to attack. He emphasized that these are the kinds of people who need a crusade, and they are dangerous. The Catholics also had similar misgivings about the abolitionists, not entirely without justification.

The Know-Nothings, also known as the American party, were explicitly anti-Catholic and anti-immigrant and won 25 percent of the vote for president in 1856. The Know-Nothings largely came out of the Whig party and went into the Republican party.

Abraham Lincoln's first vice-president was a former Know-Nothing, and Grant's two vice-presidents were also former Know-Nothings. Grant, himself, was not exactly a tolerant man: During the Civil War he issued an anti-Semitic edict barring Jews from the area under his command. As president, Grant made a speech to the Union veterans telling them they faced the danger of a new Civil War—a war between the forces of God and the forces of superstition. He was talking about a war between Protestants and Catholics.

Through much of the late nineteenth century, parts of the Republican party were explicitly anti-Catholic. Many of the most important Republican leaders in city and state politics of that period pursued anti-Catholic policies.

The slogan rum, Romanism, and rebellion, which supposedly defeated James G. Blaine in 1880, when it was used on his behalf, was a common saying. It has been singled out because it seemingly affected that election, but Blaine was more typical than not of Republican Protestant leadership of that time.

That pattern was broken in the 1890s by Mark Hanna and William McKinley. Hanna, the political boss of the Republican party, saw the possibility of recruiting immigrant and Catholic support and worked hard to shift the party's whole image around. In 1896, the Democratic nomination of a person of a fundamentalist Protestant background, William Jennings Bryan, contributed to this shift. Many Catholics did vote for McKinley, and the tie of the Republican party to anti-Catholicism was broken for a time.

The linkage of Protestant moralism with anti-Catholicism and anti-Semitism continued into the 1920s with the Ku Klux Klan. The Ku Klux Klan was very much a movement of Protestant morality, not just racial or religious bigotry. Studies of the Klan of the 1920s show that they were much more concerned about adulterers and divorcees than about Catholics and Jews. The people beaten up by the Klansmen tended to be those who engaged in moral indiscretion, rather than those who belonged to minority groups they did not like. The Klansmen also tried to enforce Prohibition and other moralistic measures.

We all tend to emphasize what we like and forget the parts of history we do not like, but the Klan and the Know-Nothings came out of the same pattern of Protestant sectarianism that led to the antiwar movement of the 1960s and 1970s. They all reflect Protestant moralism —this notion that we must do what is right. When we try to enforce the right, we become involved with the social movements that flow from this moralism.

Many of the people in the movements of the sixties were Catholics, Jews, or atheists, and some of them would be outraged to be told that their behavior is as American as apple pie. Engaging in these movements is not new and anti-American; it is very American to be involved in a massive antiwar movement. They might be even more outraged to be told that they were behaving in religious terms, and particularly in Protestant sectarian terms. I am not suggesting any direct impulse. They were behaving as Americans, and America has been deeply affected by its Protestant sectarian heritage.

In respect to socialism, that heritage has operated to inhibit the possibility of a strong political movement. There was a great divide in American history in the 1930s, when the emphasis on individualism, antistatism, and the strong approval of competition were badly shaken, and a strong element of welfarism was introduced. The support for this tended to come disproportionately from Catholic and Jewish and other non-Protestant elements within the society. Still, there are many of a Protestant sectarian background who thoroughly accept this change.

President Carter obviously accepts it, and he can only be described in Protestant sectarian terms. His politics derive from a peculiar inversion of the more general American political relationships created in the South among whites and blacks as a result of slavery and emancipation. The Southern whites who were pushed into the Democratic party constitute the great exception to the correlation between pietistic religion and the Republicans. The relationship of competitive individualism to pietistic Protestantism still exists in 1978, and the support for welfare still has stronger support in the Catholic and Jewish communities than the Protestant community.

Majority Coalitions and Minority Moralism

Religion, as I see it, has been and continues to be a major determinant of American political and social orientations. If conditions were somehow appropriate to create a Labor or a Social Democratic Labor party in the United States, or if the Democratic party moves towards a more social democratic pattern in the European sense, then the social relationships that exist in England or in Australia will evolve here, too. The Protestants are less likely to be part of this movement than are the Catholics and Jews, who are more communitarian.

In what is still a country with a Protestant majority, however, that orientation can not hope to win elections without the support of many Protestants, which it receives elsewhere more than it does in the United States. In this context, one finds the enormous continuing significance of religion in explaining our political behavior.

In our political history, the Democratic party has always had somewhat similar sociological correlates of support, and it has maintained continuity as a coalition party. The non-Democratic parties—that is, the more conservative parties, such as the Federalists, the Whigs, and now the Republicans—have had more difficulty maintaining themselves and have broken up, dissolved, and reorganized. One would think that the dominant political tendency in the country would be the one allied to Protestant denominationalism—to American individualism, competitiveness, and so on. Apart from the post-Civil War period, however, this has been the weaker political tendency.

One of its problems is that it draws its roots from pietistic Protestantism and Protestant moralism. The Federalists broke down, to some considerable degree, because Alexander Hamilton and others did not understand the coalition party politics required by the American system at its birth. They presented urban oriented policies that could not appeal to the majority of the people, who were farmers. Hamilton saw, correctly, that the future of the country lay in industrial growth and urbanization, and this was the direction that he wanted to go. He wanted the government to help commerce, but he wanted that when 90 percent of the population were farmers. Without a strong rural base, there could be no strong second party during the early nineteenth century. The Federalists, in effect, did not even try to secure the support of a majority in any realistic terms. They happened to be principled and right, but they were wrong, politically.

The Whigs also broke up. The northern Whigs included many Protestant moralists and antislavery forces. Some people did not like them and broke off to form third parties, like the Free Soil party and the Liberty party. The southern Whigs were planters and proslavery.

The northern Democrats included many who were antislavery. There were many Jacksonians among the Democrats. The southern Democrats were proslavery. Yet, the Democratic party managed to hang together. The Whigs broke up, disintegrated around the slavery issue. The Whigs opposed the Mexican War. Lincoln—who was a Whig Congressman in 1848—voted against that war, as did many other Whigs.

While the Whig party contained as many politicians—in the invidious sense of the term—as did the Democrats, I think it is still fair to say that there was more principle in the Whig party than in the Democratic party.

Down to the present, I think that this has remained true about the two parties. One may not like the principles of the Republican party, but many Republicans would rather say the truth than win elections. And many Democrats would rather win elections than say the truth.

I am talking relatively, not absolutely, and historically, not about any given time period. The party of Richard Nixon or Spiro Agnew, can hardly claim any advantage in virtue.

Now we have a Democratic president who tells us that he always tells the truth and that he never lies, and I would not want to say that he is lying when he says this.

Nevertheless, the traditional pattern of the two parties remains roughly true, to some degree, reflecting their underlying base. This may be one reason why the Republicans today are in trouble in the way the Whigs and the Federalists were once in trouble.

Bill Brock, the national chairman of the Republican party, is the kind of man who wants to win elections, but he also appears to think he has people around him who would rather adopt attitudes and positions that they consider moralistic and true. Although I would emphasize that this explanation is necessarily overly simplistic and exaggerated, I think it carries some validity in regard to the differences between the political tendencies.

The Legitimacy of Business in the United States

The United States is the Protestant country par excellence—no other country is as Protestant as the United States. When Max Weber in his *Protestant Ethic and the Spirit of Capitalism* wanted to illustrate the Protestant ethic and the capitalist spirit, he chose American examples. It is among American Protestants and American businessmen that he found the most extreme examples of the Protestant ethic, even though it was John Calvin in Europe who presumably started it. Ben Franklin was for Weber the great exponent of the pure essence of the Protestant ethic—the concentration on rationalism, on the accumulation of money, on investment, on asceticism, and the like—all of which Weber saw as necessary for the development of capitalism.

We have had the kind of culture most conducive to the emergence of a pure capitalist society. We not only had the right religious component, but we lacked the feudal and the agrarian traditions that dominated European society. In a way, businessmen and the business spirit has been more legitimate in the United States than in other countries.

One problem that capitalists have faced in Europe—apart from having strong communist and socialist movements against them—is that the conservatives have never liked them. Businessmen were never as legitimate in Britain or in Germany as in the United States. The traditional European upper class has remained the upper class and has looked down on the bourgeoisie and on their pedestrian emphasis on moneymaking, their crass materialism. The royal courts in Berlin and in London did not welcome them but regarded them as a necessary evil rather than a positive good. Businessmen did not have the highest status in society; they were not considered leaders of very legitimate undertakings.

Only in America were businessmen at the top of the heap. Only here were they considered to be engaged in the most prestigious activity in the society. Business was not a prestigious pursuit in Britain, Germany, Russia, or Italy. It remained the most esteemed activity for a long period in the United States, though that period may have come to an end some time ago. Opinion poll data clearly indicate that Americans do not regard moneymaking and economic activity, per se, as the highest order of human activity.

Although there are problems with the prestige or status of the moneymakers—the leaders of industry in the United States—it is important to reiterate that from a comparative perspective this has been the capitalist country, as well as the Protestant country, par excellence. That fact has contributed both to the ideological orientation of American businessmen, their commitment to laissez-faire liberalism, as well as to their being more self-confident than European business ever was.

European businessmen were always trying to assimilate to the upper class, which was antibusiness. An interesting example of this is given by Friedrich Engels, Marx's great collaborator, in an introduction to *Socialism: Utopian and Scientific*, which he wrote in the 1890s. Engels happened to be a businessman, a manufacturer in Manchester, and he supported Marx economically during a large part of his life. Engels describes in this introduction how he and Marx could never understand why, in Britain—which, for much of the nineteenth century was the leading capitalist country, where the British capitalists were the dominant economic and, therefore, political ruling class—why the old landed aristocracy still dominated politics. They were puzzled by the fact that Britain still had an aristocratic society, which retained a great deal of power through the Conservative party. It seemed a contradiction that the British capitalists had not taken over the country.

Engels says he finally understood the phenomenon when he went to a dinner of the Young Men's Board of Trade, which was something like a Rotary Club or a Chamber of Commerce, in the town of Bradford. A Liberal minister who had just left the cabinet gave a speech to his fellow businessmen about his experiences in London. He told them they all should learn French. Why? Because French was the language of the court. He reported how embarrassed he had been at not being able to speak French, and also at not having proper manners, and how this had inhibited him. Engels realized then that even though the bourgeoisie had the economic power, they felt inferior to the aristocracy; that status was a power force. He did not put it in these terms, but, essentially, he was saying that they felt inferior, ashamed, or crude. This sense of inferiority was why they did not take over the country as Marxist theory prescribed they should do.

The psychological subordination that the business classes felt toward the aristocracy in Europe did not exist in this country. The business classes were the elite of America; they ran it. They were secure in their status, and, therefore, they could speak up. They could advance their cause in pure form, as the Republican party has done for much of modern history.

For a long time, the Republican party was the dominant party for at least two reasons. One was its post–Civil War advantage, being the party of the Union, of the Grand Army of the Republic—a sort of bonus for having been on the right side on that great divide of American history.

In addition, the Republicans were on the right side of an issue which Hamilton had enunciated prematurely, which the conservatives advanced during all of the nineteenth century—they were the party of growth. They were the party of industrial development. They were the party of American expansion. The Democrats were the inhibiting party, the party that was reacting against the strains of growth, defending the interest of various groups that felt injured by industrialization, as well as of the less privileged.

The Republicans were identified with American prosperity and increased status, and this, in part, gave them a majority from the Civil War period on. In fact, the GOP even grew after 1896, when Mark Hanna brought many Catholics into the party. The Republican advantage lasted until the Great Depression, which undermined the legitimacy of the business classes with whom they were identified.

In this post–New Deal period, now that we have made a shift to a welfare state orientation, it is the Republicans who are the reacting party, who retain an outmoded ideology. It is now the Republicans who refuse to acknowledge change and hold on to the old values, not simply out of self-interest, but with a moralistic passion.

The problem of many Republicans is not that they are self-interested—everybody is self-interested—but that they are true believers. They have the capacity to believe that theirs is the way of God, the way of righteousness, that it is Americanism. They no longer are good politicians. They are not flexible enough.

The Predicament of Capitalism in the United States

We are in a mixed situation. On one hand, we are the only country without a socialist movement. Poll data dealing with attitudes toward business and the American economic system indicate overwhelming support for free enterprise and competitive business society among the American public, even among American liberals, when the questions are put in the most general form.

On the other hand, the same polls reveal a lack of confidence in the leaders of big business and other powerful institutions. The public is suspicious that businesses, particularly major corporations, misuse their power. In spite of the popular belief that government is inefficient and wasteful, the public supports regulation of business, designed to protect consumers and workers. The people also believe that labor unions, though viewed as frequently corrupt and internally autocratic, are necessary to protect workers from being unfairly exploited by their employers. Capitalism, though seen as far superior to socialism as a productive economic system, no longer possesses unchallenged legitimacy. The new intelligentsia drawn from the college educated sees business as crass, overly materialistic, uninterested in the public good.

The decline in the status of capitalism has not resulted in increased support for socialism. Socialism, which is no longer an untried utopian solution, is regarded as a thorough failure; it is not attractive any more; it does not work in all sorts of places, and everybody knows it. The socialist movement is weaker than ever in the United States;

labor is also weak in the United States; and, in a curious way, so is capitalism, as compared with its past.

This is not to say that General Motors or AT&T is in trouble, or will be nationalized or be taken over by the workers tomorrow— though the pension funds may be a way in which the workers will take them over. But capitalism is much less legitimate today than it used to be in America. This may be why this country has a sense of malaise. Everybody thinks he has fallen, nobody thinks he has risen, and the country has declined internationally.

This may be the kind of mood or situation that is preliminary to a new movement, because people do have a need to believe. Americans particularly believe in virtue; they believe that they are virtuous. And when they do not feel this way, they look around for a way to regain their belief in the country. Somebody may come around tomorrow, or ten years from now, and give them some new sense of virtue, though I see no such person on the horizon now.

The movements of the 1960s were prototypally American insofar as they reflect not only egalitarian values, but also moralistic concerns. Most Americans, when they feel something is right, believe they have to act out their sentiments, whether these be civil rights, or women's rights, or antiwar, or anti-Catholicism, or whatever. These moralistic movements carry with them an element of intolerance that constitutes a threat to the stability of the polity.

So far, we have always survived periods of instability. The reason we have survived them lies in the nature of our parties. Our parties have been flexible enough to absorb protest movements continually, whether they are racist or egalitarian.

We responded to or co-opted two movements in the 1960s. We absorbed the antiwar movement, and we also absorbed George Wallace and his white racists in the two-party system. We might like one and not the other, but the party system handled both. If it had left one out in the cold, the system would have been in trouble.

I have one last comment on the topic of socialism. I will make it by citing Ed Flynn, who was the Democratic boss of the Bronx at a time when it meant a lot more than it does now. He also succeeded Jim Farley as chairman of the National Democratic party. The Bronx was a heavily Democratic area because its two largest constituent bodies were Jews and Irish and other Catholics. There were almost no Republicans in the Bronx. The election contests in the 1920s and early 1930s were between the socialists and the Democrats, not between the Republicans and the Democrats. More recently, they have been between the Liberals and the Democrats, though the ethnic composition of the area has changed some.

In his book, *You're the Boss*—the "you" being the voters—Flynn writes that he could never understand why so many Jews insisted on supporting the Socialist party. He said if they wanted socialism, all they had to do was come to the Democrats, who were ready to do whatever the people want to get elected. If they wanted socialism, he said, the Democrats would give them socialism.

While that may be an exaggeration of the reality, it is also the truth about the opportunism of the American political system, and particularly of the Democratic party.

Discussion

QUESTION: Building on some of the work that Michael Novak and others have done on ethnicity, would it be possible to discern distinct ethnic/religious strands in the socialist tradition, a Jewish socialist strand, a Protestant socialist strand, and a Catholic socialist strand?

PROFESSOR LIPSET: In regard to the ethnic components of socialism, the American socialist movement in the nineteenth century was very largely German. In fact, it was conducted almost entirely in the German language.

The two places the socialists had most electoral success in the United States were on New York's Lower East Side, with the Jews, and in Milwaukee, with the Germans. The brewers union was socialist, and it was German. The garment unions were socialist, and they were Jewish. There were, of course, other groups besides these two, such as WASP farmers in Oklahoma. A Protestant socialist strand—for example, in Norman Thomas, and to some extent, in Eugene Debs— suggests that a religious, rather than Marxian, sectarianism was also operative. Catholic socialism, in the sense in which you use the word, has existed for a long time. As I noted earlier, many of the anti-socialist Catholic groups before World War I were actually social-democratic in their orientation. They were anticapitalist, pro–co-op, and pro-union.

QUESTION: We seem to be taking for granted, without any analysis, that there was something called American socialism which was very good; that it would have made this a far better country if it had prevailed; but that it could not prevail because of all the variables that you have illustrated for us. Perhaps it failed for lack of something good to offer the people.

Another point I want to make is that I suspect the American socialists underestimated the instinctive intelligence of the ordinary man. They tended to come in from the outside, to reform a movement which had fostered self-reliance on the part of the average working man. It is no accident that the American labor movement, until quite recently, had a strong suspicion of intellectuals, of people who thought they were smarter than the workers, and who might manipulate the movement for their own purposes. This is why the communists were expelled from the CIO in the 1940s.

PROFESSOR LIPSET: Your point is very well taken. Did socialism have something good to offer? What is it about the United States that made us depart from the pattern in most other industrial countries, where the workers have supported some kind of socialist, communist, or labor party movement?

The question is not so much whether socialism had something good to offer, but what made America "exceptional." What factors inhibited class consciousness in the United States? The answer lies in the conflict between socialist and American values, as well as in the unique character of American social class relations, as emphasized by Tocqueville.

QUESTION: I wonder if you would agree that, in Protestant individualism, there is also a kind of egalitarianism: the religion of the common man, the interpretation of the scripture for oneself, the congregational form of government, the antistatism.

PROFESSOR LIPSET: Yes, and the moralism of the Republican party, when it has been successful, has included at least an element of equalitarian appeal. In Kentucky, for example, John Sherman Cooper has been the most successful vote-getter in recent memory. He has had a populist appeal. He was in favor of black equality as early as 1948. One can be moralistic with both an individualistic and an equalitarian concern.

It seems to me the Republican party is not presently recruiting the kind of idealistic Republicans it needs. Is there room for moralistic and idealistic Republicans who stand for civil rights and some mixture of egalitarianism and individualism?

It really worries me that America may be moving away from "coalition" parties to "ideological" parties. The most impressive recent Republican politician was, of course, Dwight Eisenhower. While Eisenhower, ideologically, was very much a conservative Republican, he had compassion—concern for the underdog, for the blacks, and for others, even when he had no real program for them. In more recent years, some Republicans have become so passionate about the issue of state control over business, that all these other concerns have disappeared.

Even President Johnson's War on Poverty was expressed in very "Republican" terms, not in socialist terms. It was presented as a way of equalizing the race for success and competition, as the American way. The emphasis was on equality of opportunity.

Do you know the reason California has a $5 billion surplus? It is because of Ronald Reagan. And what did Ronald Reagan do? He increased the income tax and made it more progressive. He thought the progressive income tax was a fairer tax than the property tax and the sales tax. But somehow, no one ever hears about this. I have never heard the statement that the Republican party stands for a progressive income tax because it is a more equitable tax than the sales tax or the property tax—which it is, I think. If the Republicans would go around saying this, it would do something to the image of the party. After all, for a long time, the Republican party was a people's party in its own self-image. Today it has become too ideological for its own good.

QUESTION: Why has the Republican party gone this way? Is there an inordinate influence of newly rich, or "new business," who are perhaps not as socially conscious and full of ideals as the old rich?

PROFESSOR LIPSET: First, I have emphasized that pietistic-moralistic Protestantism is the cultural style of Republicans, and fosters an ideological orientation. Beyond that, the weaker the party gets, the larger the proportion in the party of ideological purists. This can create a vicious cycle of isolation. The very concept of coalition connotes opportunism.

Republicans do not have the kind of machine politician typified by Mayor Daley of Chicago. In spite of the decline of the boss system, he played an important role even in the most recent years. There was a first-rate article about Daley by Andrew Greeley in the *Bulletin of the Atomic Scientists* in February 1973. I think it should be required reading in every introductory political science course. To Daley the task of politics was to get one vote more than your opponents. And how is that done? Daley believed that politics is the art of giving people what they want in return for their votes. Nothing prevented the blacks of Chicago from voting for him, or the Jews, or the Greeks, or the labor movement people. They all voted for him. He got 70 percent. What did the Mayor do? He went to each group and, in effect, said, "What's the most important issue for you?" Then he went back to them and said, "Look, unless we give such-and-such group this, I can't give you what you want," and to the others vice versa. And this worked. He ran Chicago more efficiently than anybody else. In a 1968 survey,

Chicago turned out to be the city in which the police were most popular, where there were fewer complaints about unfair treatment by the police, and that was after the Democratic Convention. Incidentally, the height requirement to be a cop in Chicago is 5-foot-2. In every other place it's 5-8 or more. Why is it 5-foot-2 in Chicago? Puerto Ricans are short people. At one time the Puerto Ricans went to the Mayor and said the height requirement kept them off the police force. The Mayor told them they had a good point, and it became 5-foot-2. That's politics. And that's why 70 percent voted for the Mayor. He saw politics as the art of building coalitions.

It is this sort of thinking which, I think, the Republican and Democratic parties need, as against moralistic ideology. One of the reasons why Jimmy Carter is doing so badly is that his government is not a coalition. One part of the party is in administrative control, the New Politics wing. They are antagonizing people of all other persuasions. When we have too many moralists in both parties, we are in trouble.

Commentary

Monsignor George Higgins
Social Action Department, U.S. Catholic Conference

You described a certain type of Protestant individualistic reformer—or a certain type of Republican—as being more interested in telling the truth than in winning elections. I have the feeling that was probably also true of the socialists in the United States. One can be moralistic about social virtues as well as individual virtues. A certain type of small town Protestant can be moralistic about the social values, without even realizing it, just as he is about adultery or drink. And I suspect that many Catholic workers had a strong instinctive reaction to that, which had little to do with what their bishops said about the religious problem in socialism. Those workers came from a different culture, which was not quite as moralistic in the same sense.

I suppose we have never had a more moralistic man in the history of the United States than Norman Thomas. He was a preacher who left the pulpit, but carried his moralism into the social field. I suppose he wanted to win elections, but he never really gave anybody the idea that he did. He almost seemed to enjoy moralizing, whereas a politician like Ed Flynn would rather die than moralize if it interfered with winning an election. There is a great cultural difference there.

On the question of the influence of Catholics in holding back socialism in the labor movement, I think Mark Carson—who wrote the first book on the subject—exaggerated it because he did not quite understand how the church operates. He attributed much more significance than I would, as an insider, to pastoral letters from bishops and to occasional statements from priests. We have had many examples in recent times of pastoral letters that had no influence.

A combination of factors were at work. Samuel Gompers, who started out as a socialist, was not taken away from socialism either by his rabbinical leaders or by any influence of the Catholic church. He adapted to what he considered to be the realities and the needs of his time. Not that it was a perfect choice, but any other choice at that time might have been far less perfect. Socialists tend to think in terms of perfection rather than of what is feasible in a messy situation—and the American labor tradition has been extremely messy.

One of the ways neoconservatives differ from others is in the emphasis they put on the family and on freedom of education—that is, on parents having freedom of education. Coming from different traditions, they have a suspicion of universalism, in the bad sense of the word.

Many Catholic immigrants, particularly the Irish, brought that suspicion with them. They would have had it even if the American bishops had said nothing about socialism. The universalist approach of some highly intellectual socialists threatened certain values that these immigrants instinctively felt were not to be tampered with. These values included the stability of the family and freedom of education. No one had to give them a pastoral letter on that. The socialists were speaking a language on those issues that the immigrant Irish instinctively mistrusted, perhaps for sound reasons.

In the general discussion of why we do not have socialism, there seems to be the hidden premise that socialism had something very good to offer, that it did not succeed only because of these variables in our culture. That begs the question whether or not socialism had anything to offer in the American scene. Perhaps one reason it failed in the United States was that it had little to offer. Milwaukee had socialist mayors for a long time, but it was no different after it had a socialist mayor than before, except the government might have been more honest. So far as the poor were concerned, the socialist mayor in Milwaukee probably did no more for the people than a more opportunistic politician would have done.

Another of the failures of the American socialists, I suspect, was that they underestimated the instinctive intelligence of the ordinary man. They tended to come in from the outside to reform the movement. For a variety of historical reasons, however, a kind of self-reliance had developed in the average working man in our country that was not typical of Europe. It is no accident that the American labor movement, until quite recently, had a strong suspicion of intellectuals; they had a suspicion of people who thought they were smarter than the workers and were going to manipulate the movement for their own purposes.

There is an argument now as to why the communists were expelled from the CIO in the 1940s. I was at every major meeting at which that was discussed, and I was present when they were formally ejected, but I don't remember the scene as it is described by intellectuals today. They never seem to capture the notion that the working people, who had formed their own unions and who believed in a measure of union democracy, simply would not tolerate outsiders who wanted to manipulate the movement for their own purposes.

In many liberal books about that phase, there is a myth that—if it had not been for the intransigence, the stupidity, and the Cold War mentality of Catholics, in cooperation with people like Walter Reuther—we would have a far more liberal and open-ended labor movement today.

I don't believe it. I saw no great social program by the communists. They sold out on every economic issue to suit the needs of the Soviet Union. They favored a speed up when the Soviet Union favored one and opposed it when the Soviet Union did, and they reversed their position overnight. They didn't even have to wait for instructions. They did it by instinct.

The American workers have a very healthy suspicion of outsiders with an ideology who want to use the movement for their own purposes. That suspicion would have existed with regard to socialism in the United States quite apart from anything the church said.

Response
Seymour Martin Lipset

I agree with about 90 percent of what you said—so much so, in fact, that I may have to rewrite parts of a chapter dealing with immigrants and socialists in a book I am writing. Your stress on the basic sociological factors and values, apart from what the leadership said, is extremely well-taken. In a sense, the Socialist party was like the Republicans in its moralistic orientation, and it was culturally different in style and in language from that of the Catholic workers, many of whom were immigrants. We know how little attention is paid to pastoral letters and speeches today, and we have no reason to think it was different in 1900. But there were also organizations, such as the Militia of Christ—conscious efforts to build antisocialist factions in unions where the socialists had factions.

In the white commonwealth countries—Australia, New Zealand, and Britain—the Labour parties draw disproportionately from Catholic workers. While all three of those parties have played down socialism, they were still Protestant led. The British Labour party had many Protestant moralists in its leadership but was still able to recruit Catholic workers.

Marx anticipated that as industrialization advanced the working class would become socialist, and somehow, that has become the norm. The problem is, why doesn't the United States follow the pattern of most other industrial countries where the workers have supported some kind of Socialist, Communist, or Labor party movement. It is a question not so much of whether they had something good to offer, but of what inhibited class consciousness. The weakness of the American labor movement reflects the weakness of conscious class relationships in our society.

Another factor in this picture of Catholic immigrants, is the link between the Democratic party and the trade unions. In Catholic working class areas, leaders of the trade unions and of the Democratic party grew up in the same block and knew each other. When the socialists called the politicians "reactionaries," the people realized they were talking about their best friends, the ones they went to parochial school with. If the workers needed a favor, or if they needed support in a strike, they just asked for it, and that was that.

There was a meshing of the urban Democratic machine and the labor movement, and even the unorganized workers, that the socialists were trying to break, but it was an unbreakable system. In a more recent period, Ed Flynn and Mayor Daley reflected the kind of politics that was particularly responsive to ethnic organizations. The ethnic communities could not be broken to create a new movement.

One last comment ought to be made in the context of the moralism not only of the Republican party but also of business in this country, as reflected in the reaction to labor law reform. The labor law reform bill was a very mild, moderate bill, seeking to help this weak labor movement to grow, particularly in the South. It was certainly no threat to the power or influence of American business in the society. But the entire business community made it a *cause célèbre*. It became a moralistic crusade for the Chamber of Commerce and the NAM and the Business Roundtable. Not a single prominent businessman came out for labor law reform. I think this was a mistake. The business community needs alliances with the labor movement; but in reaction to the conflict, a number of labor leaders have said that the coalitions they have had with business are finished. They had been having legitimate, long-term good relations with the companies that now say unions are the worst possible thing for American society. Many of these businessmen do not believe that, but they got themselves caught up in a crusade, which, I think, will have bad effects.

Capitalism and Socialism: Empirical Facts

Peter Berger

The basic theme of this conference is the ethical assessment of a fundamental alternative in the modern world, the alternative between capitalist and socialist systems.

Defining the Concepts

Before anything else, I should give my own definition of those terms. In this particular instance, I suffer from a professional shortcoming of being a sociologist, in that I do not particularly like either/or definitions. I tend to think of the empirical world as a rather messy affair, in which it is very difficult to find pure cases of anything. Everything is in some kind of continuum, in which it is very difficult to make clear-cut divisions. I think this is very true here. Those familiar with social-science thinking know Max Weber's theory of ideal types, which can be paraphrased into very non-Germanic English by saying that the world is a very messy affair and concepts do not walk around on two legs. In any case, it seems to me that the terms "capitalism" and "socialism," if defined with any degree of intellectual elegance, refer to two phenomena which, as such, do not exist in the empirical world today. A pure capitalist system would be one in which the basic goods available in the society are distributed solely by means of market mechanisms. A socialist system would be one in which the same goods are distributed through a system of political allocation.

Incidentally, it is interesting that while the human race has shown enormous imaginativeness in thinking up different arrangements—take the mind-boggling variety of sexual and kinship institutions in human history, for example—it has been rather unimaginative about economic systems. Most of them are modifications of those two ideas.

It seems clear that in the contemporary world there is no pure market system. Nor is there a system, even in radically socialist places, of complete political allocation. Thus, the two conceptual constructions can be very elegant and very clear, but in the empirical realm, societies range on some sort of continuum, coming closer either to one or to the

85

other pole. If we say, for example, that the United States is a capitalist society while the Soviet Union is a socialist one, the concepts become messy again as soon as we look closely at the reality. That is, neither society fits the elegant concept.

Political allocation is a tremendously important element of the American socioeconomic system and that of any other so-called capitalist society. On the other hand, whole sectors of the so-called socialist economies seem to operate by market mechanisms.

Take one dramatic case: Soviet agriculture as a whole would collapse immediately if it were not for the—as it were—subterranean market system which keeps it going. Until a few years ago, people thought that in China it was very different. It is now becoming fairly clear that things are not that different in China.

The empirical situation in the contemporary world is that we have an economic system which people refer to as world capitalism, though it is certainly not a pure market system. It is politically modified in different ways in different countries, as in Switzerland and Sweden for example (to take two very different cases within Western Europe). This international system interacts with a growing number of socialist systems, which, again, are modified in a variety of ways. In other words, we are talking about two basic overall alternatives, market mechanisms of distribution as against political mechanisms. So much for the matter of definition.

Capitalism under Assault

A fundamental point is that the basic *cultural* fact in Western societies, leaving aside the Third World and those societies that consider themselves socialist, is that capitalism is under assault. In terms of the intellectual elites of the Western world, the present mood is certainly not pro-capitalist, though it may be arguable to what extent it is socialist. It is very critical of capitalism in all of its manifestations. This anticapitalist mood can be conveniently looked at in terms of six charges commonly made against capitalism. For each of these six charges, there is a correspondingly positive view of the socialist alternatives. Before proceeding, however, we should rule out any comparison between *existing capitalist societies* and *ideal socialist ones*. This is, I think, the common practice of many of those who criticize capitalism. There are endless discussions of the alleged evils of American society, West European society, Brazilian society, and other so-called capitalist societies, whose empirical features, such as they may be, are compared with an ideal. That, I think, is intellectually inadmissible. It is not inadmissible to compare empirical facts with an ideal. That is part of the eternal thrust of the human mind toward the divine, or whatever it may be called. Far be it from me to say one should not do this, but it must be done *both ways*. If facts are to be compared with ideals, then socialist facts must also be compared with ideals. If an ideal socialism is to be discussed, then an ideal capitalism must also be discussed.

The whole metaphysics of what constitutes "true" socialism is an endlessly fascinating topic. With each empirical disappointment, there was always some true socialism somewhere else. The issue cannot be discussed this way. *When facts are compared with facts and when facts are compared with ideals, they must be compared in the same way across the board, as it were.*

The Inequality of Capitalism

In intellectual discussion in Western countries today, one of the most common charges against capitalism is that it fosters inequality. Capitalism is a system which is said to produce inequality. By contrast, socialism is said to be egalitarian.

Now, even the sharpest critics of capitalism in the Western world generally stipulate its immense productivity and its capacity to generate wealth. I am not aware of any important socialist critic of Western societies that has seriously challenged this proposition. In this respect, they are very much in the tradition of Marx himself, who wrote almost poetic passages about the productive miracle of capitalism.

This is a rather important point in any discussion of inequality, particularly in regard to the ethical questions involved. For example, in the United States between 1940 and 1950 the real income (that is, in standardized dollars) rose 176 percent among unskilled workers, 172 percent among skilled workers, 111 percent among white-collar workers, and 95 percent among proprietors and managers. (There are many sources for these data. The one I took preparing these remarks is a rather useful book by Harold Hodges, *Social Stratification*, published in 1964.) The enormous increase in income—in just plain money available to people—is even more impressive over a longer time span, than just one decade. We have had an enormous increase in the standard of living of almost all strata of the population in Western societies, and particularly in the United States. There are very similar data from Western Europe (and, indeed, from Eastern Europe, though they are less dramatic there).

In view of this, it is not surprising that the critics of Western societies increasingly raise the question not of poverty but of equality. On the facts of equality, there is widespread agreement, even among people who are very positive about the Western system, that no dramatic changes have occurred either in income differentials or in social mobility. Nearly everyone in this society is better off than before in absolute terms, but inequalities persist in fairly stubborn forms. If income distribution is seen as a layer cake, there still are more or less the same number of people in each layer, but every one of the layers now has more income. Nevertheless, the gaps between the layers have not changed significantly, nor have the chances of individuals to climb from one stratum to a higher one (which is what sociologists mean by social mobility rates). One economist has called these facts the tyranny of the bell-shaped curve of income distribution.

A number of distortions result from this way of looking at income distribution. The key question, of course, is what is being compared with what? If the inequalities of contemporary American society are compared with an egalitarian ideal, they look horrendous, as they must. An empirical reality always compares unfavorably with an ideal. If contemporary American society is compared with the past—that is, its own past—the progress is rather remarkable. Again, that is very hard to deny. It is interesting to compare existing inequalities in American society with inequalities in other societies in the world, especially in the societies that call themselves socialist. Statistics on income distributions for the United States (as well as for other Western societies) include old people, young people, and female heads of households. If these three categories are removed from the income distribution statistics of the United States, the picture is much more egalitarian. Irving Kristol has discussed such matters rather persuasively in his recent collection of essays, *Two Cheers for Capitalism.*

Now, please do not misunderstand me. I am not saying that our income distribution is something to be celebrated. In fact, I am not at all in the habit of celebrating capitalism. In regard to the first category, that of old people, for example, it is troublesome enough to suffer from getting old without experiencing a rapid decline in income and what sociologists call downward social mobility. As our population ages, that deplorable fact will become a greater and greater social problem.

In the same way, it is not good that there should be no place in the labor force for large numbers of young people or that female heads of household should be paid less than male heads of household. In each of those three cases, however, we are dealing with problems that have nothing to do with capitalism. That, I think, is an important point.

Another point to be made about Western societies is that the income distribution statistics ignore payments and services from the mechanisms of the welfare state. Edgar Browning's *Redistribution and the Welfare System* published by AEI in 1975, calculates some of these benefits and the amounts are impressive. The basic fact is that we do not calculate as income what people receive from the state. If we did calculate as income what poor people receive simply by virtue of being citizens of a society that has a welfare state with its various mechanisms of redistribution, we would see a different picture. Needless to say, it would be much more egalitarian.

For comparison, we should look at the so-called socialist systems in Europe. The others are hardly relevant, for fairly obvious reasons. It does not make sense to compare the United States with North Korea; it does make sense to compare, say, East Germany with West Germany, or for that matter, the United States and the Soviet Union, in terms of industrial and economic development. At first, the figures from the socialist systems seem more egalitarian. But there are two very important facts that are systematically left out of income distribution figures that come from those countries. One is the virtual absence of an income tax. I have a number of friends who are recent and not so recent refugees from Eastern Europe. One of the real traumas they have had upon coming to Western countries is that they suddenly find themselves shelling out an enormous percentage of their income in taxes. Taxes are rather significant (that fact need not be emphasized to people in an income bracket similar to mine, and equally unable to cheat).

Income distribution statistics from socialist countries also systematically ignore the miscellaneous "perks" of higher income positions, such as apartments, purchasing possibilities, vacations, and what not. These facts, if added into the mix, of course, indicate a much more inegalitarian distribution.

To sum up, the inequality in capitalist societies is greatly exaggerated, as is the equality in existing socialist systems. What the *ideals* of capitalism and socialism might be is a question that does not concern us at the moment.

Exploitation of the Third World

A charge commonly made against capitalist societies is that capitalist wealth is based on exploitation of the Third World and that socialism is liberation from such exploitation.

On this issue, Lenin's theory of imperialism, published in 1917,

89

is still relevant. It is also relevant that Lenin published this theory of imperialism at the point when imperialism, as he defined it, ceased to exist. Nevertheless the theory has been tremendously potent in various manifestations to this day. An extremely useful book by Benjamin Cohen, *The Question of Imperialism* (1973) contains a good critique of Lenin's imperialism theory and the various theories derived from it.

On the basis of a strong interest during the last decade in questions of modernization and development in the Third World, let me only express my opinion that both the original theory and its later derivations are weak, both historically and in contemporary terms. That the nascent capitalist powers of the West exploited countries in what is now called the Third World is, of course, true. There is no question about that. What is less clear is that this exploitation and colonial dominance contributed much to the economic development of Western countries. The evidence for the Marxist view is very weak indeed. In contemporary terms, the notion that our wealth is based on their poverty is even weaker. In a way, the truth is more depressing. The truth is that if most of the Third World disappeared under the ocean tomorrow, it would make little difference to us. I find that morally more depressing than the Marxist notion of exploitation.

Equally dubious, it seems to me, is the proposition that socialism would end the exploitation, by ending the dependency on the world capitalist system. I see no reason at all to believe this assumption. Countries that are highly developed industrially tend to strike good bargains for themselves with countries that are less developed. Conversely, when rich countries and poor countries deal with each other economically, the poor countries tend to get the worse bargain. I think there is strong evidence for that proposition. Also, under modern conditions it is not easy for a poor country to join the rank of rich countries (though it is not impossible, and some are doing it successfully). But these relations, again, have nothing to do with whether the rich countries are capitalist or socialist.

Two other observations should be made. First, exploitation is by no means the only form of economic relations possible between rich and poor countries. Many relations are beneficial to the poor countries. Second, socialist countries are just as capable of exploitation as are capitalist countries.

Various types of relationships are possible here. A rich capitalist country can exploit a poor capitalist country, and that does happen. Poor capitalist countries can relate to each other in various unsatisfactory ways. (When I became interested in Latin America, a Mexican economist tried to explain certain things that I did not understand too well by saying, "Well, essentially, the relations between Latin American countries are like three people who keep selling two oranges to each other.")

Poor socialist countries also relate to each other. There are not too many cases of this at the moment, though Cambodia and Vietnam provide an interesting case. But much more relevant to the present discussion are cases of rich socialist countries exploiting poor socialist countries. The relationship of the Soviet Union to various countries that are economically dependent upon it is, I think, the most important case in point.

All of this could be expanded at great length, but the basic point is simple: socialism is not a necessary solution to the problems of the poverty and exploitation of nations.

International Oppression and Liberation

A third charge, which is commonly made, is that capitalism is linked to a system of international oppression and that, again by contrast, socialism is linked to various movements of people liberating themselves from oppression. Although this allegation is related to the charge of exploitation, particularly the exploitation of the Third World, its emphasis is less on economic exploitation than on the support by Western states, as well as by multinational corporations, of oppressive political regimes. I would not for a moment dispute that this exploitation has, in fact, taken place and still takes place. However oppression is defined, a number of regimes in the world that clearly are oppressive by any sane criterion are being supported by Western governments or by multinational corporations.

It would be useful to adopt a statistical approach and to be as specific as possible. To discuss oppression in general terms is meaningless. One should talk about specific matters, such as torture or starvation.

I think it is oppressive to live in a society in which the police routinely torture prisoners. I think it is also oppressive if people starve to death or even if they suffer from a high level of malnutrition. Such specificity is useful in discussing oppression.

As far as torture is concerned, the socialist societies are more oppressive than the capitalist societies, according to all the facts I know. In one part of the world I try to keep up with, Latin America, there is not merely an occasional use of torture but rather routine use of it on political prisoners. That, I think, is the real issue. In these terms, probably the worst country in Latin America is Uruguay, and the second worst is Cuba. Only then would we come to Brazil and Chile. In terms

91

of torture, the general charge against capitalism does not hold. (For a statistical approach to this question, I would recommend the annual reports of Freedom House, as well as the reports of Amnesty International and other human rights groups.) In terms of starvation, also, the charge against capitalism does not hold. One of the most important facts about Soviet socialism is that in more than half a century, this economic system has simply not succeeded in becoming agriculturally productive. The Soviet Union seems fanatically determined to make its agriculture as unproductive as possible. Until just a few years ago, the general opinion in the West was that the Chinese had solved their own agricultural problem. I thought so myself. When I wrote my book on models of development and development ideology, *Pyramids of Sacrifice*, which was published in 1975, I was very critical of the Chinese, but I said that they seem to have solved the problem of starvation. Well, we now know that they have done no such thing, and we know it not from sources hostile to the Chinese government but from the Chinese government itself, though it blames the Gang of Four for the entire problem. Actually, the Chinese aggravated the problem by instituting a socialist system of agriculture, just as the Russians did. As a result, large numbers of Chinese starved to death, and some are starving even today. Western visitors, of course, are not taken to the areas in which this happens.

One could go on with other specific points. I would suggest that in terms of human misery the world is a very depressing place. But a map of human misery fails to support the identification of capitalism with oppression.

Domestic Oppression

A fourth charge is that capitalism is also oppressive domestically, again by contrast with socialism. Once more, we must ask, What does domestic oppression mean? With regard to anything remotely connected with political rights, in the sense either of democratic institutions or of what we now call human rights, the reverse is the case. One charge often subsumed under this notion of domestic oppression is that of racism. Capitalism, in the United States and elsewhere, supposedly has fostered racism and continues to do so.

Again, let me stipulate that there has been horrible treatment of other races in American history and the history of the Western world. Let me also stipulate that Western societies have not solved this problem in its entirety. An almost incredible revolution in race relations has taken place, however, in American society and other Western societies. I know of no other society in the world of which this is true. This revolution has been most dramatic in the South, but it has occurred not only in the South. Other societies, which have a rhetoric of racial equality and racial emancipation, have systematic, or institutionalized, forms of racial discrimination that would be unthinkable in the United States or any other Western country. The treatment of their racial minorities by the Chinese today may be cited here.

Another common charge concerns the treatment of women. Again, real rather than rhetorical advances in the rights of women have been made almost exclusively in Western societies.

Materialism

Capitalism is supposed to foster materialist values, while socialism is somehow supposed to evoke the less materialist instincts in human beings. Apart from the irony of this proposition in that Marxism understands itself as being a materialist philosophy, is it really correct that Western capitalist societies are more materialistic? I know of very little evidence to that effect. Again, it helps to put the question in concrete form. Two issues are often cited under this heading—the environment and consumerism, or consumerist values. One notion is that capitalist societies tend to plunder the environment and to be destructive of nature, and the other is that false values are fostered where people are interested in nothing but material possessions. Again, it seems to me the facts almost precisely contradict the charge. The only countries in the world with any kind of systematic concern for the environment are in the West. The present nuclear controversy is a dramatic illustration of this. Where are people demonstrating against nuclear energy? In Western countries. There is no likelihood of this happening anywhere else. Where is there legislation protecting the environment? I am not concerned here whether such legislation is good, bad, or indifferent; the fact is, it is enacted only in Western capitalist societies.

The notion that capitalism is in some peculiar way inimical to the environment is absurd. The case that modern industries or technologies are inimical to the environment would be much more interesting to discuss. But that has nothing to do with whether a society is more capitalist or socialist in its organization.

As to consumerism, I have been in a good many parts of the world, and I know of no human society in which people are not interested in possessions. And the poor are much more interested in posessions than are the rich. I know of very few societies in which there is as much concern with idealistic causes, concerns, and values as there is in the West, especially in the United States. This has less to do with

93

our being such wonderful people than with our affluence. We already have so many material things that we can afford to be concerned with ideals. Precisely that affluence, though, is the result of our capitalist system.

Alienation and Solidarity

The final charge is that capitalism is supposed to encourage individualism and competitiveness, and therefore feelings of alienation or anomie. By contrast, socialism is supposed to reaffirm belonging of some sort and collective solidarity.

Here, I think, is the only one of the six charges on which a good argument can be made. The values of individualism and competition are intrinsically linked—historically and in the present—to the capitalist economy and social system. Conversely, at a very profound level of values, socialism is, has been, and continues to be a protest against that. The appeal of the socialist vision has much to do with its rejection of these values of individualism and competitiveness. How one assesses this in ethical terms, of course, is another question, but I think the empirical charge is probably correct.

Discussion

QUESTION: You are speaking of capitalism and socialism, but I am not convinced that this distinction is very meaningful. There is an old joke in Czechoslovakia: "What is the difference between capitalism and socialism? Capitalism is the exploitation of man by man; socialism is the other way around." I think we should speak instead of the American system and the Soviet system. Then we have two complete social systems to compare. Otherwise we are speaking about two systems that do not actually exist, and we have to try artificially to determine which is one and which is the other. Doing that leads to ways of thinking that deform the real issue, and we will come to false conclusions.

PROFESSOR BERGER: I agree that when one uses the words "capitalism" or "socialism" there should be quotation marks around them—as I explained at the beginning of my presentation—but for shorthand, one can say capitalist or socialist and know which societies one is speaking about. In my mind, taking certain goods out of the market system and making them subject to political allocation is a step in the direction of a socialist ideal.

The problem is that very few socialist thinkers are grappling with the fact that as the system of political allocation is increased, the classes of people who benefit from that system of political allocation and who have an interest in certain inequalities also increase. One can imagine a type of socialism in which this is not the case, but it is hard to imagine that it could exist.

In other words, the Soviet case is not that unexpected. Granted that there are peculiar aspects of Russian history to consider, and that socialism in Western Europe would probably look different. However, some of the basic tendencies would have to be there, and that is an internal contradiction (pardon the Marxist expression) of socialism, which in my opinion is not resolvable. The relative importance of market mechanisms as an allocation instrument is that it does not have this particular contradiction, whatever other problems it may have.

QUESTION: It seems that there is confusion in not distinguishing the kinds of socialism one encounters in the democratic countries and the kind of socialism one encounters in the Eastern bloc, where there is no popular influence over the decisions made by government bureaucrats. In the former, the question of which goods should be allocated politically is decided in the course of political debate, in the democratic culture at large, and the argument that political allocation is leading to totalitarianism, if it is done by democratic means, has absolutely no validity. After all, we are not tempted to make the United States more like the Soviet Union, but perhaps more like Denmark, or Sweden, or Germany, or Switzerland.

PROFESSOR BERGER: Frankly, when I wrote this, I had in mind the anticapitalist wave in the Western intelligentsia. They do not look to Sweden or West Germany. They look to East Germany, or Yugoslavia, or Mozambique. I agree with you that more interesting comparisons can be made with countries which are similar to us but a little further toward the political allocation pole.

Even if more equality is achieved through democratic means, however, it is done through an enormous expansion of the political mechanism that allocates, and that is what I am afraid of. I am not afraid of egalitarianism; it is the political consequences of an egalitarian thrust that I fear, because, for reasons I have already mentioned, that thrust tends to be totalitarian.

Capitalism and Socialism: Ethical Assessment

Peter Berger

The empirical facts about the contemporary world indicate that the capitalist societies—an ambiguous term, but we know which societies we are talking about—cannot objectively be considered bad either in the contemporary world or historically. There is much that is morally reprehensible in the Western world, and some of it has to do with capitalism. There are evil men doing ugly things in the board rooms of American corporations. Let us concede all of that.

Nevertheless, if one looks around the world today for hope, in terms of the values held by most people—where can one look? In terms of humanity, compassion, of justice or of innovativeness or daring, mostly in the societies of the West is there anything like hope.

The basic fact, in my own mind, in the contemporary world, is that we have a shrinking number of societies in which there is such hope. They are increasingly surrounded by various forms of totalitarianism, most of which consider themselves to be socialist. As I understand the concepts, they are quite accurately described as socialist or, as more toward the socialist pole than we are.

The profound mood of anticapitalism in the very societies that benefit from this kind of socioeconomic arrangement, therefore, requires explanation. Also to be explained is the fascination with a socialist mystique, the empirical realizations of which are, almost without exception, morally and humanly depressing. The fact that this viewpoint is concentrated in the cultural-intellectual elites of Western societies particularly requires explanation. There are two reasons for this phenomenon, and both of them have ethical implications.

The Problems of Modernization

The first reason has to do with the complexities and discontents of the modernization process. Modernization has brought a breakdown of the kind of community and solidarity within which human beings have lived through most of history. Incidentally, the pre-modern community should not be idealized or romanticized; some of this kind of solidarity was quite oppressive. But, at least people knew who they were, who they belonged to, and what the operative values in life were supposed to be. This was the case for most people most of the time; today it is true for fewer and fewer people.

This process of modernization and the alienation that goes with it historically has been linked to capitalism, and that linkage cannot be denied. A fundamental error of Marxism—one made by Marx himself and continued in every Marxist approach—is to see problems of modernization exclusively as problems of capitalism. In terms of classical logic, it is the fallacy of *pars pro toto*; in other words, a part of the phenomenon is seen as the exclusive cause.

The reason why the socialist vision has such persistent appeal, is that it is a vision of a restored community. It is a kind of world in which people will again know who they are and with whom they belong and will have operative values in common.

It is almost impossible not to sympathize with such a vision. Unfortunately, I am quite persuaded that in the modern world—a world that requires vast technological and bureaucratic support systems to keep the population alive, let alone affluent—such a vision cannot be realized. The fundamental contradiction of socialism (and I deliberately use a Marxist term here) is that every empirical attempt to realize its vision of solidarity has resulted in alienations far worse than it protested against in the first place.

The ethical implication of this contradiction is, to my mind, fairly simple. One could refer here to Max Weber's classical distinction between an ethic of absolute ends and an ethic of responsibility: morality and ethics can be seen either as the pursuit of visions of perfection or as a quest for what is possible within certain circumstances. I am almost fanatically in favor of the second as against the first. The quest of visions of perfection in human history, virtually without exception, has ended in disaster, and more so in this century, I think, than in any preceding one.

Certainly in a Judeo-Christian perspective, morality means to try to do the best with what one is given in a particular place and time, rather than to give up those possibilities of improvement in favor of a redemptive vision of total solidarity, total justice, or whatever. The reasons why socialism appears as a solution to the problems of modernization, and why it is a false appearance, have been developed at considerable length in a book I wrote with Brigitte Berger and Hausfried Kellner, *The Homeless Mind: Modernization and Consciousness* (1973).

The Self-Interest of the Cultural-Intellectual Elites

The socialist vision appeals because it is profoundly inspiring, and the nature of that inspiration can be fully analyzed. The second reason why the socialist vision appeals particularly to people in the cultural-intellectual elites of Western countries is that it is in their interest. I use the term "interest" in the most vulgar possible sense, with respect to the struggle for power and privilege.

On this point, I have nothing original to say. On the first issue I may have made some original contributions, but on this one, I am persuaded by what other people, particularly Irving Kristol, have said.

Fritz Machlup, the economist, used the term "knowledge-industry" for the first time, in the 1960s. Referring to the same phenomenon, some people have called it the second industrial revolution, while Daniel Bell, for example, has said we are actually moving into a postindustrial society. They all refer to the fact that, when a certain level of technology is reached, fewer and fewer people are employed in the production and distribution of goods, and more and more people are involved in administration and services. At the same time, more and more people are involved not in the production or distribution of things, but in the production and distribution of symbols—that is, in the knowledge industry. They are not simply the intellectuals: they compose a much broader group. Within this group, the intellectuals may be compared to the "captains of industry" in the group that comprises small businessmen and traveling salesmen.

There is a lively discussion going on today whether these people should or should not be called a "class." I think they should be called a class. In any case, whether they are called a class or anything else, they are people with particular interests. A German sociologist, Helmut Schelsky, summed up the interests of intellectuals nicely, except that I would apply his terms, not just to intellectuals, but to the entire class. Schelsky said the interests of the intellectuals are—and I will use the German terms, which are not easily translated—*Belehrung, Betreuung, Beplanung. Belehrung* means indoctrination, *Beplanung* means planning, *Betreuung* means caring for other people. In an essay I used the terms "beteaching," "beplanning," and "becaring," which suggests what these terms evoke, despite the poor English. In other words, this class is concerned with teaching other people how they should live, administering agencies that take care of other people's lives, and planning for the whole society as it moves into the future. Even in Western societies, these activities are largely in the public sector. That is, they are activities which thrive, or are perceived as thriving, on increases in the political allocation mechanism of the society.

To make this more concrete, the environmental issue may be taken as an example. In terms of the conventional wisdom among college-educated Americans today, there are on the one hand the special interests, which are by and large industrial; they are making a profit out of polluting the atmosphere and befouling the rivers. And then, on the other hand, there are the various upright defenders of the general welfare, like Ralph Nader and people of that sort; they have no personal interests in the matters, but are motivated only by morality, fighting the evil forces to save our clean air.

The conventional wisdom in this matter is, of course, nonsense. Let us concede that industry does not want to increase its costs by having to install antipollution devices in its plants. Let us even concede this in terms of the more radical statement that some industries have a vested interest in polluting the atmosphere, while alleging that they do not pollute the atmosphere.

The knowledge class also has a vested interest, in alleging that the air *is* dirty. Furthermore, it has a vested interest in creating institutions which, supposedly, regulate air pollution. The Environmental Protection Agency is a prime example of a governmental agency that provides power and privilege to members of the knowledge class. Whether this or that industry is in fact polluting the atmosphere (say, from the point of view of a physicist) is a different question and one in which I have no professional competence whatsoever. What I *do* know is that the people who say the atmosphere is being polluted have just as much of a vested interest as the people who say it is not being polluted.

The example can be carried across the board in terms of political and social issues today. The notion that the anticapitalist viewpoint is somehow virginally free of vested interest is, perhaps, the nonsense most in need of debunking in American public discourse today. This notion may not necessarily be wrong in every instance, but in the business of ethics, one must always ask what the person making a report may hope to gain from it. With an understanding of the class dynamics of contemporary Western society, it is not very difficult to answer that question, not just for industry, but also for Mr. Nader and other people who are supposedly concerned only with the general welfare of the people.

The knowledge class, or the new class, has a vested interest in perceiving Western societies as being very bad, because every important project to reform or revolutionize the status quo in Western societies is likely to increase in the power and privilege of this class. In other words, their ethical claim is suspect—though no more and no less than that of the other class.

The Statistical Relationship between Capitalism and Democracy

Let me come back to the issue of the ethical assessment of these matters and focus on the relation of capitalism to liberal democracy. Again, a statistical approach is useful, in these matters; something like the Freedom House reports are a good tool. In the world today, there is a checkerboard of societies, some of which are democratic. Not only do they have a formal process of elections, recognized opposition parties, and peaceful changes of government, but also, what is more important, there are institutional guarantees for human rights and liberties, which the government cannot whimsically change from one moment to the next.

Now, in this checkered world picture, there are some facts of fundamental interest. There is not a single democracy in the world today that does not belong to what, loosely speaking, can be called the world capitalist system—not one.

Within that world capitalist system, there are a number of societies that are not democratic, by any reasonable standard; and are violating human rights and liberties. That must be conceded. But no society that can be called democratic exists outside what was called the Free World during the Cold War (a term that was not as obfuscating as some people now think).

To put the same thing in negative terms, among those countries that can be called socialist, there is not a single country in which there is democracy. There is not a single country in which human rights and human liberties are even remotely protected against whimsical changes by the state. I find it fascinating that Western intellectuals, who have, to my mind, psychotic hopes for nations like Angola or Mozambique (let alone Vietnam, or North Korea), seem to have no interest whatsoever in the one socialist country that shows some promise along these lines. The rights I have mentioned are in better shape in Yugoslavia, a socialist country by any reasonable criterion, than anywhere else in the socialist world, though they are certainly in far worse shape there than in any country to the west.

This relationship between capitalism on the one hand and political democracy on the other is of immense ethical significance. The statistical picture becomes even more interesting when the category of totalitarianism is introduced. The inability to perceive what totalitarianism is is perhaps the most serious of the various delusions and dementias of Western intellectuals.

Confusion on this point can be found even in the rhetoric of American government, especially in that of the Carter administration, but also in earlier administrations. Democracies are constantly contrasted with dictatorships, as if all dictatorships were of the same sort. They are not at all.

An important distinction has to be made between totalitarian regimes and authoritarian regimes, both of which, of course, are dictatorships and not democracies. Hannah Arendt explained the difference in her *Origins of Totalitarianism* (1951). An authoritarian regime is one which does not permit political opposition. Brazil, for example, permits a little opposition but not much. The Philippines, South Korea, and Spain under Franco are other examples. A totalitarian system *not only* permits no political opposition, but also insists upon the political control of every institution in the society, including the family, education, religion, and so forth. That is the meaning of totalitarianism, a term that was coined, incidentally, not by its enemies but by those who wanted to foster it; namely, it is a term that comes from Nazi Germany. Goebbels, I think, invented the term "totalitarianism," and he thought it was a great thing that the brotherhood of the German nation would embrace everybody and every institution within the Nazi state.

This distinction may seem abstract, but it is not abstract at all. Anyone who has had any experience living in countries of these two types knows the difference in his bones. In an authoritarian regime, the probability is that people will be left alone if they keep their mouths shut. If they engage in political opposition, they get into trouble, and the trouble can be extreme; they can be tortured, and they may be shot. But if they shut up, if they engage in no activities inimical to the state, they can live with some peace. That is the essence of an authoritarian system. That is *not* the essence of a totalitarian system. It is not enough that the people shut up, and it is not enough that they do not oppose the government. Everything they do must be politically organized, by the party, by the state—where they worship (or if they do worship), their relationship with their children, their place of work—everything is mobilized by the central political authority of the society.

That is totalitarianism, and that, in my view, is the most overwhelming problem in the twentieth century. It is not poverty, which is an old problem; and it is not salvation, also an old problem. And it is not equality. The overwhelming moral problem of our time is the phenomenon of totalitarianism, which is new. There was never anything like totalitarianism in the past, for the simple reason that political authority did not have the technical means for this kind of control in the past.

To what extent Nazi Germany can be called a right wing or a left wing society, or a socialist or a capitalist society, is a very interesting question which I cannot pursue at this moment. But Nazi Germany, thank God, no longer exists. In the contemporary world, all totalitarian societies are socialist societies. In the contemporary world, not a single totalitarian society is part of the world capitalist system. Authoritarian societies are a part of it, but not totalitarian societies. Now, this, it seems to me, has ethical implications of enormous scope.

I have slummed around in all kinds of unsavory countries, particularly in the Third World. As long as an authoritarian society is not yet totalitarian, it can be empirically demonstrated that there is hope for revolutionary change. Once a totalitarian system has been imposed, that hope, it seems, comes pretty close to zero.

As Hannah Arendt pointed out, not a single totalitarian system of the twentieth century has been overthrown from within. Nazi Germany, of course, was overthrown from without, by war. There are modifications here and there of totalitarian systems; but their structure seems to have an incredible durability. These structures are survival-prone because of the control mechanisms available to them.

For concrete examples, compare Cuba and Uruguay, or compare Vietnam today with South Vietnam under the Thieu regime. Compare North Korea with South Korea; compare China with Taiwan. To compare these under the heading of "dictatorships" is absolutely crazy. If one neighbor were occasionally to slap his children while another tortured them and kept them locked and starving in the cellar, if both neighbors were equated as "child abusers" *that* would be somewhat similar to lumping together all these countries under the heading "dictatorships."

Please do not misunderstand me to be saying that everything in South Korea, for example, is great, or that South Korea is a democratic country. Comparing its human rights and human liberties with those of North Korea, however, is roughly equivalent to comparing Switzerland with the Empire of Ghengis Khan. In North Korea, one would never know that a dissident was in prison. He would disappear without a trace, and Amnesty International and Western liberal newspapermen would never be able to interview him, nor would his family or friends ever know what happened to him.

The statistical correlation of these phenomena with the world capitalist system is not accidental. In my mind, there is no mystery why it happens this way.

Socialism, whatever else it means, necessitates an increase in the sector of the society that makes political allocations. Whatever else it does, empirically socialism increases the power of government. The already enormously powerful reality of the modern state becomes even more powerful. In view of what human beings are (and I am afraid I am very Lutheran in my view of that), it is not surprising that such an increase in power should be misused. And the notion that the enormous power implied in socialism would be used benignly is not realistic.

The Totalitarian Future

As I see the world, its prospects are not very good. The chances for the survival of anything we call decency are questionable. We are probably moving into an age of increasing conflict, increasing scarcities, increasing tyranny, and, in fact, a steady advance of the totalitarian sectors of the earth. What ideological colors it will have—whether it calls itself Marxist-Leninist, or whether it is some new upsurge of fascist-type nationalism—is irrelevant.

Social and political totalitarianism has, I am very much afraid, a bright future. Important segments of the intellectual and cultural elite of the Western world—the very ones who should offer some hope— tend to despise their own societies and to look for hope in places like North Korea, Mozambique, and God knows where. That this should be the case at such a moment in history is, in terms of ethics, an obscenity. It is something that a future age (if we leave any records for future historians to read) will see as one of the great cases of collective psychosis in human history.

A few years ago I was in Denmark, where I had never been before. Some of my books had come out in Danish, and the publisher wanted me to talk at various universities so I traveled all over Denmark. The country is delightful, the Danes are very congenial people, and I had a very good time. By any sane criterion, this is a decent society. There is virtually no poverty in Denmark. There is a welfare state, how-ever much one may criticize it, which does take care of virtually every serious problem people have—sickness, disability, whatever. It is a society with few minorities, but such as it has, are treated admirably (foreign workers, for example). If there is a place that is a decent society, it is Denmark.

Then I talked to the intellectuals, and with a straight face, with no sense of irony, with no sense of the madness of what they were saying, I heard them say again and again: "Denmark is like the Third Reich," "We live in a fascist society," "We live in a society which is humanly intolerable."

At one university, there was a campaign under way for students to volunteer to do work in a socialist country. It was something like the Venceremos Brigades of American students who volunteered to work in Cuba. Cuba is a bit too far from Denmark, however, so these students were going to Albania. There were posters all over the campus about Albania, and the well-scrubbed young Danes were lining up to work on the railroad in Albania. What is Albania? It calls itself Marxist-Leninist; it is, in fact, a kind of medieval tyranny. In comparison with other nations in Europe, it is almost a kind of Mongol regime. It is the one country in the world, as far as I know, where infant baptism is a crime, where all worship is prohibited, not only in public, but also in private. A person is thrown in jail if caught praying. That is Albania—a place of tyranny, of incredible poverty.

That was an ideal for these Danish intellectuals. That may be regarded as an extreme case, but it is no more extreme than the succession of utopias these people have acclaimed since the 1930s. One has the feeling one is reading a report from a psychiatric hospital.

It seems to me that those people who regard our society as intolerable—those who are looking for a revolution that derives its inspiration from Russia or China or wherever—are engaged not only in an intellectual mistake, but in a moral offense. I think it will weigh heavily on the Day of Judgment, if there is a Day of Judgment (and I take it that people in this room, like myself, incline to the view that there is). On such a Day of Judgment we will be called to account, and we will be called to account for having missed that moment in history in which we could do something about decency, compassion, and justice. We missed it in favor of a dream that satisfied our own aspirations, and to some extent our own interests. We missed the moment to pursue a dream of impossibility. In serving a dream of impossibility, we abandon the possibilities for improving the human condition that, in fact, are available to us.

Discussion

QUESTION: The way in which you have described the New Class could leave the impression it is univocal, that the people in it all tend to do the same thing. In just the academic community, however, there are some who are in favor of the status quo, some who are reformers, and some who are radicals. Among my colleagues, I know people whose mentalities I would describe as aristocratic, some archaic, some reformist—in short, a great variety. The fear that lurks in the back of my mind is one of premature generalization.

Let me give an example. Wherever I travel, I read all of the local newspapers, and while certain intellectual writers in journalism on the Eastern Seaboard may be said to belong to the New Class, in a pejorative sense, that description simply does not fit the press in most parts of the nation. In other words, I have the uneasy feeling that a great deal of attention is given to the New York intellectual scene and that premature generalizations are made from that. Even when one looks there, I find it difficult to see the New York *Times*, or the Washington *Post*, as vanguards of anticapitalism.

PROFESSOR BERGER: Class consciousness is a statistical matter. In other words, there is a frequency distribution of certain values and beliefs. In any particular class, there is a certain preponderance of a certain kind of consciousness, but it is not overpowering. There are always some who go against it for one reason or another. To come to the point at issue, anticapitalism, in some shape or form, has a very high frequency distribution among knowledge class members. It is not absolute but it is certainly predictable, statistically.

Now, if you are saying that we need more empirical data, I agree with you. The whole concept of a New Class is new, and we need more data. On the other hand, you say that the world does not consist of New York. Of course, neither does it consist of Detroit. Yet when looking at the manufacture and distribution of motor cars, it is Detroit we have to be concerned with, not our local car salesman. In the same way, there are centers for the production and distribution of symbols. There is a media power complex which can be definitely located, consisting of the three networks, the two major news magazines, and a number of metropolitan newspapers. I am not saying that flaming socialists surround these institutions, but their points of view, broadly speaking, tend to the left, on both international and domestic issues. This media complex is related to knowledge-class interests much more than are the small town newspapers.

Finally, I did not say that the socialist vision is appealing exclusively because of these class interests. That is one important factor. I spent more time on it than on other factors because I think it is less known.

QUESTION: There are two points I would like to make. First, I was intrigued by your distinction between authoritarian and totalitarian social organization. Using your own illuminating terminology, it might be wise to compare the political totalitarianism of the so-called socialist countries with what might be termed the "economic totalitarianism" of the West. In other words, we have a political freedom which is certainly undreamed of in Albania, for instance, but with regard to economic life, there is a certain totalitarianism exercised here, in that so much emphasis is placed on the market system and on economies of scale as a way of measuring things. A member of a country who is considered totally as a citizen of that country, as in, say, revolutionary China, certainly has his humanity denied to a certain extent. However, if one's totality is defined as an employee or as a consumer, then I think his humanity is also denied.

Secondly, it appears that much confusion is raised by an equivocation in your use of the word "capitalism," sometimes referring to Western liberal society and sometimes referring to a particular kind of economic system connected with private capital. Much of what we value in Western society—trade unionism, the ecological movement, and so forth—is the result not of capitalism as an economic system but of social criticism of the excesses of that economic system. Capitalism, as an economic system, certainly does not generate the environmental movement—no more than it generated the labor movement. To say otherwise is to completely dismiss the fact that those movements arose as adversary movements, against tendencies in the economic realm.

PROFESSOR BERGER: In regard to your first comment, there are obviously some things to which you point which are empirically there—for instance, the permeation of life by certain kinds of advertising—but to

107

compare that to totalitarianism strikes me as very strange. No one is being coerced to consume all of these things. Suppose that we do live in a society in which people are bombarded with messages which, if taken seriously, would make them profit-hungry and overly mobile. There is an enormous difference between that and a political structure which coerces, with terrible sanctions, the individual to organize his life according to the wishes of the government. In Vietnam a peasant has no choice; whether he moves or stays, and where he moves is determined by the government. If someone is offered more money for a job in a different part of the country, is he being forced to move? I don't see any comparison.

This relates directly to your second comment. You mentioned adversary movements which are discouraged by the captains of industry. What I find interesting is that in a capitalist economy, such adversary movements have a chance to appear. I do not think that is accidental. If we are interested in humane values—economic rights, civil liberties, cultural innovation—then we need an enormous interest in the institutionalization of adversary relations, and those are correlated with capitalism in a way which does not exist in the socialist ideal, let alone the present realities of socialist countries.

Seven Theological Facets

Michael Novak

One of my former graduate students visited not long ago, and wrote to a friend about her visit: "I obtained one of the rarest commodities in the world, an unpublished thought of Michael Novak." You are about to receive what will soon become a most common commodity, one of my published thoughts. I will divide my remarks into seven parts.

1. The Call of God

Some of you will remember that the *Summa* of Thomas Aquinas has the structural shape of an hourglass, the world issuing forth from God, and the world returning to God, passing through at the central point Jesus, the Christ. This *Imago Christi* is for him the central metaphor for the entire universe. To talk about the shape of a political or an economic order is to look for a way to fulfill the vocation of the universe, to find the way the human race may best return to God. The commandment of God which has been the best observed of all the commandments, is recorded in Genesis as, "Be fruitful, multiply and fill the earth." If only we had fulfilled all the other commandments as thoroughly! Our obedience to this command has been so exemplary as now to constitute a danger.

The course of fulfilling that commandment, however, required, in relatively recent history, some extraordinary strides which we now take for granted. It required mastery over many forms of illness, extreme poverty, and all those other dangers that for most of recorded history made *under*-population the chief threat to the human race.

The human race experienced for much of its short life on this planet a fairly precarious existence. In Siena, the most beautiful village of Italy, one can still mark out with one's own feet the outlines of the cathedral that was to have been built there. The present structure—still the second or third largest in the world—forms but one arm of what was projected. The unfinished foundations of the original plan remain. During the years of construction, the population of Siena was decimated by the Plague and the city's growth was aborted.

A degree of mastery over illness; the delay of death; and the consequent multiplication of the world's populations—all these victories over harsh nature have occurred only in the modern period. The habits of science and technical practicality nourished under democratic capitalism made these victories possible.

A few theological remarks. Only three religions among all the world religions have taught that the salvation of human beings requires responsibility for the making of history. Salvation is seen by these religions not as an escape from history, but as the building up of God's kingdom, to speak metaphorically, or the humanizing of the earth, making what was perceived to be a hostile planet into a planet friendly to the human race. Judaism, Christianity, and Islam, the religions of Abraham, are *historical*, uniquely so, in that they take history seriously. That is an important point.

The second important point to make about the perception of God's call in these religions is that the call is communal. The task of salvation is one in which we must, in brotherly and sisterly fashion, lay our shoulders to the wheel together. Our salvation is not merely individual, and the call does not merely come to us one by one. It comes to the entire communities of which we are a part—Judaism, Christianity, Islam.

Thirdly, in all three of these historical religions, the very principle of the possibility of history is respected; namely, the appeal of God to the individual conscience, the freedom of the individual conscience.

It is because each human individual is a source of liberty, a source of decision, that history is possible. Otherwise, there is only nature, only necessity. Because each of us is an originating source of imagination and action, and because God appeals to that spark of the divine that is within each, the cosmological image and the image of the individual are patterned on one another. As the cosmos is historical, so the individual is free.

The principle of history is liberty. The liberty of human beings, individually, to imagine a vision, to conceive plans, and to execute actions, creates the possibility of history.

2. The Contributions of Socialism

It is important to notice the contributions socialism has made to our conception of life, and especially to our religious social vision in the United States. Since others addressing this conference have been critical of socialism, I think it is especially important to bring out these contributions.

First, socialism has a major advantage over capitalism because its basic texts supply, explicitly and immediately, a moral vision. Whereas capitalist writings tend to limit themselves to economic man, a cunning abstraction from human life useful for economic considerations, socialist writings, by and large, tend to be holistic and to assume the form of moral philosophy. From the beginning, socialists have described a moral vision, and tried to imagine a society within which certain moral values are preserved. That is an important advantage.

A second advantage of socialism over capitalism lies in its stress on sociality and fraternity—an important corrective of the Anglo-Scot tradition. Few American books celebrate this ideal. Wilson Carey McWilliams, Jr., has done so in *The Idea of Fraternity in America.* That book stands as virtually the sole study of the fraternal spirit in America.

Most of the writings of our tradition have, by contrast, emphasized the role of the individual. Few have pointed out that, in actual practice, we are a most fraternal society, as may be seen in the cooperation required to raise barns and houses on the frontier as well as the ease with which we perform that most American act, establishing committees.

We are an astonishingly social people. One of the contributions of the writings of socialists in the United States was that they redressed an intellectual imbalance by bringing out the importance of human sociality. Socialists imported theoretical concepts designed to emphasize the ways in which a proper analysis of human life requires attention to the communal and the social, as well as to the individual. America needed this contribution.

A related contribution was to bring American religion, too, to social consciousness—to expand the Anglo-Scot tradition of individualism to include social consciousness even in our understanding of religion.

The third contribution of socialism to the United States was to add to the antifeudal impulse of the culture some theory, structure, and weight. Most would speak of an "egalitarian" impulse, but it seems more accurate to say antifeudal. I say that because, in the contemporary period, a number of socialist writers—I cite Irving Howe—have emphasized that our idea of equality under socialism must not be too naive. By equality, socialism does not mean that each individual will be paid by the same wage rate, or that all work ought to be equally rewarded financially. That, Howe says, would be a naive view of socialism. There are differences of talent and function in the human world, as in every part of nature, and in a just and, above all, creative social order, these differences would be rewarded, according to a socialist vision.

A last remark. Many of the criticisms Irving Kristol made of socialism as a form of gnosis can also be made of the ideology that accompanied the rise of capitalism. Social Darwinism, the raw abstraction of economic man, and other doctrines about the rise of capitalism were equally false in their estimates of human nature. The myth of the dynamo, which to Henry Adams in his book on Mont Saint-Michel and Chartres had replaced the myth of the virgin, exalted the notion that progress is our most important product, that we may achieve a "better world through chemistry." This myth, too, has gnostic elements.

Thus, part of our task, insofar as we would wish to rescue socialism and to rescue capitalism is to save both sides equally from gnosticism. Neither socialist nor capitalist thought is adequate to the realities which we have experienced and from within which we cry out for new theories. Both need revision.

3. The Trinitarian American System

What I mean by a trinitarian system is that there are three working systems here that must function well together for the system, as a whole, to be healthy. These are the political system, the economic system, and the cultural system (I am borrowing this, of course, from Daniel Bell's *The Cultural Contradictions of Capitalism*). Our system, the system under which we live in the United States and for which we do not have an adequate name, is in terms of its political component a democracy. In its second component, the economic, it relies quite heavily, but not totally, on enterprise. It is, thirdly, a liberal culture.

Writers on our subject tend to take up the first two of these systems and to treat them rather well, but in isolation from one another. The economists have written rather well of the economic system, but their writings are unsatisfactory when compared with one's own experience, because we do not live merely in an economic system. The political scientists have written rather well of political democracy and the way in which the United States is both like and unlike other democracies. Not many have made all the connections between the political system and the economic system.

The least developed of all elements in our theory, however, is the cultural system. How and in what ways does our cultural system mesh with our political system and our economic system? How and in what ways does our culture undermine those systems, or do they undermine it? The humanists and the more humanistically inclined social scientists have not kept up their end of the investigation. They have lacked sufficient economic and political consciousness to keep up the intellectual standing of their own area of responsibility.

Thus, our understanding of ourselves is sadly deficient. We have an inferior understanding of the cultural dimensions of the economic and political systems in which we live.

Our system, then, is trinitarian. By contrast, socialism is monistic. The impulse within socialism is to collapse all three of these systems into one; a single monistic system in which the harmony of the political, the economic, and the cultural sound one note.

It may be true that social democrats alert to that danger would want to insist that socialism, too, needs to be a trinitarian system, with the political order and the economic order and the cultural order each remaining independent. They, too, may desire a pluralistic system, in which each part, while working with the others, nevertheless, represents a check and balance on them. But this is difficult when the "public" sphere, which in practice is the political organism, determines everything.

Socialism, as a program, is continually being revised. It is important to keep speaking of socialism as a vision, a moral vision, encompassing economic, political, and cultural life, because the specifics of the socialist program have been profoundly modified. Virtually all the classic characteristics of a socialist system have been abandoned by socialists over the last sixty years. The notion that the socialist movement is distinguished by being international and antinationalist has been abandoned. The notion that socialism ought to be monocentric, that it ought to move forward as one movement with a single center, and that the Soviet Union is the single voice of the socialist movement, has long since been abandoned.

The notion that the favored technique of a socialist government is the nationalization of industry has been abandoned. The Swedish Prime Minister Olof Palme, on his last visit to the United States, said that nationalization by and large does not work, and that socialists would be silly to commit themselves to it, except in special cases where it does show promise of success. Finally, the firmly entrenched notion that what distinguishes socialism is a program of welfare benefits may also be radically modified as we gain greater experience with the implications of building a complete welfare system; implications of expense and bureaucratization.

I repeat, it seems important to think of socialism rather more as a vision, emphasizing the sociality of human responsibility for the social and political order, than as a set of specific historical programs, or a mere mechanism of political allocation.

4. The Theology of Incarnation

We must examine the Jewish-Christian culture, within which capitalism, in recent times, was incarnated. Capitalism is not very old. Probably three or four hundred years is a generous estimate of its actual functioning life. It has thrived on a relatively small portion of the planet, for its first eight or nine generations, largely in Jewish-Christian cultures.

This cultural system, within which the economic system of capitalism was inserted, set certain limits and controls upon that system. Capitalism might have been very different in some other setting. It is often forgotten that Adam Smith envisaged three books, not one. One was the study of the political system, one of the moral system, and only the third (*The Wealth of Nations*) of the economic system. He intended them to be read as one.

There was, in the Anglo-Scottish world of the seventeenth, eighteenth, and nineteenth centuries, almost uniquely in world history a high intellectual emphasis on the individual. In most parts of the world, human beings do not perceive themselves primarily as individuals, but primarily as members of families and groups. Eric Voegelin points out that Plato was the first writer to record an act of individual self-consciousness. There an individual, Socrates, for the first time imagined himself governed by laws and rules separate from those governing his community, to such an extent that he could be obliged in conscience to violate the rules of the community. When the community condemned him to death, Socrates could obey in some peace, because he still shared the older form of consciousness, that the community had its rights. He left unresolved, in some tension, the rights of the individual over against the rights of society.

Individual consciousness did not emerge equally everywhere on earth. It would be wrong to think that all around this planet human beings imagine themselves to be individuals, or would understand that commercial that says a certain hair rinse will "free the true woman within you." What if there is no unique individual inside? In any case, a high sense of the individual—of the "rights of Englishmen"—was extraordinarily highly developed in few parts of the world.

There also existed in English culture—perhaps less in theory than in fact—a very strong sense of community responsibility, of stewardship, including concerns for welfare. Someone in the community—very often the church organization, quite often the family—was responsible for the crippled uncle or the child that was retarded or the grandparents no longer able to work. The community, Jewish and Christian, like many other communities in the world, could not merely abandon such persons. The community recognized a religious responsibility to care for the needy and the poor. Jewish and Christian communities had a strong sense of family life, though it was not often articulated in essays, treatises, and books. The family was regarded as a sacred institution, as a metaphor of the relationship of God with the world, as an instrument of creativity, sharing in the creative action of God.

Apart from such cultural notions, the sudden introducton of the capitalist system, a powerful new instrument for generating wealth, would have caused enormous dislocations, and perhaps totally destroyed western society. And, as a matter of historical fact, the introduction of capitalism came very close to doing just that.

The introduction of a free market mechanism, respecting individuals apart from ties of kinship, seems to fulfill the Jewish-Christian emphasis on the individual, but it wreaked havoc with the schemes of community, welfare, and family by which prior Jewish-Christian cultures had lived.

The economic component of the system, in short, began to undercut—and to this very day continues to undercut—the other two components of the system. There are tendencies within the economic sector that generate desires, fulfill desires, and generate still more desires, so as to make plausible the notion that the pursuit of liberty is the pursuit of hedonism. These tendencies undercut the habits of discipline, saving, and restraint which make possible the accumulation of capital, wise investment for the future, and the continued health of the economic system. Thus, one part of the system can unleash forces that weaken the other two.

Reciprocally—and this comment may help to explain why I have a certain aversion to what Kristol, Berger, and others have called the new class—the spread in the cultural sector of the system of ideas hostile to family, hostile to local communities, hostile to the kind of ascetic, disciplined interior life required for Jewish and Christian development may also undercut the political and economic systems. Because of the spread of malicious, nihilistic, and destructive ideas in the cultural sector, because of the spread of hedonism or other abuses, the disciplines required for a democratic politics become quite difficult to maintain.

In short, the Jewish-Christian cultural system nourished specific values for nearly three thousand years. These values modified, and were modified by, the successive economic systems in western history. Today, after having been assaulted by several generations of hostile thinkers, the cultural preconditions for the health of the economic and the political components may be undermined. One can imagine, for example, that a generation from now, more and more people will not want to work. Even today with a little bit of luck and a little help from their friends, people can live until thirty without ever holding a job, going from fellowship to fellowship and, alternately working for a little while and going on unemployment. Anyone who really wants to, can live like a kid until the age of fifty. A striking number of people in our society already alternate between work and paid unemployment in such a way that they work only half or less than half of the time. They have no great ambition to be powerful or rich. They are content to enjoy the sun; they collect their unemployment checks in Aspen. One can imagine that spirit spreading. Every aspect of our system would then begin to suffer the consequences: in workmanship, in the reliability of products, in capital formation, in skills and disciplines of many kinds.

This should be enough, by way of example, to suggest that our tripartite system might be destroyed through the economic order, through the political order, or through the cultural order.

5. Jewish-Christian Values in Capitalism

I have already mentioned that the presence of socialists in our midst has brought about a recognition of some of the deficiencies of the capitalist ideology. What specific values in capitalist ideology and in capitalist practice did the Jewish-Christian culture respond to affirmatively? In the same way, one might ask, What values were there in feudalism that Judaism and Christianity could embrace? And they did embrace them; since they had no alternative, they made the best they could of feudalism. Similarly, in eastern Europe and in some other places, there are strong efforts by theologians, philosophers, novelists, and writers to make the best that can be made out of socialism. The question I am raising is, What values might a Jewish-Christian culture affirm in capitalism?

There is a preparatory point that should be made. From a Jewish-Christian perspective, no social and political order represents *the* way. Judaism and Christianity are wanderers' religions, always *in*, but not *of*, the world. No matter how much we would embrace any one system, we would always be prepared to imagine that there is a better one, and that this system must be abandoned, and that the march must be begun again in yet another direction. So we must be cautious in thinking that capitalism or socialism or any other alternative might be the fulfillment of Judaism or Christianity. We are a pilgrim people.

The first characteristic of capitalism that is reassuring to a Jewish-

Christian culture is its sense of experiment, openness, and innovation, which is captured by the word "enterprise."

The fundamental intellectual and social gamble proposed by the first exponents of capitalism was as follows: if a society will liberate private individuals to pursue their own self-interests and to invest their own resources—and allow them to take the rewards with the risks—it will generate the greatest burst of imagination and creativity the world has ever seen. It will experience a great leap forward. Capitalism—they said—will free human imagination and human intelligence as they have never been free before. To do so, they argued, is socially of greater utility than is any effort to manage the economy by the state, by the king, by the chancellor of the exchequer, or by committees. To permit individuals to win such rewards through the market is also less costly, because individuals risk their own resources, not those of the state treasury.

I want to draw attention to the fact that the gamble concerned imagination. It is astonishing to contemplate that this gamble was taken in the British Isles—a nation so small in population, and so remote, and one not particularly favored in climate or national resources. In a short space of time it achieved a staggering explosion of adventure, of imagination, and of achievement.

It is that history-making function, that explosion, that capacity to alter history, that, I think, has properly excited the Jewish and Christian imagination. The inventiveness of God is respected through respecting the inventiveness of human beings.

A second attractive feature of the capitalist ideology was that it emphasized the humbleness of the human race. It emphasized—not that we are a community of saints, or even of brothers and sisters, because we are not so yet—but, rather, that we are a community of sinners. Capitalist ideology is depressing to read. Its economics has been called "the dismal science," because it takes human beings quite in their weakness. It follows the paradox of Isaiah and of Christ, that redemption should come in the most unlikely spot, through the weakest and the poorest of persons, as in the carpenter from a very poor and undeveloped part of the Roman Empire. In a related way, capitalist thinkers discovered the dynamic energy to change the face of history not where it might be expected, in human nobility, grandeur, and moral consciousness, but in human self-interest. In the pettiest and narrowest and meanest part of human behavior lies the source of creative energy —a magnificent and, I think, absolutely Jewish and Christian, insight. Where no one would choose to look the jewels are to be found. It is a rather humbling insight about human nature that we must accept human beings in their sinfulness rather than in their grandeur. At the heart of Christianity, according to Leon Bloy, lies the sinner. At the heart of capitalist creativity lies self-interest.

This self-interest must be understood in a rather large sense. It is not just the self-interest of the individual that is important, although a fresh recognition of individual self-interest was one of the great contributions the immigrants to the United States added to Anglo-Saxon moralism, as Professor Lipset has noted. His lecture made me recall that marvelous sentiment of Finley Peter Dunne's Mr. Dooley, "When a fella says 'Taint the money, it's the principle,' it's the money." Well, in the same way, it is not only self-interest that is at stake here. The larger point concerns the role of evil in history. Teilhard de Chardin points out the incredible numbers of species of living things which have disappeared since the recorded beginnings of the universe. Forms of life have been thrown up in profusion on this planet. Many species had to die for every one that lived; millions of individuals died so that the species might live. One of the things the paleontologist notices is the prodigality of the Creator, who raised up and destroyed so many living things, in order that those which were to prosper and to live might survive.

We live in a world, after all, which has been and is harsh to human beings. There, too, capitalism has had a not pleasant, but harsh, sense of reality that runs counter to the niceness which a certain kind of Christianity tends to place over life. Capitalism builds the sense that, in Biblical terms, a kind of cosmic pessimism is not entirely out of keeping with human reality. The recognition of the whole dimension of evil is implicit in capitalism, despite its often false rhetoric of optimism and progress and betterment.

Thirdly, the capitalist order was a value-conferring order. Under the aegis of capitalism, tremendous value was conferred upon parts of nature which had never been valued before. Black liquid lay under the sands of Araby for thousands of years, and even was known to lie there, but it had only limited value until a civilization was erected that found a way to use that oil, and conferred tremendous wealth on the territories under which that oil lay. So it is, with any number of metals, minerals, sound waves, light rays: humble elements of nature, which never were valued before, were made objects of value, and objects of human betterment.

It is as though creation was left in an unfinished state, as though human beings were called forth to be co-creators and to discover values in what nature itself wasted, polluted, destroyed, and abandoned recklessly: things awaited human beings for a recognition of their value and the invention of ways to make them things of value.

To put this point the other way, there is a not-niceness in nature. The pollution of one thing by another, the destructiveness wrought by one part of nature upon another part of nature, was not first brought about by human intervention, and it was not first brought about by industrialization. Nature was raw and cruel to nature long before human beings intervened. It may be doubted whether human beings have ever done one-tenth of the polluting to nature that nature has done to itself. There is infinitely more methane gas—poisonous in one respect, and damaging to the environment—generated by the swamps of Florida and other parts of the United States than by all the automobile pollution of all places on this planet. In our superhuman efforts to be nice and to feel guilty, we sometimes try to take all the credit for pollution, improperly.

The fourth value Jewish-Christian culture has recognized in capitalism comes under the theological symbolism of light—the reliance of this economic and political order on the values of intelligence and invention. Recall the Royal Societies of invention developed in our history, the emphasis on the advancement of science, the suggestion boxes in the factories, the patent offices. Tremendous pride, joy, and pleasure in invention have spread through our society.

Every year, my family and I return to my wife's home in Iowa. We have often witnessed auto races. The old cars ride out before the grandstand, and thousands cheer while young fellows compete to see who can wreck other cars and stay unwrecked the longest. Some see this as a terrible celebration of destruction. It is just the opposite: it is the most marvelous celebration of resurrection. Each of those cars has been destroyed countless times and resurrected by young fellows working until five in the morning to bring them back into shape for the next week's events. This pride taken in the farm country in being able, by human intelligence and human resourcefulness, to make impossible things possible, to make things run, is impressive. And during the Bicentennial celebration there, as they trotted out the wooden plows and the wagons with wooden wheels from a hundred years ago, with hardly any metal on anything, we realized that Iowa was an undeveloped country, in the period of our grandparents.

The inventiveness of those people led to today's staggering two-story tractors with air conditioning, miniature television sets, and hi-fis. It is absolutely astonishing, the valuation placed upon intelligence applied to daily activities that has been encouraged in this culture.

Once launched into the world, this became a very high value, and it is no longer the property of capitalism only. Yet it was the capitalist order that first saw the enormous social value of practical intelligence.

6. The Problems of Industrial and of Welfare Capitalism

The problem of industrial capitalism, the earlier form of our society, was that the ideology of the time was individualistic, paternalistic, and blithely optimistic about the benefits of progress. I have just completed writing the story of a labor struggle in northeastern Pennsylvania, in the coal fields of 1897, and the massacre of some fifty striking miners.[1] The story of the coal operators is quite marvelous. They were poor boys who first saw the special value of anthracite coal, invented ways to make it burn, invented ways to get it out of the ground, invented machinery to handle lots of it quickly, dug the most incredible tunnels, developed all kinds of new gears, cutters, and gadgets, and found ways of transporting the coal quickly to markets. Two or three men did it, brilliant men. To read about their philosophy of life and their philosophy of themselves is, on the one hand, terribly impressive and, on the other, very depressing.

Their attitude towards their workers was one of paternalism, at best, and in certain ways, it was harsh and callous. Yet they felt pride that they, by their imagination and efforts, had made possible the economic uplifting of all the people of the valley. They could see how much better life had become than it had been when they entered the valley. This mix of their own sense of humane accomplishment and their own callousness provided an ideology much too narrow, though not entirely ugly, with which the United States might enter the twentieth century.

Concerning the problems of welfare capitalism at the present time, we still lack adequate theory, intelligence, symbol, imagination. In 1935, John Dewey wrote a little book called *Liberalism and Social Action*, in which he argued that there have been four ages of liberalism in the past, in every one of which liberalism was opposed to the state. Yet now, for the first time, he argued, liberals should entertain a different attitude towards the state and the central government. They should enter a new age of liberalism. According to this new attitude, they should cease regarding the state as a moral enemy and regard the state not merely as a neutral force, but as a force for moral good.

In the context of the time, and given the emergency of the time,

---

[1] *The Guns of Lattimer* (New York: Basic Books, 1978).

I think many of us would agree that Dewey's was a proper, helpful, and creative intellectual step. Dewey provided a theory—and later, with Reinhold Niebuhr and others, helped to found Americans for Democractic Action and the Liberal party in New York—which provided a vehicle for experiments in economic and political policy, together with an intelligible philosophy for carrying forward their purposes. Dewey and his followers achieved a great deal of good.

Their theory was verified by its fruits. By regarding the federal government as a friend instead of as an enemy, a great deal of good was accomplished for average, ordinary Americans. In the year 1900, over half of the people of the United States were living below levels of subsistence. By 1932, not many were better off. If it were not for their accomplishment, I sometimes think that I would still be working in the mills or mines of western Pennsylvania, and many of us would be working on farms, and our families would still be trying to pay off mortgages. Many of us who are here in this room would still be living in exiguous poverty. (There are frustrations to academic living, but I keep reminding myself, it beats heavy lifting.)

Much of the progress our nation has made is attributable to the adjustments made in the economic and political order by the New Deal. We are beneficiaries of that Deal. However, when we turn toward state bureaucracy, there are penalties to be paid. Slowly but surely there comes a point at which increments in state activity become more and more marginal and have less and less benefit. Indeed, increments in state activity begin to have destructive consequences. Part of our problem is that the solution that did indeed once work now seems to have reached the point where it, itself, has become a problem or a danger. There is too much state, too much bureaucracy, too much loss of liberty and vitality, too much paternalism, too much encouragement to the prudes and the moralists among us, who have become our nannies. (I become infuriated when I sit down in my automobile and Ralph Nader buzzes at me for half a minute.)

7. A Different Arrangement in the Future

How might we begin to orient ourselves philosophically and culturally toward a different adjustment of political, economic, and cultural systems, so that we might be able to save the best in the vision of socialism, and the best in the vision of capitalism?

I have been attracted by the notion which Professor Eugen Loebl and Mr. Stephen Roman have put forward in *The Responsible Society* of trying to imagine this state functioning less as the actor in the future drama and more as the regent.[2] The superiority of the socialist dream was that it inspired human beings, especially in their communal responsibility and their vision of a just society. Socialism has spoken better to the heart than capitalism has. Let us try to save that. Let us also try to save the superior capitalist sense of sin, the capitalist sense that self-interest can be redeemed, not by trying to repress it or deny it, but by trying to give it expression in a system of checks and balances.

We must save where we can the power of self-interest and of incentives. We must also try to save the superiority of the capitalist sense of enterprise, of imagination, of invention. It is in these areas that our system seems to be superior to the Soviet system. They do many things very well, but we seem to have so many more technological breakthroughs, which they then try to buy from us. That, I think, is the subject of Solzhenitsyn's complaint; that where their system breaks down, we keep coming to its rescue.

How can we promote enterprise while expanding nonbureaucratic welfare? We need to maintain the sense of welfare and responsibility, while trying to find ways to do so nonbureaucratically. I really don't know how that can be done, though I think this is the right question. When in the future will we find a philosophy, a theory, and a set of programs that promote enterprise, imagination, and risk and encourage private groups to do things, while caring for the poor more than we do now? We must do it in a better and less expensive way, a way that creates less self-interest among the bureaucrats who administer the programs, so that we do not create a new force of oppression as we try to alleviate a problem.

I have been attracted by Professor Loebl's notion that the state might function not as the agent—doing everything through its own offices—so much as the provider of capital, the regent. Suppose that the state provided capital to people with which they could do things while operating in a system of enterprise. That is, they would draw loans from the government, the same way they now draw loans from banks, and they would pay back those loans at different degrees of interest for different purposes.

If the state wanted to encourage, say, home ownership, it might provide the money at a very favorable rate of interest for a time. Or if the state wanted to provide employment in the ghettos, it might provide capital to employ the young men and women of the ghetto in that most obvious of tasks, repairing the potholes, and painting the wood and sanding the floors of some of the best housing in America, in its old

---

[2] *The Responsible Society* (New York: Regina Ryan, Two Continents, 1978).

neighborhoods. Then, as workers finished this work, enough money would be made to repay the loans to the government, and the funds would be reinvested in other projects. I am not enough of an economist to be able to weigh the value of Loebl's ideas, but their attraction to a theologian must be obvious.

Discussion

QUESTION: You and others are saying that we have moved from a political situation in which social welfare programs were proscriptive, to a situation in which they are prescriptive. That is one of the prescriptive tendencies that Kevin Phillips has condemned in what he calls the "balkanization of America." A lot of interest groups are now demanding recognition, including black groups, feminist groups, and mediating structures. Phillips says this effort to develop or encourage small segments of society is tending to break the United States apart. Is there a danger in terms of fragmenting the culture to a pathological degree?

PROFESSOR NOVAK: In a short answer, yes. The trick is to develop a common culture which is truly common; that is, in which every voice feels as though it is legitimate, and it is, at least to some extent, being heard. We can err on either side. We can prematurely create a unity in which different elements are left out, as, for example, when we describe the American character in terms of the upper-class Northeasterner. On the other hand, people can sheer off in different directions, and fail to come together. I think Kevin Phillips misses the most important point, though. One of the unique things at the present moment is not the emphasis on differences—but the insistence of so many groups on declaring rights.

Now, the problem with declaring rights is that to do so is to ask for much more than tolerance. If we declare rights, we are imposing obligations on others. I have no problem whatever in expanding, for example, the dimensions of tolerance for homosexuals. But I resist strongly the notion that it is a right to which I must now defer on moral grounds. Different interests can be pursued without raising them to the level of rights.

QUESTION: There is one aspect of capitalism that I think is necessary to look upon as Christians—that is, the idea of how much is enough.

If the good life is the simple life, then what is good is only pertinent if one knows how much is enough. In the United States people have lost sight of what is enough, and therefore they are no longer particularly aware of what is good. If we are still caught in this idea of continued economic growth, sooner or later a nemesis will destroy whatever we do have.

PROFESSOR NOVAK: I agree with your principles. The first point is that there are always many more Americans than we think who settle for enough. I remember my father turning down a promotion that would have brought more money and opportunity. It required traveling, and he wanted to spend more time with his family. I suspect in everybody's family, out of every four people there are three who did something like that.

In addition, we all have come to face the limitations of resources, which are teaching us that there are limits to growth. When I grew up in Johnstown, Pennsylvania, a purple red dust filled the sky between the valleys and settled on the leaves of all the trees. It was regarded as a sign of our superiority over the Indians who, after all, did not know about the iron ore and coal. It came as a shock to me when our county was listed as the second poorest in Appalachia, and the seventh most polluted county in the United States. We had always thought we were at the front edge of human progress.

Thirdly, I notice that the end of the myth of unlimited progress has been awfully hard on this generation. Can the students now in college feel they will go farther than their fathers did? And is it worth it if they do? Younger people have a much more marked sense of failure than Americans are accustomed to, a sense of limits. Reality itself is teaching Americans a wisdom which we were not required to learn before from the openness of the frontier.

QUESTION: Could you clarify the concept of liberal culture that you find going along with political democracy and the economics of enterprise? I think of people like Sir Francis Bacon, Voltaire, John Stuart Mill, and John Dewey. It is hard for me to think of the liberal tradition as embodying the Judeo-Christian tradition. On the whole, there seems to be a tension there.

PROFESSOR NOVAK: Like Louis Hartz, I think it is fair to call our culture liberal. I think our people have a remarkable sense of liberality. Even with respect to race relations, ordinary people are having the most incredible patience with many daily frustrations. In all income groups, the percentage of blacks going to college is slightly higher than the percentage of whites. And, of course, it is being done through scholarships; 70 percent of the black students are on scholarships, compared with 50 percent of the whites. The American people know that, and there is no big protest about it. There is some resentment, but our people remain a very liberal and generous people, on a whole set of indices. There is a notable intellectual tension in liberalism between its atheistic or agnostic wing and its religious wing. Both these traditions learn from and rely upon each other. Bertrand Russell was asked on what grounds in his own philosophy could he base compassion. He said explicitly that this was a value he recognized had come into the world through a religious genius, Jesus, and had been taught in the culture. On the whole, Russell found it a good thing. Russell was quite willing, explicitly, to borrow from Christianity something he needed to make his system go. I would say of our atheists and agnostics that the mythic component of their philosophies is Judeo-Christian. Conversely, Jews and Christians have learned the self-criticism and the analytic ways of their critics. Some have argued that the source of a great deal of our vitality is that we have such checks and balances both in the cultural sphere and in the religious sphere. The atheists and the agnostics are not allowed to go as far as their own logic would take them, and the religious people are not allowed to get away with obfuscations and sentimentalities.

QUESTION: I quite agree with your contention that we have not a good enough understanding of American culture, as a culture. To gain a better understanding of our culture, should we have a research program in which observers from other parts of the world, trained in anthropology, sociology, and so on, would be brought to the United States and allowed to do the same kind of observation which we so readily do in other cultures?

PROFESSOR NOVAK: Well, actually this is often done. Father Bruckberger did this twenty years ago. Jacques Maritain did it. Gunnar Myrdal was brought here to do this. Jean-François Revel has recently done it. It is often done, and it does work, up to a point. But our civilization is so various and so complicated that we can see only a part of it at a time.

QUESTION: One thing we can learn from looking at political history is that, under both Republican and Democratic administrations, there has been a steady growth of bureaucracy and growth of the state. Is it inevitable? Can we only hope to humanize it?

PROFESSOR NOVAK: My perception is Eastern European in the sense that not much good has happened in that part of Europe in a thousand years. My initial perception of reality is that everything is impossible, the world looks bleak, and there is no way to turn the tide. So what's new?

Perhaps this tide toward ubiquitous government cannot be turned. On the other hand, its costs become clearer and clearer, and more and more people from different points on the compass perceive those costs. If someone were able to articulate this situation well and find the right politics for it, he would succeed. In order to succeed, so many things have to go right. But we can take some comfort from the notion that reality folds back on itself. Reality teaches.

QUESTION: I think I heard a rather novel theological interpretation of the possible virtues of capitalism. With regard to your attempt to show some kind of a parallelism between the Christian conception of the sinner, and the capitalist conception of self-interest, I feel very much disturbed. What about the principle of self-transcendence, that grace whereby the sinner should be converted in the image of Christ to become the new man? Where do you find self-interest transcended in the interest of the community?

PROFESSOR NOVAK: All across the United States and Great Britain, there are icons and pictures of businessmen who are praised and given social acclaim not simply because they became rich, not simply because they followed their self-interest, but because that self-interest was transmuted into philanthropy, or some contribution for the benefit of humankind. There are a hundred examples: the service organizations, the lectures on stewardship, the sense that being rich is not a sufficient justification for a life. This is, I think, the way in which this civilization has tried to make self-interest redemptive. It is, also, I think, very good theology in that it does not teach us that the sinner is ever truly born again, in the complete sense. It keeps focusing our eye on the fact that self-interest persists, even when we have done good, even when we have made a contribution.

There are two kinds of redemption of self-interest at stake. One is the notion that, having pursued self-interest, one can then make a contribution. But, more than that, the very conception of pursuing self-interest is regarded as something productive. Capitalism will not work through hedonism. Capitalism will only work if there is willingness to save, to provide, to invest in productive ways. And that is the way in which self-interest becomes redeemable. Capitalism is a system which depends upon taking something that is ignoble about human nature, but pervasive, and making out of it something noble, or at least something productive. Within the culture, we do have our churches, we do have our literature; the economic order is not the only agency of redemption. But I have also been trying to draw a more narrow point: that even in the economic order there is a small form of redemption.

The Islamic Doctrine of Economics and Contemporary Economic Thought

Muhammad Abdul-Rauf

The economic doctrine of Islam is closely related to and is part of the Islamic concept of life. This concept is based on a network of interrelated concepts of God, of humanity, of man's relationship to God, man's position in the universe, and the relationship of man to his fellow men. At this time—when the world of business and industry is crying out for ethical safeguards against large-scale corruption, and when widespread pollution and the shortage of energy pose a threat to humanity—the moral teachings of Islam can provide not only the ethical guidelines needed for effective control of economic behavior but also compelling motivation for international cooperation in the efforts toward the salvation of humanity.

Economics, in my opinion, is not a value-free, pure science; it is a division of social studies. Economic behavior is human action aiming at the satisfaction of human needs, and it is bound to generate emotional vibrations. As such, it can be assessed and measured in moral terms. The notion that economic behavior is neutral has led to undue emphasis on material success, controlled only by the so-called invisible hand and resulting in the rise of the ruthless entrepreneur and the merciless exploitation of the weak.

The Islamic Religion

Some remarks about the Islamic religion may serve as background to the subject under discussion.

Islam was first pronounced through the Prophet Muhammad in Mecca in 610 A.D. For the next thirteen years, the Prophet had to struggle against the polytheist inhabitants of that town, a trading class of aristocrats who exploited for their selfish interests a large number of serfs and slaves and rejected Muhammad's egalitarian teachings as vigorously as they did his monotheistic beliefs. Tribal solidarity committed Muhammad's clan to protect his life, and this alone saved his

129

neck. When his enemies intrigued to circumvent tribal protection, Muhammad found refuge in the agricultural community of Medina, almost 300 miles away, where his teachings met lesser resistance.

In Medina, the first community of Islam, the Islamic city-state was established with the Prophet himself as its temporal head. With the basic ideology of Islam well entrenched, legislative guidance developed, aiming at the best possible results in all spheres of life, including the social, economic, and political domains. At the death of the Prophet in 632, the Holy Book of Islam, the Qur'ān, had been completely revealed. It incorporates the basic guidance of Islam and is believed to be God's own word. Preserved in the hearts of thousands of the Prophet's disciples and also recorded in writing during his lifetime, the Qur'ān was soon duplicated for wide distribution. As a source of Islamic guidance, the Qur'ān was supplemented by the *Sunna* (way), the reported words and actions of the Prophet, which run into tens of thousands of records, known as *hadīths* (traditions). Both these literary works have always been acknowledged as the primary sources of guidance for Muslims on all aspects of life.

As the Islamic state expanded and incorporated most of the territories then known, Muslim leadership was confronted with innumerable problems, which they resolved with an amazing degree of efficiency. As a result, the Islamic legal system emerged, known as *Fiqh* or *Shariʻa*, based primarily on the Qur'ān and the hadīth records. Muslim jurists sought to answer every conceivable question and organized their findings into several categories—dealing first with the details of the ritual duties then with all types of human interactions, including what may be regarded as commercial law, personal law, and criminal law. If an answer could not be found in the Qur'ān or Sunna, resort was made to the principle of analogy. The consensus of the first generation of Muslims on any matter was recognized as a fourth authority.

Based on the ideologies of Islam, the Islamic world has survived for many centuries, and its steadily increasing population is now said to approach one billion. It has been able to operate effectively throughout the ages and in all places under the Shariʻa law, generating a splendid civilization in its early history. Despite the savage wars of the Mongol hordes, the Crusades, and then the European colonialism, the Islamic world endured. This survival bears witness to the existence of a working and adaptable concept of economy.

Islamic guidance permeates all aspects of human life and divides all human behavior into five moral categories: obligatory, merely desirable, forbidden, merely undesirable, and neutral. The judgment depends on how the activity bears on religion, human life, mind, descent, and property. A careful analysis of the guidance reveals the following principles:

• Islam's goal is to guide man in his quest for salvation in the hereafter through fulfillment of the purpose of human existence on earth.

• The purpose of human existence is to serve God both inwardly and outwardly—by internal acknowledgment of God's magnificence and supremacy and by awareness of His presence, His munificence, and His call for human progress and righteousness, and by external compliance with God's teachings pertaining to ritual and nonritual activities.

• The divine ritual guidance is to be accepted as given; it does not leave room for human choice or modification because it is the pre-scribed method in which the Creator wishes His human creatures to express their devotion to Him. The guidance covers the ritual declara-tion of God's uncompromisable unity and uniqueness and the validity of the mission of His Prophets and their scriptures. It also includes instructions pertaining to prayer, almsgiving, fasting, and pilgrimage to Mecca. Acknowledgment of these truths and compliance with these teachings inspires and reinforces correct orientation, certainty, a mean-ingful concept of life, and hope for the future. In short, Islamic guidance meets the spiritual and psychological needs of the individual and makes him a better social being.

• The nonritual divine guidance covers the domestic, social, aesthetic, political, judicial, and economic areas of human activities. It does not confine man to a single course with no choice, nor does it leave him a victim of uncontrolled greed, human vagaries, and stubbornness. It grants man a wide range of choices and creativity, motivates him to satisfy his physical and psychological needs in progressive processes, but seeks to protect him from evil. In the particular area of economics, this is achieved in three ways: (1) A set of basic values—*hudūd Allāh* (the boundaries of God)—motivates and delineates the area of per-missible economic action. These values should not be violated or trans-gressed, but within those limits man is free, indeed urged, to use his intellectual and physical endowments for the betterment of his life and his society. (2) Along with this value system Islam provides general guidelines that serve as a chart or a compass for steering man through the large area of human freedom in the sphere of the economic activities. (3) Man is also given a set of divine ordinances, some urging specific actions to promote the well-being of humanity and others warning against certain damaging factors. These specific injunctions are the foundations on which the Islamic framework of economics rests.

In the light of this analysis, the Islamic concept of economics may be defined as a framework for motivated but free human action within the Islamic value system. That action must respect specific ordinances pertaining to economic life and take into account the spiritual and material needs of the individual and his society in a balanced and harmonized way.

The Relevant Value System

The relevant values that delineate the economic framework prescribed in Islam include complete commitment to God, the Creator and Provider of all ecological resources, and constant awareness of His presence even in the depth of material engagement: "O you who have believed, let not [your occupation with] your wealth nor your children distract you from the remembrance of God. Whosoever can be so distracted are indeed the losers."[1] "Serve God as if you see Him; for if you do not see Him He sees you."[2]

Another value is appreciation of the wealth and all the ecological resources provided by God for the satisfaction of human needs. Wealth, a favor from God, is to be sensibly treated, not abused, destroyed, or wasted, or laid idle. Resources are given in abundance, though scarcity is caused by human limitation. Man has to develop greater knowledge and skills and should endeavor to explore, to discover, and to exploit these resources in moderation for his own best interest. God could have made all our needs easily accessible in unlimited abundance; but without the economic challenges man would be idle, dull, and given to criminality. "If God were to enlarge the Provision for His servants they would surely rebel in the earth, but He sends down by measure as He wills. Surely, He is Knowing and Aware of His bondsmen."[3]

Wealth is to be regarded as a means, not a final goal. It is a means of satisfying needs, of providing sustenance—in moderation—for survival, for a limited term of life on earth, leading to a more meaningful and lasting life hereafter. In treating wealth otherwise, man

---

[1] Qur'ān 63:9.

[2] This is a *hadīth* related by Muslim ibn Majjāj, *Sahīh* (Cairo: Halabī Press, n.d.), vol. 1, p. 22.

[3] Qur'ān 42:27.

becomes materialistic, selfish, ruthless, and greedy and yet can never be satisfied. "Whosoever makes material success his uppermost goal, God will make [the threat of] poverty ever present under his eyes."[4]

In the last analysis, real ownership of wealth, consumable or productive, belongs to God. Man's temporal possession is limited and is granted by God; man is merely a "trustee" for a term. Realization of this dual ownership mitigates against selfish and dishonest tendencies that often result from the deceitful notion of absolute ownership.

Although we are created equal, and no one may claim inherent merit over another, yet we are created with different talents and are bound to attain different degrees of success. It is a duty to accept our fortune, not to despair or to be resentful, although we are to struggle as hard as we can for our best interest: "And He [God], has made you the viceroys in the earth, and raised some of you over the other [in fortune] in order to test you in the gifts He has given you."[5] "If God had so willed, He would have made you one nation, but [His plan is] to test you in what He has given you. So strive for good things as in a race. To God is your return, all of you; when He will show you the truth concerning your diversity."[6]

Implicit in the notion of "trusteeship" and testing through wealth and worldly success is the idea that material superiority does not entail higher merit. All people are created equal, as equal as the teeth of a comb. Righteousness is the criterion that raises the rank of a person with God.[7]

As a corollary of human equality, all people are equally entitled to the same set of human rights. These include:

- *Haqq al-Hayāh* (the right to live): Encroachment on this right is a grave sin, next to disbelief in God, and entitles the family of the victim to claim capital punishment.

- *Haqq al-Hurriyyah* (the right of liberty): Encroachment on this birthright is dehumanizing to its victim.

- *Haqq al-Tamalluk* (the right of ownership): This right can be legitimately earned through labor or it can be received as a gift or as a share in inheritance. It is subject to certain restraints including payment of alms and charitable obligations.

---

[4] Muhammad Ibn Yazīd Ibn Mājah, *Sunan* (Cairo, 1952), vol. 2, p. 1375.

[5] Qur'ān 6:165.

[6] Qur'ān 11:118.

[7] Qur'ān 49:13; see also Muhammad Abdul-Rauf, *The Islamic View of Women and the Family* (New York: Robert Speller and Sons, 1977), pp. 21–22.

- *Haqq al-Karāmah* (the right to dignity): This is another birthright that entitles each individual to respectful treatment.

- *Haqq al-'Ilm* (the right, even obligation, of education): This right leads to invention and greater production.

All that happens, including the outcome of our own planning and efforts, comes about only in accordance with God's will. This Islamic doctrine is known as *qadar* or *qismah*. We are to plan the course of our activities carefully and exert enough effort and energy to achieve our goal, yet the desired ends also need the blessing of God. Our planning and effort are not the only factors that count.

Two things emerge from this doctrine. Since achievement of our goals needs our planning and efforts as well as the blessing of God, a Muslim should not neglect his duty of working hard to earn a living. Heaven, so to speak, does not rain gold or silver; it has to be earned the hard way. Negligence, on the pretext that whatever has been predestined for us shall come no matter what we do, is condemned as lazy *tawākul*, "forsaking one's duty." Hard work accompanied by the belief in the role of the divine hand is known as sensible *tawakkul*, "pursuing our ends through regular measures while conscious of the need of the blessings of God."

On the other hand, should we occasionally fail to reach our goal, we as Muslims surrender and resign ourselves to our fortune and accept it as an act of God without resentment or despair. We should renew our efforts in hope and faith in God. This belief spurs a Muslim to exert his effort toward worldly success and sustains him at times of difficulty and hardship. It inspires him with a sense of satisfaction and contentedness, a virtue of great merit in Islam.

Various Needs to be Harmonized

In addition to the above value system demarcating the area of free economic action, the Islamic economic framework is delineated by the call to uphold the Islamic virtues of truth, honesty in dealings, respect for the rights of others, pursuit of moderation, sacrifice, and hard work. These virtues should guide a Muslim in his economic struggle through the processes of acquisition, production, distribution, and consumption. He legitimately acquires the means to live through his labor and hard work. He knows that idleness and apathy are discouraged in his religion, which leaves nothing unexplained, even the manner of eating and dressing. He scrupulously avoids all suspicious sources of income and never attempts to thwart the efforts of his fellowmen.

Moderation is the Muslim's guide in all situations. He is advised by the Prophet: "Eat and drink. Dress yourself well and give away in charity. But there should be no extravagance or arrogance."[8]

The individual's possessiveness and his concern to satisfy his personal needs have to harmonize with his obligations to his society—his family, his tribe, his neighbors, and the state of which he is a citizen. The needs of the individual and those of his society are intrinsically interdependent. Apart from his obligations to his family, a Muslim is not to let his neighbor smell his cooking without letting him share it, nor should he let his children play outside with new toys unless he has presented his neighbor's children with similar toys. In addition to the payment of prescribed alms, a Muslim has to hand over to the state whatever it may demand from him and must respect its policy, which has to be in the interest of all its citizens including himself. On the other hand, society must offer the individual security, protect his life and his property, and respect his dignity—alive and dead.[9]

The Islamic welfare economy is not based upon increasing the aggregate welfare of the community by encouraging the individual to maximize his own interest and be indifferent to the interest of others. It is based upon the bond of universal brotherhood in which the individual, in seeking to benefit himself, avoids malevolence to another. The Prophet stated: "No person may become a perfectly true believer unless he loves for others what he loves for himself."[10] "A Muslim is he who causes no harm to another, neither by hand nor by tongue."[11]

The spiritual aspirations of the individual must harmonize with his material endeavors. While the individual is admittedly a biological organism and a social entity with sets of basic and acquired needs, he is a psychological being with a divine heart. As such, although he is compelled to meet his biological and social urges, he is moved by his divine element and yearns to reach a state of spiritual elevation.

The word for religion in the Qur'ānic tongue is *dīn*, a term which connotes a whole way of life. Religion is not merely a private matter, nor does it touch only the periphery of individual lives; it is both private and public, and permeates the whole fabric of society. Economic pursuits are meritorious, leading not only to material sustenance but also

---

[8] Muhammad Ibn Ismā'īl al-Bukhārī, *Sahīh*, 4 vols. (Cairo: Halabī Press, n.d.), vol. 4, p. 15; see also, Ahmad Ibn Hanbal, *Al-Musnad*, 6 vols. (Cairo, 1933) vol. 4, p. 132.

[9] A dead person is entitled to a decent funeral service, which includes a mandatory full washing, shrouding, prayer service, and respectable burial.

[10] Bukhārī, *Sahīh*, vol. 1, p. 7.

[11] Ibid., pp. 6–7.

to God's pleasure. Thus economic pursuits cannot be separated from the spiritual objective—let alone be elevated over it—nor should they be separated from the religious content and become purely materialistic. In his economic pursuits, a Muslim's objective is to meet not only his material needs but also his social obligations, whereby he hopes to improve his position with God.

Islam seeks neither monastic indifference to physical needs nor indulgence in sensual pleasure and the maximum satisfaction of human wants. It is for moderation—not for either extreme. A want is a painful and disquieting experience; its satisfaction brings relief and leads to peaceful equilibrium. Relief is best achieved through reasonable moderate satisfaction. Maximizing satisfaction—overeating and luxurious living—results in complications and causes other wants. Hence the Qur'ān and the Prophet blame extravagance and praise moderation. The Qur'ān reads:

> And the sky, He has raised,
> And the balance He has placed
> That you may not transgress the balance.
> And establish the balance equitably and do not
> fall short in balancing.[12]

And the Prophet said: "The child of Adam never fills a container more harmful for him than his own stomach. If he must fill it, let him fill only one third with food, leaving one third for water and one third for breathing."[13]

To observe the principle of justice and fair dealing is the overall absorbing teaching of Islam dominating human interactions. This principle was mentioned above with other Islamic virtues, but it is treated separately because of its special importance. Injustice is condemned in most severe terms. The Qur'ān reads: "And if you judge between mankind, do so with justice,"[14] and, "whoso among you commits injustice, We shall let him taste a great punishment."[15] The Prophet said: "Injustice is darknesses on the Day of Resurrection."[16]

Not only does the individual have to be just in his economic dealings with his fellow men, but the state also has to be just and fair in dealing with its citizens. State interference should be minimal and is allowed only for compelling reasons. Uncalled-for repressive meas-

---

12 Qur'ān, 55:7–9.
13 Bukhārī, *Sahīh*, vol. 4, p. 15.
14 Qur'ān 4:58.
15 Qur'ān 25:19.
16 Bukhārī, *Sahīh*, vol. 2, p. 42.

ures may not be used. Ideally, the state's function should be restricted to the administration of publicly owned properties, the conduct of national economic affairs that are beyond the jurisdiction of its citizenry, and general supervision of the market to protect against malpractices such as hoarding of food, inflated prices, and deceit. Such supervision is exemplified by the traditional post of *muhtasib*, who checked the weights and measures used in the marketplaces and looked into cases of fraudulent practices.

The Ten Commandments of Islamic Economics

Apart from the set of values discussed earlier, which demarcate the large area of freedom of economic action, and the above guidelines which serve as a compass in charting the course of sail, Islam provides specific ordinances. Some are positive injunctions which serve as sources of energy or fuel for the economic boat; others are prohibitions that point out dangerous spots which might wreck the boat. These ordinances may be called the "Ten Commandments" of the Islamic economic system.

1. The first is the payment of the *zakāt*, an almsgiving duty, amounting to 2.5 percent annually on income and saving. Ten percent is due on an agricultural harvest if irrigation was at no cost and no effort to the farmer; otherwise, only 5 percent is due. Zakāt also applies to commercial goods, some categories of livestock, excavated treasures, and mined wealth. Zakāt ideally would be collected by the state treasury. Otherwise, the individuals responsible have to distribute it themselves, as is the case today in most Muslim territories. In either case, zakāt has to be given to the destitute, to zakāt collectors, to those who fall in debt to make peace, and to wayfarers or to assist in preaching the faith, in freeing slaves, and in the struggle for Islam. Unlike modern taxation, zakāt is a flat rate and does not rise exuberantly on an ascending scale. Thus it does not discourage working for greater gain, nor is it exposed to evasive or dishonest measures. Equity is achieved by encouraging voluntary charities, *sadaqāt*, which assure seven hundredfold rewards with God. Moreover, in case of need, the state may levy some taxes on the richer.

2. The maintenance costs for certain categories of relatives must be paid—particularly for one's wife, needy parent, female children till they marry, and male children till the age of puberty. The wife's right to maintenance is due whether or not she has financial resources of her own.

3. The obligation of charitable assistance to one's kin, to one's

neighbors, to orphans, and to the needy is denoted by the term *haqq*,[17] which is an emphatic word meaning, "an inalienable right." Charity is better paid in a concealed manner, however, so as not to embarass the receiver. He is also to be treated politely.

4. Working hard to earn one's own living and the living of dependents is highly praised. Food so earned is the most blessed, and the hand that toils will never burn in hellfire. Struggle for living is believed to be as meritorious as the struggle for the faith; and the hand that gives is better in the sight of God than the hand that takes. For Muslims, however, "labor" and "work," which are praised in the Qur'ān hundreds of times, are identical. Thus we are all workers and laborers, even though one may be employed or an employer, one deriving wages and another a profit.

5. A worker, manufacturer, administrator, or whoever should exert the utmost effort to make his product as perfect as possible. It is related that the Prophet said: "God verily likes to see any one of you, when he does something, to make it as perfect as he possibly can."[18]

6. The conditions laid down in the Shari'a law for the validity of business and financial transactions must be fulfilled. These laws make the transfer of goods safe and easy and facilitate the conclusion of economic transactions between the contracting parties. They also ensure the absence of vagueness or misunderstanding—whether the transaction is a contract of sale, partnership, employment, cooperative agriculture or irrigation, or anything else. In the final analysis, the goal is to reduce the causes of social tension or litigations and promote an optimal climate of peace. Writing down the terms of financial agreements is strongly recommended. The legal requirements as stipulated by the jurists pertain to the contracting parties, the commodity being transacted, the price involved, and the terms of the contract conveying the mutual acceptance by both parties, the wording of which should be categorical and unambiguous. The parties should be responsible free agents of sound mind; the commodity should be clearly specified, truly owned by the seller, and accessible and deliverable; and the price also has to be made specific. Goods so transacted have to be of economic value Islamically; therefore, contracts involving legally unconsumable material such as wine, pork, or polluting matter are not valid.

7. Pledges, trusts, and terms concluded with other parties must be kept. The Qur'ān reads: "O you who believe, violate not [your covenant with] God and His Messenger, or the pledges amongst you."[19] "Let

---

17 Qur'ān 51:19 and 70:24.
18 Suyūti, *al-Jāmi' al-Saghīr* (Beirut, 1970), vol. 2, p. 144 (Hadīth no. 1876).
19 Qur'ān 8:27.

him who has been trusted [with anything] be true to his trust."[20] "Verily God commands you to return the trusts to their owners."[21]

8. The ordinances pertaining to the distribution of the estate of a deceased person among his heirs must be respected as laid down in the Qur'ān.[22] The heirs include the deceased person's surviving spouse, surviving parent or parents, and all surviving children. In the absence of a father or male child, brothers and sisters may share the estate. In some cases, paternal uncles and cousins may also have a share. A person may not make a will which deprives one of his heirs or which favors one heir over another, nor may he make a will involving more than a third of his estate.

9. Usury is among the serious sins, and all usurious practices should be avoided. Debate over the question of earning a fixed interest on deposits in financial houses has subsided with the availability of un-debatable alternatives with no fixed interest, such as investment in the newly formulated Islamic banks, discussed below. Arguments that interest encourages the practice of saving or that interest is a compensation or reward for voluntary restraint from overspending have been exploded. The individual is impelled to save by a deep desire for financial security, and Islam itself encourages saving. "To leave your heirs self-sufficient is better than letting them be a social liability—stretching their hands begging."[23] There are also those who save but do not invest in interest-bearing saving accounts. Moreover, although interest is claimed to be a reward for abstention, a rich man who saves cannot be described as sacrificing to the same degree as a low-income saver. Nor does this theory explain why wealthy persons charge exuberant rates of interest on loans.

Prohibition of usury has to be understood in the light of the Islamic philosophy of wealth and the legitimate ways of acquiring it. Earning should not involve the exploitation or the hardship of others and should be in keeping with the spirit of brotherhood and cooperation. Condemnation of usury is in keeping with the Islamic prohibition of earning without effort or risk and with the cooperative spirit it promotes. Usury is a form of hoarding because it may impede the function of money as a tool in the exchange of goods, and it is inconsistent with the principle of human equality.[24] The Qur'ān reads: "And what-

[20] Qur'ān 2:283.

[21] Qur'ān 4:58.

[22] Qur'ān 4:11–12 and 176.

[23] Ibn Mājah, *Sunan*, vol. 2, p. 904.

[24] Morroe Berger, *The Arab World Today* (New York: Doubleday, 1964), p. 52, speaks of this dimension as follows: "The Koranic prohibition against the taking

ever you give to invest and increase your wealth through usury is not an increase with Allāh. But what you give in charity for the sake of God, such givers are those who receive multiple blessings and rewards."[25]

10. Last but not least, there must be respect for other peoples' property and abstention from unproductive malpractices, profiteering activities, and disruptive transgressions, such as robbery, extortion, deceiving, gambling, hoarding, monopoly, and distributing harmful drugs or pornographic material. Earning through expediency and manipulation of the law—now common in our daily life—is not legitimate. The Prophet once said: "It may happen that one of disputing parties is more effective in presenting his case than the other. If I should judge in his favor [under the effect of his deceptive presentation], let him know that what he gets is a piece of the Hellfire."[26] Even when the judgment is made by the Prophet himself on the basis of deceptive evidence, it does not justify the resulting earning. Control emanates from the Muslim's innner conscience and his awareness of the watchful eye of God, not the fear of the court and its agencies from which one can easily escape.

These ten ordinances, or "Ten Commandments," give the Islamic system of economics its distinctive character. The underlying concept is that the economic community is like an organic body, in which each cell grows and contributes to the well-being of the other cells. The Prophet is related to have said: "The believers in their mutual love and concern are like one body; if a part of it complains the other parts call each other to come to its assistance, sharing its pain and sleeplessness."[27]

Ideal and Application

The ideal Islamic concept of economics described above was fully implemented in early Islam under the guidance and leadership of the Prophet in Medina. It successfully survived the severe test it encountered shortly after the death of the Prophet when nations with different cultures and backgrounds came within the fold of the state. The wisdom of the early caliphs and their advisers and their long experience

---

of interest (not merely usury) is likewise an example of this devotion to the principle of equality, for it involves an increase (or riba, the technical term for interest) in one's possessions at the cost of another."

[25] Qur'ān 30:39.

[26] Ibn Mājah, *Sunan*, vol. 2, p. 777.

[27] Bukhārī, *Sahīh*, vol. 4, p. 33.

with the Prophet helped them meet the challenge effectively. They used their judgment and the tool of analogy, but were always within the boundaries of the Qur'ān.

The Islamic values and injunctions pertaining to economic behavior continued to guide succeeding Muslim generations, particularly at the grass-roots level of Muslim society. Islamic beliefs were inculcated and internalized by the recitation of relevant Qur'ānic verses and the repetition of popular phrases such as those praising the virtue of relying on God and emphasizing God's possession of all that is in heaven and the earth and the return of everything unto Him.

Guided by this system, Muslims held together the political reins of a vast empire, started an efficient postal service, struck coins (the golden dinār and silver dirham), built roads, canals, palaces, castles, and cities, and left behind magnificent landmarks. Muslims set up professional and trade guilds which cooperated in various parts of the Islamic world and organized and developed their various skills in each locality. Their artifacts fill Islamic museums in the Muslim capitals, and their international trade left some traces in European culture, including the terms "traffic" and "tariff."

Various factors have caused Muslims to move away from the model set by the Prophet and the early caliphate, and the spirit of sacrifice and generosity inspired by these values and injunctions has been progressively conquered by the powerful corruptive forces of possessiveness and love for wealth, particularly among the ruling and influential classes. The major factors which crippled the Islamic economy and finally led to the current confusion were:

- Political upheavals, starting with the introduction of the dynastic concept in Islam, concentrated power and curruptive influences among certain families and their entourages, and this was inherited by succeeding generations.

- The widespread devastations of the Mongol wars and the Crusades erased cities, demolished libraries and schools, and eliminated scholars.

- Ascetic tendencies arose, fed by the oppressive climate and reinforced by some misguided Sūfī doctrines.

- European colonialism in recent centuries caused the fragmentation of the Muslim world and the loss of Islamic identity. Muslims were compelled to abandon their heritage in favor of European institutions and were gradually imbued with divisive nationalistic tendencies.

Current Pressures and Response

When the world of Islam regained its sovereignty, it found itself fragmented into separate nations laboring under heavy burdens of inequity. Each of these units is now struggling toward economic solvency and responding in one way or another to the pressure from two competing systems: capitalism and socialism. Because of socialism's attractive claim of egalitarianism and the discouraging association of capitalism with Western imperialism, modified varieties of socialism are making inroads in most Muslim countries. This process of pressure and response has led to debates and even to heated disputes over the question of which of the two systems is more compatible with Islam. The Islamic doctrine of economics permits degrees of individual freedom and state intervention but leaves the determination of these degrees to the wisdom and consciences of those involved, who should take current conditions into account. This flexibility has made Islamic economics open to alternative options within its framework.

Faced with a great deal of external pressure and intricately entangled in economies that have been imposed on their land for centuries and that are based on alien values, the Islamic people have responded in three ways. First, the "centralists" or traditionalists believe that Islam can meet the challenge intact. Second, there are those who turn to the East. Oblivious to the alienation of capitalism and socialism from the spiritual life and to the materialistic goals of both systems, some naive elements claim that Islam, on account of its principle of social justice, is a socialist system. Similarly confused, others turn to the West and advocate capitalism on the ground that it permits ownership—a sacred right in Islam—and promotes free private enterprise, which is more compatible with the Islamic doctrine of individual responsibility.

The story of Abu Dharr, a notable Companion of the Prophet, caught the attention of the advocates of socialism and even of its radical form, Marxism. In the region of Syria during the reign of the third caliph, Abu Dharr was alarmed by the misuse of the treasury funds and the luxurious life pursued by the Umayyad ruler in Damascus. Abu Dharr advocated that any surplus of income over needs be given immediately to charity, and he substantiated his views by several *hadīths* he attributed to the Prophet. According to one of these, while walking in the outskirts of Medina the Prophet told Abu Dharr: "Should this mountain of 'Uhud be turned into gold for me, I would not wish that the nightfall comes before I have disposed of it all in charity except two carats."[28]

The Umayyad governor of Syria feared unrest as a result of Abu Dharr's vigorous criticism and complained to the caliph. The caliph summoned Abu Dharr to Medina but failed to dissuade him, and thus banished him to a lonely hamlet where he soon died. A fatwa (religious ruling), given in the early 1950s by al-Azhar, the leading theological school, supported the opinion of the caliph over that of Abu Dharr.

I do believe in Abu Dharr's teaching, but that was not communism or socialism as such. It was a call for the loftiest level of charity. The strong protest of Abu Dharr was provoked by nepotism and the misuse of Muslim funds. I also believe in the caliph's view that a person can retain the surplus of his earning so long as he meets all his obligations. The Qur'ān teaches that the righteous in Paradise will be divided into two grades: *Ahl al-Yamīn*, those on the right of the Divine Throne; and *al-Muqarrabūn*,[29] fewer but superior in rank, who will be closer to God, so rewarded because of their greater sacrifices.

Islamic Banks and Muslim Common Market

The traditionalists or centralists, who aspire to restore Islam to its original purity and escape from alien influences, have attempted to prove the suitability and adaptability of the Islamic doctrine of economics to the needs of modern times. They developed a concept of interest-free financial houses, often called Islamic Banks, modeled on the successful experiment in Mit-Ghamr, an Egyptian Delta town, in the mid-1960s. The first major project of this type was started in Dubai in March 1975 after long study and investigation. The immediate success of the Dubai experience has led to a series of these banks elsewhere.[30]

The sponsors of these banks argue that the Islamic banks are not much different from the familiar Western banks which permeate Muslim countries. The only difference is that they are not based on fixed rates of interest on loans or on deposits, which, from their point of view, are usurious under the Shari'a law. The regular banks, they argue, not only deal in money but also invest in agricultural, industrial, commercial, and human projects. Therefore, Islamic banks can deal and invest in such projects but without the use of usurious interest rates.

---

[28] Abū Hāmid al-Ghazzālī, *Revival of Religious Sciences* (Cairo: Subaih Press, 1958), vol. 3, p. 230.

[29] Qur'ān 56:7–11.

[30] This pattern has been repeated in Saudi Arabia, Kuwait, Sudan, and Egypt and is being developed in Jordan and Bahrain.

Broadly speaking, these Islamic banks maintain three types of account: (1) nonprofit accounts with a very small minimum deposit from which withdrawal can be made at any time; (2) profit-sharing deposit accounts with a modest minimum balance, from which withdrawal can be made annually (or at shorter intervals); and (3) social services funds, consisting of gifts, from which payments are made in emergencies such as accidents involving participants.[31] The profit made by these banks is said to be enormous for both profit-sharing depositors and stockholders.

In this new category of financial institutions is the Islamic Development Bank, started two years ago under the auspices of the Permanent Islamic Secretariat of the Foreign Ministers' Conference with headquarters in Jedda, Saudi Arabia. The only difference is that it is an intergovernmental institution to promote economic cooperation among Muslim countries in accordance with the Shari'a law. Among the activities of the Islamic Development Bank are:

- participating in capital for projects

- extending loans to institutions and productive projects in member countries

- extending financial assistance in various forms for economic growth and social progress

- helping in international trade between member countries and in the production of commodities

- extending technical assistance, particularly in training personnel, in economic development, research, banking, and other economic activities in accordance with Shari'a.[32]

Related to this subject of international economic cooperation is a project now being worked out to create an Islamic Common Market, also under the auspices of the Permanent Islamic Secretariat. A memorandum on the subject was submitted to the ninth session of the Islamic Conference of Foreign Ministers held in Dakar, Senegal, in Jumāda 1398 A.H. (April 1978).[33]

---

[31] Ahmad al-Najjār, *Interest-Free Banks* (Cairo: Sa'ādah Press, 1972), p. 51; see also Tal'at Abū Zahrah, "Concept of Islamic Banks," *al-Hidāyah* (Bahrain), March 1978, pp. 6–10.

[32] "The Islamic Development Bank," *Akhbār al-'Alam al-Islāmī* (Mecca), April 1978, p. 41.

[33] "Muslim Common Market," *The Muslim World* (Karachi), May and June 1978.

Islam versus Capitalism and Socialism

While these developments are taking place, supported by certain influential elements, the debate—violent in certain areas—rages over Islam versus socialism, Marxism, and capitalism.

As indicated in the earlier discussion, Islam has some affinities with both socialism and capitalism, but it departs from each in certain basic ingredients of its own. Islam is not so rigid or so radical, so tough or so cruel, nor is it so materialistic or so limited. Treatment of the economic life is only one part of its comprehensive totality. Its flexible framework can be applied to both simple and complex societies, to a gathering economy, to a pastoral economy, and to agricultural and industrial economies.

Capitalism idolizes the individual, regards his personal freedom as a sacred and precious gift, trusts him with the task of maximizing production, and forbids state interference in the entrepreneur's initiative; socialism goes to the other extreme, however, insisting on state control of the national means of production—land, mines, industries, and human resources. It usurps the individual's liberty of economic action, denies him the chance to exercise his initiative, kills his incentive to work hard for greater personal gain, and deprives him of much of his dignity. While capitalism is a decentralized system that provides the individual with unlimited room for dynamism, imaginative ambition, inventiveness, and improvement, socialism is a centralized system that is to a great degree static. The state administers the existing means of production and controls the will of the masses. Yet capitalistic ideas breed selfishness, cruel individualism, and greed and are bound to create a climate of loneliness and isolation. The atmosphere of severe competitiveness is bound to lead to deep tension and depression, resulting in domestic instability, criminality, corruption on a large scale, and a deep fear of insecurity since there can be no limit to selfish ambitions. Unbridled socialism, on the other hand, is capricious, transgressive, and dehumanizing and has also led to widespread corruption and nepotism. Socialism owes its rise to envy, jealousy, and dissatisfaction; in its extreme form it therefore calls for class struggles and the elimination of the vanquished class. The ideal of both systems is simply materialistic, with little or no concern for the spiritual needs of the individual. In its evolution, Western economic thought has struggled at various stages with the ideals of the Christian church and has abandoned spiritual thinking and resorted to exclusively pragmatic reasoning.

In contrast, the Islamic system, believed to be divinely prescribed, aims at satisfying immediate material needs and maximizing production within the available means, as well as at meeting the spiritual needs of the individual. In his materialistic endeavors, a Muslim feels that he is manipulating the means of production put at his disposal by his Lord. He is required to subdue the natural resources that have been made accessible, and he never ceases to remember God in his heart or to praise Him in gratitude even in the middle of his material pursuits. In his striving for material gain, he feels that he is complying with the ordinances of God and anticipates double rewards—a profit in hand and a reward in Paradise.

Not unlike capitalism, Islam believes in human freedom and individual liberty and encourages the entrepreneur's initiative. Yet, it does not resent limited state intervention when necessary, as a lever against boundless greed and corruption and at times of a special need.

The Islamic system takes into account certain essential moral objectives that call for social justice based on mutual responsibility. The moral content of Islamic economics is given great emphasis, and one can easily see the reason. Mankind was created with a possessive instinct, an insatiable thirst for accumulating wealth, and a tendency to cling to possessions; thus incentives are needed not to inflame these urges but to control them. The moral stress which outweighs the call for economic fulfillment compares with the greater emphasis laid on filial duties than on parental obligations.

The economic problem, in the Islamic cultural milieu, is not scarcity of commodities nor lack of efficient organization of the means and sources of production and distribution. Rather the problem lies with man and human greed. Islam confronts the problem and prescribes the remedy through softening human greed and elevating the human soul, calling for social justice and mutual responsibilities in the pattern described above.

As the Qur'ān often draws to our attention, man is provided with abundance, both in heaven and on earth. This abundance should be put to good use, not abused, wasted, damaged, hoarded, or monopolized. Even in making the ablution required before prayers, a Muslim is forbidden to increase the washing unnecessarily beyond three times, even if he happens to be beside an ocean. Wasting water is a sin. Overspending is a sin. "Eat and drink," the Qur'ān commands, "and be not extravagant."[34] The Qur'ān also praises "those who, when they spend, do not exceed the limits nor do they be mean but strike a path in

---

[34] Qur'ān 7:31.

between."[35] It also reads: "Tie not your hand to your neck nor do you widely open it all the way."[36] And the Prophet warned: "No person shall cross the path [leading to Paradise] unless he has answered successfully these questions: How he had used the time for the duration of his life; how he had used the vigor of his youth; and how he had earned his wealth and how he had spent it."[37]

A conscientious Muslim has to satisfy himself that whenever he spends he does it in a way that does not displease God. Muslims can be horrified to see someone throw a piece of bread into the drain or step on a grain of corn or any kind of foodstuff. Polluting any part of the environment is a sin. Hence the prohibition of responding to the natural urge in or beside a sea, a river, a pool, or a well or under a tree, or on the road or in open frequented places. Now the large-scale pollution by modern heavy industries is certainly a cardinal sin.

Like capitalism, Islam fully acknowledges the right of ownership and entitles each to the fruits of his or her labor. The state is to protect this right of its subjects, Muslim and non-Muslim alike. This is reflected in the terms of the treaties concluded by the Prophet himself as well as by the early caliphs in which protection of this right was assured to non-Muslim communities living within the Islamic state.[38] They assured the protection of non-Muslim citizens, their lives, their churches, and their properties. Yet, an owner should be aware of the fact that, in the last analysis, all wealth, including land, is truly owned by God. The human owner is merely an agent trusted with the wealth to handle it righteously and is accountable for the way he has managed it.

Two Islamic injunctions work against the concentration of wealth in a few hands: the obligation of zakāt, the annual payment of alms in income and savings, in trade commodities, in crops, and in certain other properties; and haqq, the right of the poor to receive charity. The law of inheritance, which breaks up the estate of a deceased person among all the heirs (normally numerous), also works in this direction. Moreover, as already indicated, since ownership ceases on a person's death, he is restrained from making a will involving more than a third of his estate.

---

[35] Qur'ān 25:67.

[36] Qur'ān 17:29.

[37] Muhammad Ibn 'Isā, al-Trimidhī, al-Jāmi' al-Sahih (Cairo: Misriyyah Press, 1930), vol. 7, p. 101.

[38] Alfred Guillaume, The Life of Muhammad (London: Oxford University Press, 1955), p. 231; see also Muhammad Ibn Jarīr al-Tabarī, Ta'rīkh (Cairo: Ma'ārif Press, 1970), vol. 3, p. 609 and vol. 4, p. 109.

Conclusion

To recapitulate the major points of Islamic beliefs as they affect the Islamic economic system: God has created humankind and deposited him on this planet, from which he was created, in order to test him, particularly in economic pursuits. God has deposited in the environment enormous resources for the sustenance of man, most of which have to be explored and exploited, developed, grown, and manufactured before they can be distributed for consumption. In all these processes, man is to be guided by the intellectual power with which he is endowed, apart from his physical strength, and he is free to make choices subject only to certain limits. These limits have been divinely laid down for mankind's best interest, to provide for the special psychological and spiritual needs which distinguish him from the nonintellectual animal kingdom.

Islam recognizes the existence of an economic problem which lies not in the scarcity of consumable goods but in the shortcomings of man, who is so created that he must fulfill the needs of his animal nature. These needs impel man's economic activities and creativity. The goal of the moral concept of economics is to balance man's needs as an animal with his needs as a spiritual being. In the harmony between these two aspects lies man's true and perpetual happiness—no matter what the degree of his material success might be. Thus Islamic economics is a framework of a value system which defines the boundaries of the free area of, and provides a sensible motivation for, economic action. Within these limits, economic action is steered by the concept of a fair balance between the human and spiritual needs and between the individual and social obligations. The economic framework is further delineated and more specifically illuminated by a set of ten injunctions, the "Ten Commandments of Islamic economics."

According to Muslims, the moral economic concept I have endeavored to describe is not made by mortals but is based on divine revelation. As such, it is perpetual and universally applicable, since a divine teaching is timeless and spaceless and recognizes no boundaries. The concepts of conservatism versus modernism and progressive versus reactionary are alien in a truly Islamic context, as much as the dichotomy of sacred and profane, and of church and state. Divine guidance is never outdated but always suitable, adaptable, and applicable. One of its features is that it does not and should not lead to hardship: "And God has not imposed any hardship upon you," the Qur'ān declared.[39]

---

[39] Qur'ān 22:78.

Islam, like many other religions, concerns itself with man's ultimate salvation in the hereafter, but unlike many of them it is equally concerned with man's worldly success. In the words of Christopher Wren, writing recently on the world of Islam, although in a different context: "Mohammed [he should have said God] laid out in the Koran detailed secular as well as religious injunctions for his followers, covering personal, social and political relationships and both civil and criminal law, making it virtually impossible to confine Islam to spiritual matters."[40] (The implied dichotomy of secular and religious is Wren's concept.)

A moral content seems to be inherent in all types of human behavior, including economic behavior. Even capitalism and socialism, often thought to be purely economic concepts, seem to have their moral roots. The laissez faire philosophy of capitalism sought to restore the rights of the individual and assert his liberty; and socialism sought to release the laboring class from oppressive exploitation. As such, each sought to achieve economic justice. Yet, each was a one-sided, unbalanced expression of justice. Man is at once an individual and a social creature; and the ideal society is one in which both his individuality and his sociality are duly recognized and mutually harmonized.

Economic justice, however, cannot be achieved in a vacuum or in a climate morally lacking in other areas. Economic justice, to be truly attained, has to be a part of a total moral code. And a moral code, to be truly operative, in my opinion, has to derive its authority from an ever present, conscious, and infallible power that cares for the well-being of mankind. Islam provides this comprehensive moral code that rests on the authority of a power immensely beyond that of the mortals. Recognition of God is, therefore, the central nonnegotiable truth of our moral code, a recognition that not only provides moral guidance but also fosters certainty, comfort, and a sense of direction.

At no time did the dynamics of the Islamic doctrine of economics lose its vitality—although it may have appeared to do so as a result of colonial domination. In spite of severe challenges, the revival of these dynamics is manifesting itself in the phenomena of the Islamic banking system and the call for the creation of an Islamic common market.

---

[40] Christopher S. Wren, "The Moslem World Rekindles Its Militancy," *New York Times,* June 18, 1978.

Discussion

QUESTION: Ten years ago, when I was teaching in a small desert town in Iran, one of the phrases that I found particularly difficult to understand was the phrase *in sha'a 'llāh*, which essentially translates "if God wills." One would say, for example, "class will meet tomorrow, in sha'a 'llāh." As an American, it seemed strange to me to have the future so consciously dependent upon God.

A few months later, a severe earthquake destroyed a neighboring town, and 10,000 people were killed—as we say in the West—"by an act of God." Then I realized a certain ethnocentricity in my not understanding the phrase.

I'm beginning to think that a prime motivation of the capitalistic spirit is to assure or guarantee one's future. That is, instead of recalling that one's future is dependent on God, one relies on the accumulation of capital, investment, planning, and insurance, to control the future. From the Islamic perspective, isn't this considered blasphemous?

PROFESSOR RAUF: The phrase *in sha'a 'llāh* is a polite statement that is on the tongue of all Muslims. It is an indication of our belief in our depedence upon God, even though we have some power to determine our future. It gives a Muslim assurance and helps him to accept calamities, such as the one you mentioned. However, it does not mean that one should not plan or work for the future. In fact, there is a saying: "Prepare for this world as if you are living forever, but work for the next world as if you are dying tomorrow." In other words, depend on God but do not make this an excuse for not doing or planning. In this sense, the spirit of capitalism would agree, to a great degree, with the Islamic spirit. Muslims are amazed, however, when Westerners speak in merely economic terms, as if mankind were made only to succeed economically. For a Muslim, wealth is a means, not an end; as a vehicle for survival it has only a temporal function. The fundamental goal is to avoid evoking the displeasure of God.

QUESTION: For several days we have been hearing that our society has come too far away from Christian teachings and values. Today you have explained to us the Islamic teachings concerning economics. Is there not a similar concern about people not following the Islamic traditions? You mentioned that some Muslims are depositing money in Western, interest-giving banks. Doesn't this indicate an individualistic tendency which would be in conflict with Islamic law?

PROFESSOR RAUF: As I said at the beginning, I am seeking to explain the Islamic doctrine of economics as an ideal. I do not pretend that these values or guidelines have always been maintained in Islamic society universally. There are many individuals who violate Islamic law and put their money in a bank with interest-bearing accounts. But it is avoided by many others, who deposit their money in the new Islamic banks, for example.

It is true, the economic pursuit in modern times has raised many questions for the Muslim world, in areas such as interest-bearing deposits, life insurance, and many others. These have been and are still being much discussed within the context of Islamic law.

QUESTION: Aren't there many Muslim students studying business in the United States who are learning an approach to economics which conflicts with Islamic traditions?

PROFESSOR RAUF: Many Muslim students have been coming to the West to study various subjects for many decades. Those in economics have developed their own studies of what they call Islamic economics. Their literature shows the parallels between modern economics and the concepts of economics in the Islamic religion. Many of these scholars who have studied in the West write, in discipline and detail, about the dangers and evils that arise from the bank interest system and speak in praise of the Islamic teachings against the taking of interest.

QUESTION: Do you think there is any correlation between the rather generous foreign aid of Muslim countries to development in other lands and the policies toward almsgiving in the Muslim faith?

PROFESSOR RAUF: Zakāt is an individual duty. The payment is either collected by the state for its projects in the interest of society as a whole, or the individual gives it directly to the poor. Whether foreign aid from a Muslim country relates to the notion of zakāt depends on the intention of those who give the money. If it is their intention to pay it as a zakāt on the revenue from their minerals, it could be considered as such.

The Success of the American Economic System

Ben J. Wattenberg

I doubt that it is possible to say anything new or different about this subject that has not already been presented at this conference. But I will go ahead in any event to examine briefly, if possible, the success, such as it is, of the American system of economics. You might later choose to debate whether it is a capitalist or a welfare state, or a mixed economy. In discussing the American system I will resort, where possible in this ideological setting, to facts. And we will see if perhaps such facts as are available—or at least that I know of—have some relevance to the discussion.

We have heard a lot about the negative side of the American economic system in recent years, and with some merit. It has been a time of two recessions, of inflation, stagflation, and so on. We have heard that the country endures poverty, is ravished by inflation, has a declining standard of living and blatantly high levels of unemployment; that multinational corporations are some sort of an evil and spreading disease; that big business is unresponsive to the consumer and surely unresponsive to the society; that this system rapes the environment, and so on—surely, a wide array of charges. I thought it would be useful to examine some of the facts that seem relevant to those charges in perhaps a neutral way, if that is possible. Then perhaps we can discuss whether this American economic system under which we all live is a moral system.

The Problem of Inflation

The number one problem in America today, as recorded by the public opinion polls, is inflation. We have had two months of double-digit inflation; that is, about 11 percent. We have had several years of inflation running between 5 and 7.5 or 8 percent, which is abnormally high by American historical standards. Anyone who would deny that this level of inflation has eroded American purchasing power and the American standard of living would simply be wrong, because it has.

On the other hand, the charge has surfaced that our standard of living is declining because of inflation, two recessions, and, of course, the very nature of capitalism in the modern world. This charge is not the same as saying that inflation has eroded some of our purchasing power, which it surely has.

To my knowledge, having looked through a wide array of statistical data, I find that it is simply not true that the American standard of living has been declining in the last decade or so. The real income in the United States is up per family, per person—no matter how it is measured—after discounting for such ravages of inflation as are appropriate through the consumer price index.

Interestingly enough, the charge that real income has been declining is made by both liberals and conservatives, for a variety of political, polemical, and rhetorical reasons. Both seem to have a vested interest right now in saying that this economy does not work.

In the political community there is an old axiom that when liberals want to set up a firing squad, they form a circle. For forty years our society has been largely dominated by liberal activists and new-deal type economics. Now, for some reason, liberals seem to have a vested interest in saying that the system does not work. Their clarion call is, "We have failed. Let us continue." I have great difficulty in figuring out exactly what their motive is, but I think we are familiar with that kind of rhetoric.

The conservatives, of course, like to say that the economy is not working because we have been spending too much money, and we have to cut back and live within our means. But in fact the standard of living in the last ten years has been going up, though at about half the rate that it was going up in the previous decade. The 1960s were a boom decade throughout the developed world. Especially in the United States it was a time of quickly advancing prosperity sheathed by only minimal amounts of inflationary erosion. The real per capita income in this country was going up about 4 percent a year, and in the last seven or eight years, it has been going up a little less than 2 percent a year. There has been some erosion because of sometimes baffling economic phenomena. But that is all it has been—an erosion of a rate that is still headed north. That is an important fact that people tend to forget.

In the European countries, the less-developed countries, and the developed countries, including Japan, there has been talk about the great economic miseries they have been going through in recent years. But despite the recession, unemployment, and inflation, their real standard of living also has been going up—though admittedly at a much slower rate than previously. The question is whether, for example, the 9, 10, and 11 percent annual growth rates that Japan had in the 1950s and early 1960s are really sustainable over an extended period of time. When those numbers are extrapolated the curve doubles back on itself it goes up so fast; it is like compound interest. The same question applies to the German, Italian, and French growth rates. At certain periods they were 5 or 6 percent, remarkably high and perhaps unsustainable. These countries started from the very low base of a wiped-out, war-ravished economy and were able to grow very rapidly. In a more mature industrial society, however, is it realistic to expect 4, 5, and 6 percent growth rates? The only answer I know is that nobody knows the answer. History will have to play itself out.

Employment and Unemployment

Unemployment statistics have been very much in the news in the last couple of years. The first thing that one must acknowledge, if one has any sensibilities at all, is that unemployment is a real and tragic problem. Anybody who has ever been out of a job, or thought of being out of a job, knows how scary that can be. And nothing that I am about to say is to be construed as diminishing the idea that unemployment is a deeply unfortunate human circumstance. It is, however, perhaps useful to put unemployment into a numerical perspective that might give us a sense of what it is we are talking about.

People say that the unemployment rate is going up, yet there are some other rates that are of interest. For example, the number of people employed has been soaring in this country. As the baby-boom youngsters become of job-holding age they are looking for work and, for the most part, finding it. This is not a planned economic feat, but this society is absorbing about 4 million new workers every year in just those teenage brackets. That is a lot of new workers, and the economy is absorbing them with only some trouble. Moreover, although unemployment rates are high, the percentage of the population employed is about four percentage points higher than it has ever been in this country.

The percentage—which is not what the unemployment rate indicates, although many people think it is—is at an all time high for some simple unplanned reason. There are a disproportionate number of young people and a disproportionate number of women moving into the labor force. In an era when we are told that the work ethic is diminishing and that we have a high unemployment rate, it is useful to note that greater percentages of people are working now than ever before in the history of this republic.

That leaves us with the unemployment rate, which is at about 5.7

percent right now. Some of the economists at the American Enterprise Institute choose to say that that is close to full employment, and I have come around to the belief that they are probably close to right. I will go through the numbers and suggest why it is that I have come to that belief.

It was not close to full employment when, during the middle of the recession, unemployment was 8 percent, or 7.5 percent, or 7 percent. We have always regarded 4 to 4.5 percent unemployment in this country as "frictional"—that is, mostly people who are voluntarily switching jobs, about 4 percent of the population. They count as unemployed because of the way the unemployment survey is conducted in this country. A telephone survey is made by the Bureau of Labor Statistics that asks, essentially, two questions: Do you have a job? And are you looking for work? If the answer to the first question is no, the second question is asked to find out the unemployment rate. The employed and the unemployed together are called, "the labor force," and the percentage of the labor force that is actively looking for work gives the unemployment rate.

In a normal situation of full employment 4 to 4.5 percent of the population is thus "unemployed" because they have voluntarily left one job and are looking for another. In addition, as I have said, a disproportionate number of women and teenagers are in the job market. Teenagers are by the nature of their social, not their economic, circumstances perennially and typically over-unemployed. They are recently out of school; they are bouncing around; they have one girlfriend, they have another girlfriend; they decide to go to California. Those who have teenaged children will recognize the situation.

To a lesser extent, a high rate of unemployment is also characteristic—at least historically—of women in the labor force because of maternity leaves and a number of other factors. The growing number of women and teenagers in the labor force explains why the economists say that 5.7 percent unemployment is pretty close to full employment, with what they call some "structural pockets." This means that there are certain categories—particularly black teenagers, for example—that have unacceptably high levels of unemployment, but they are only a small percentage of the population.

It is perhaps useful to discuss the black teenage unemployment rate because it is often abused. It is said on the radio and on television again and again that 40 percent of the black teenagers are unemployed. The definition of the unemployment rate, however, suggests that this statistic is wildly misleading.

About 60 percent of all teenagers are "not in the labor force."

155

That means that they do not have a job and are not looking for a job. Most of these 60 percent of black or white teenagers are typically housewives or full-time students, and they are not counted in these unemployment statistics. Only 40 percent of the teenagers are counted "in the labor force." A 40 percent unemployment rate among teenagers therefore refers to about 40 percent of the teenagers in the labor force, or about 16 percent of the total number of teenagers.

Of that 16 percent, half are full-time students looking for part-time work—they are not kids who are hanging around on the street corner, desperate. There are tens of thousands of such desperate young black men, and it is a terrible problem in this country; I would not say anything other than that. But in terms of magnitude, black teenagers who are out of school, out of work, and looking for full-time work constitute 8 to 10 or 12 percent of the number of black teenagers, not 40 percent. This correlates with other statistics. The percentage of black high school graduates today who go on to college is a trifle greater than that of white high school graduates. Blacks drop out of college a little earlier, they are not as likely to get a masters degree, and so on. But ten years ago a white was about seven times more likely to go on to college than was a black. Today, it is about even, and blacks are actually a little bit ahead. That is an absolutely stunning statistic, given the racial history of this country.

Again, there are substructural elements in that blacks are more likely to go to junior colleges than to four-year colleges; they are more like to go to public colleges than private colleges. Still, that is the figure, and it comes much closer to correlating with my view of what the real magnitudes of black unemployment are than the more popularly perceived notion that 40 percent of black teenagers are unemployed. And I would stress again, lest I am misunderstood, that I acknowledge that this is still a deep, and serious, and, in fact, heart-rending problem.

We are told by the Russians that socialist economies do not have unemployment, and they are right. When I was in Hungary about a decade ago, I saw an elderly, overweight woman on a street corner with a bathroom scale. Anyone who wished to be weighed could step on the bathroom scale and pay her the Hungarian equivalent of a penny, which was worth at that time about a third of a U.S. penny. Of course, she was considered employed. In the Soviet Union a few years ago I walked through Red Square in the early morning. Elderly matrons in teams of four were sweeping the square with brooms made out of wooden twigs wrapped around a handle—they are pretty efficient brooms, as a matter of fact. These women are also counted as employed, needless to say.

I do not think there are many people who would argue with the fact that Americans simply will not take this kind of job. Such jobs do not exist because they have been mechanized, but Americans would not take them if they did exist. We do not have women on street corners with bathroom scales; we have penny weighing machines. And we have big street-sweeping machines that do the same thing that the women with the sticks do. Moreover, we have something called unemployment insurance. This is a social welfare floor that we have built into this capitalist economy—which is why people call it a mixed economy, I guess.

Some of those floors, in recent years, have risen to moderately high levels; enough so that in many of the industrial states, unemployment compensation runs close to $140 a week, tax free. In Detroit, for example, in 1975, when the recession hit the auto industry some automobile workers were laid off by the heartless capitalists at Chrysler, Ford, and General Motors. Nobody wanted to buy the cars because there was a recession, though laying off these workers furthered that recession. (An Achilles heel of a capitalist society is surely that it is both cyclical and harsh.) Those unemployed auto workers went on unemployment insurance, and the balance of their normal wage, which ran up to $13,000 or $14,000 a year was paid by the subsistence fund of the United Automobile Workers, which pays benefits in the case of a layoff or a strike. It is money that is provided as part of the negotiated contract with the firm.

About 200,000 automobile workers were laid off, but they were getting as much money as they would have had if they were employed. And they were not stupid. Tens of thousands of them, with their wives and children, drove down to Orlando, Florida—it was wintertime—to observe that capitalist phenomenon, Disney World. The television networks had a big media sweep of Disney World, showing all the unemployed automobile factory workers with their families having a wonderful time on the equivalent of full pay.

Of course, the conservatives clucked and said, "This is terrible. Look at these people—it is a rip-off of the system." I did not think it was terrible. I thought that if they had to be laid off, they might as well be laid off at full pay and go down to Disney World for a few months while the situation straightened itself out.

The unemployment insurance system is of course not without abuse, but it is not a bad system to serve as one of those floors to cushion this harsh, capitalistic economic system and make it a little more humane. There are hundreds of such programs—though not all as comprehensive as unemployment insurance.

Western societies attempted to deal with the recession in another way. The Swedes kept all their employees on in the automobile factories and subsidized the factories to continue producing cars that nobody wanted. Though they did not have unemployment they had a great many cars they did not know what to do with. As I understand it, they are still trying to sell some of them.

Sooner or later, as the illustrious Milton Friedman likes to point out, there is no free lunch. One cannot continue producing cars for which there are no buyers. That is merely a temporary palliative and does not really work in the long run.

When the English faced these kinds of problems, Labour government bailed out the companies in order to preserve jobs. This and similar actions have led to an array of astonishingly inefficient English corporations that simply cannot compete in the world market in a variety of goods and services. Consequently, the English have had to sell their labor more cheaply in order to get a market for their goods. The attempt to be benevolent has ended up by diminishing, not raising, the standard of living of the English worker.

Corporate Responsiveness

It might be useful to take a look at the American corporation, and particularly at the charge that American corporations are not responsive. This seems to be one of the major charges leveled against American corporations, and I would suggest that it is not correct. American corporations, if nothing else, are extremely responsive, occasionally to a fault, in my judgment.

Several years ago *Forbes* magazine had a piece about the responsiveness of American companies. We tend to think of American corporations as ageless, mindless behemoths that go on and on in their own merry way without doing anything for society. In line with this thought, *Forbes* went back fifty years, from 1967 to 1917, and looked at the top hundred corporations in America to see which had survived and which had not. About half of them were no longer in the top hundred, and about a quarter of them had simply gone out of business. With the article, *Forbes* ran a cartoon that pictured a corporate graveyard with headstones for various defunct corporations.

I did a television show last year, called "There Is No Business like Big Business." It attempted to deal with the question, "Is big business in America responsive?" The television people wanted a visual gimmick to make the point a little more apparent than it would be in words alone. They saw the *Forbes* cartoon and talked me into doing a video vignette in which I wandered through an eerie graveyard showing headstones of dead corporate behemoths. It was an interesting scene, and I will go through some of the headstones that we showed.

One headstone was for Central Leather, which in 1917 was the twenty-fourth largest corporation in America. Its profits at that time exceeded those of Sears, Roebuck. Its net worth exceeded that of General Motors. It had put together an empire of 158 tanneries. Central Leather no longer exists, however, because a variety of different kinds of shoemaking equipment came in that it did not respond to quickly enough. Other people were able to undercut the firm, and it simply went out of business.

The next gravestone was for a company called International Mercantile Marine, which was the eleventh largest company in America in 1917, owned by a young man named J. P. Morgan—surely a man not without political influence in this country. The company needed subsidies from the Congress in order to stay afloat but it did not get them. It was undercut in large measure by foreign freighters and went out of business.

The show went through a whole series of such corporate gravestones. There was a great corporate conglomerate called American Woolen, whose executive board simply did not believe that synthetic fibers would ever amount to anything. By the time American Woolen became aware of the American consumers' demand for synthetic fibers, there wasn't any American Woolen left. Baldwin Locomotive was convinced that the diesel engine would never make it in American railroading. Of course, diesel engines did make it, but Baldwin Locomotive did not.

During World War II, Curtis-Wright built the P-40, a great zooming airplane. The firm was bigger than Boeing and bigger than Lockheed. When the war ended, the corporate managers decided that while the jet plane might be useful as a military weapon it surely had no civilian applicability and they stuck with propeller planes. By the time the managers tried to get in on jets they were unable to respond to the people who had voted with their dollars that jet airplanes were, in fact, a good thing. Curtis-Wright is not a defunct company, but it went from twenty-eighth on the list to something like 550th in a matter of about ten years.

Thus, companies that we view as immovable behemoths that can never be pushed by public opinion or by the market, are, in fact, pushed by the market, sometimes to the point of extinction.

The argument is made that Madison Avenue can sell us anything. I would suggest that anyone go to Detroit and try that particular line on the people who produced the Edsel. The Edsel had a massive advertising budget of tens of millions of dollars. Production, tool-up, and advertising costs made it a $500 million automobile, but nobody bought it. The Ford Motor Company did not go out of business—though it almost did—but the whole Edsel division went out of business.

And that, in fact, is the pattern today. Occasionally, big companies, such as W. T. Grant, still go out of business because they cannot respond to the market. But, more typically, whole product lines or whole divisions simply disappear.

Every Christmas, at its corporate Christmas party, the General Electric Company displays a so-called lemon tree. The tree is hung with all the products it put on the market that year that failed, despite the great savvy and wizardry of the marketing department, Madison Avenue, and television. GE invested tens of millions of its stockholders' dollars in products that nobody wanted to buy. Despite all of the motivational market research, GE simply was not smart enough to put out a product that people really wanted.

Although I have heard many people *not* in the advertising business say that advertising and Madison Avenue can sell anything, I have never once heard that uttered by an advertising man, because any advertising man knows it is not so. Advertising people always quote Abraham Lincoln: "You may fool all the people some of the time; you can even fool some of the people all the time; but you can't fool all of the people all the time." Many people in the advertising business are perfectly prepared to confess over a few drinks that they like to fool some of the people some of the time. It is not a particularly saintly business, and I wouldn't pretend otherwise. But they cannot sell people things that they do not want. They can try to create a desire by advertising something and that in itself, of course, is an important act. It requires capital and know-how, but then it is up to the public to say whether they are willing to spend their hard-earned dollars on it.

Some people may, of course, disagree with how these dollars are spent. They may say that the dollars in our gross national product ought not to be spent on deodorants; they ought to be spent on social workers. But our society does not work—for the moment, anyway—according to the dictates of great social scientists, bureaucrats, and economists. I imagine John Kenneth Galbraith as a man who would like to tell us what we ought to buy and what we ought to have in the United States. That is not the way the system works, however.

Our capitalist system has been called "dollar democracy," and it is; it is democratic almost to a fault. People decide what they want to spend their dollars on and thereby make or break the fortunes of great advertising agencies and great corporations. I would just as soon live by the will of the people as by the wisdom of John Kenneth Galbraith.

It is said that this system of dollar democracy may be good for the consumer—he gets what he wants—but it is bad for society. We have come up with a way to deal with some of those ills as well. We call it taxes. We let corporations make as much money as they can and then we tax some of that money away and do good things with it.

When I was on President Johnson's White House staff, I felt that he made a mistake when, during the urban riots in the mid-1960s, he helped set up the Urban Coalition and the National Alliance of Businessmen. Johnson's idea was that businessmen were so efficient and so effective that they should rebuild inner-city New York and inner-city Detroit. He called them the dynamic renaissance men of our society and wanted to get them to heal the ills of poverty. I always felt that was a bad idea, however, although I am second to none in my admiration of the efficiency and effectiveness of businessmen within the market system, in producing toothbrushes, or automobiles, or houses.

At that time, a remarkable man named Wilbur Cohen was the secretary of health, education, and welfare. It is an impossible job but he did it about as well as it has ever been done before or since. Taxes collected from corporations and from people are redistributed by HEW, with a little bit—or a lot—taken out to run the bureaucracy, and Wilbur Cohen did an effective job of getting out social security checks, disability checks, welfare checks, and so forth.

I have met Henry Ford and I knew Wilbur Cohen quite well, but I would not particularly want to risk my own life or the life of my family in a car designed, and engineered, and produced by Wilbur Cohen. By the same token, I would surely not want a welfare system administered by Henry Ford. Each one was good at what he did but probably would have been a disaster doing the other person's job.

Not that corporations should not be good citizens—we should all be good citizens. Let them sponsor the opera or support the charities that interest them. But the burden of being the great moral agents of this society should not be put upon the business community. That is probably a governmental function.

Our system taxes profits and incomes and puts them to work in some benevolent fashion, and I think the record over the last twenty years has been rather good. According to the official definition of poverty, in the last twenty years the percentage of people in poverty in the United States has been halved, though about 9 or 10 percent of the population is sitll officially considered "in poverty." The number of people in colleges increased from about 3 million to about 12 million in about a fourteen-year period, partly because of demographics, but also because of a great increase in the percentage of the population going on to college. It represents a massive upgrading of education in this country. We inaugurated Medicare, which, for all its inflationary effects, still enables elderly people in this country to live their lives with a greater measure of dignity than before the program existed. We set in motion a set of environmental protection laws, which started out to be good and in some ways still are, though in other ways that I will talk about later, they have gone too far. In any event, we made certain welfare gains during those "Great Society" years, and they have not been rolled back in my judgment.

The Private Sector and the Public Sector

If the public sector, for all its flaws, does do some good with our income taxes, corporate or personal, the obvious next question is why the government does not do more of those sorts of good things. But what do we really want when we say that? Do we want a greater percentage of our total wealth devoted to the public sector, to these benefits, or a greater actual amount of dollars to help the poor and the unfortunate? I would rather have more dollars. I do not care very much about the percentages; I care about getting a certain amount of dollars out to people.

The argument that economists make, with a great deal of merit, I think, is that at a certain point, siphoning money out of the private sector and into the public sector through taxes stymies incentive. If too much is taken out in taxes, the people who are producing the wealth will find that it is not worthwhile to invest money in a new plant, to work over-time, or to come up with a new invention. At that point, although a greater percentage is being taxed out of the economy, there are fewer tax dollars to distribute to people who need it.

We have seen in other mixed or social-democratic economies exactly this phenomenon at work. In the United Kingdom, income taxes go up over 90 percent at the incremental top dollar. As a result there are a great many English doctors in America. They did not want to work an extra thirty hours a week if they could keep only one out of ten or one out of twenty of the extra dollars. Those kinds of punitive tax rates also engender a massive system of either barter or cheating.

In Sweden there was a well-publicized case of a woman who wrote children's books. She made the startling discovery that through a variety of criss-crossing tax regulations, her 1975 income would be taxed at the rate of 104 percent. At that rate she would end up with less than she started with, and she complained. Ingmar Bergman, the great Swedish movie director, was being taxed in the high or the mid-ninetieth percentile, and he simply left Sweden. Bjorn Borg, who is a Swede, now plays tennis out of Monte Carlo, where his official residence is. These are some of the results when more money is pushed into the public sector.

A separate problem is that many of us, for a variety of reasons and to a variety of degrees, have become somewhat disillusioned with how well the public sector is doing its job. How much waste is there? How much bloat is there? I have never met anybody in government who doesn't think that there is a great deal. Of course, I have never met anybody in corporate life who does not think there is waste and bloat there as well.

When I came to Washington in 1966, I was the chief executive officer of a one-man publishing firm, my own. Then I went to work in the White House for Lyndon Johnson, the leader of the free world. I went from the smallest business in the world to the biggest, right at the peak of power. I tried to figure out which was the less efficient of those two operations, the one-man model of great precision—my own little company—or the federal government. I decided that they were each sorely lacking in efficiency and the kind of corporate zeal that they ought to have had. When I later got into the corporate world, I found that here, too, human beings operate at high levels of inefficiency.

Another example of this phenomenon of "no free lunch" is given by Theodore H. White in his new book, *In Search of History*.[1] I recommend it to you. He is a good writer and a thoughtful person. I do not agree with everything he says, but it is an interesting book.

He recounts his life as a war correspondent in China during World War II and then as a foreign correspondent in Europe. He describes the beginnings of the Marshall Plan, whereby the United States pumped massive amounts of American dollars into the staggered and demolished European economies.

The English, being benevolent and with a very idealistic Labour government, used much of those extra Marshall Plan counterpart funds to fuel a new welfare state—national health insurance, free college education, and the whole gamut of the English social welfare system. The Germans, who were our former enemies, were not allowed to do that by the Marshall Plan administrators—though I am not sure they wanted to. They were told, in effect, that they would not get things

---

[1] Theodore H. White, *In Search of History: A Personal Expedition* (New York: Harper and Row, 1978).

free, that they would have to earn everything. We would give them some money to get back on their feet because of the threat of Soviet power and the danger of a recurrence of the economic and political situation of the 1920s, but the German people had to earn it. And they did. It was not until about ten years later that they were able to set up a social-welfare system. It was derived from real earnings, from real productivity in real factories producing real goods that people wanted, not just fabricated out of "funny money."

The lesson that White draws very clearly, is that today the German standard of living, including those social welfare floors, is about twice as high as the English because the Germans spent out of earnings. They reinvested earnings, and they operated in the real world. They did not get seduced—or were not allowed to be seduced, as the case may be—by the idea that it is enough merely to be a "good guy." We have learned again and again in this country, in every one of our attempts to be great social engineers, that the game is not that simple. Frequently, when we try to be a good guy, we end up hurting what we love about as much as if we had been its mortal enemy.

Multinational Corporations and the Third World

The multinational corporations also have been dragged through the court of public opinion. The case has been made that they exploit the Third World, that they are great imperialists, and so on.

I have only one specific point to make about the general charge that the great raping, rampaging multinationals control the world today. The simple fact is that governments are stronger than companies, and for a very simple reason: governments have armies. If there should ever be a war between a government and a company, the government would win. Even in the most lowly, least-developed country in the world, if the government should decide to start a war with the corporation, the government would always win.

One normally hears how powerful multinationals are. But countries are the more powerful instrumentalities. The corporations really have only one weapon, which is not to invest their money in a country. If, for example, a country levies taxes at 104 percent, the corporation can close its factory or open a new one. The government has the power to do whatever it wants, but the only thing the corporation can do is to go somewhere else. That is, in fact, how the equation plays itself out, again illustrating the theory that "there is no free lunch."

My experience has been that the Third World countries are busy crying "rape" at the same moment they are practicing seduction. They

164

go to the United Nations and accuse the imperialist multinational corporations of ruining their culture and plundering their fuels. At the same time, on Wall Street and elsewhere they are trying desperately to persuade American multinationals, German multinationals, Japanese multinationals, English, and Dutch, to invest in their country the megabucks accumulated from Western technology. They promise tax holidays, tax deferrals, cheap labor costs, and no unions, and they offer a long string of benefits.

This causes great consternation in the American labor movement, but the developing countries are absolutely right. They know that in the less-developed world only where imperialism has landed has prosperity come about. It is a harsh and ugly system, cruel in many ways. But the historical facts seem to be that only where Westerners, with no particularly benevolent motives, set foot, do technology, and capital, and modern marketing methods also set foot, and are markets developed for products in the Third World. The case that I would make is that of all of the great modern instrumentalities, the multinational corporation, for all its flaws, is probably the supreme agent of human betterment on this planet at this moment.

Environmentalism and the Standard of Living

The corporation also has been attacked on the ground that it is a great polluter and raper of resources. There is an element of truth to that, surely. But, again, one must ask the question, at what point does environmentalism begin to become counterproductive?

Nobody wants to live in a smoggy, sooty, disease-ridden city with dirty water and dirty air. Accordingly, environmentalists, particularly on the campuses and among young people, have captured the moral high ground with the image of being "Mr. Good-Guy." I would suggest, however, that if we examine the environmentalist activities in recent years, we would come up with a very different answer; they are not the "good guys" any more. They—in the corporate sense of "they"— are opposing nuclear power; for many years they opposed the development of offshore, outer-continental shelf oil, they opposed and delayed the Alaska oil pipeline, they are holding up dams in several states to save the snail darter and the Furbish lousewort, and they have delayed and diminished the ability to strip-mine coal. Any one of those ideas makes a certain amount of sense, like the idea that we should not have a particular food or a particular drug because it may be dangerous or carcinogenic. But taken as a whole, these ideas begin to kill the things

165

we love. They begin to diminish severely the standard of living in this country.

The environmentalists say that pollution abatement creates jobs, and it does. But Lord Keynes, of course, remarked that we can achieve full employment by employing people to dig holes and then fill them up again. And that is what a lot of environmental spending can amount to.

If we envision the economy as a pipeline, capital and technology and labor are put in one end and what is supposed to come out the other end is goods and services for people. In the middle of that pipe there is now a baffle that filters out some of that capital and technology and labor and devotes it to taking particles out of the air or to some other antipollution measure. A certain number of particles, obviously, have to come out of the air, but the costs are enormous.

If environmental spending in this country is plotted on a graph, it looks like what the economists would call a J curve. It goes up steeply, starting in about 1970 when antipollution laws began to phase in. Recently Edward Dennison at the Brookings Institution showed me some of the numbers of aggregate environmental spending in both the public and private sector. The curve looks exactly like a J, except that we have not yet reached the top. Environmental spending is at a level of about $35 billion a year. Programs started up with $10 million here and $10 million there. And as the late Everett Dirksen used to say, a billion here, a billion there, starts adding up to real money after a while. One agency estimated that half a trillion dollars will be spent in ten years, diminishing the American standard of living by about 10 percent in terms of its growth.

That is a lot of money, particularly in relation to the environmental ills that we have. We rarely stop to consider that, as Philip Handler, the president of the National Academy of Sciences, recently said, never before in the history of humankind have people been as healthy as they are today in the Western world, of which ours is surely the preeminent country.

The environmental mentality is a rich person's mentality; it is a rich person's movement. They say, in effect, that they already have theirs, so they can pull up the gangplanks. They want no growth or slow growth, and they refer to the "gross national pollution." They don't want the national parks swarming with middle-class people who, if the economy keeps flourishing, will have enough money to buy a second car and a camper trailer. And yet, for some strange reason, they are called liberals.

Part of the attack on "energy waste in America" is, in my judgment, an indirect but profound attack on the American suburb—a detached house, with an air conditioner and two cars, that needs two breadwinners to support it. It is as though something obscene suddenly came into our world right after World War II—an ugly thing called the suburb. Of course suburbia is made up of fast-food restaurants, and neon signs, and superhighways, and other unattractive things. But a house with a yard and some shrubbery, and a car, and a shopping center, and maybe a swimming pool happen to be what most people in America want, and, in fact, what most people around the world want.

The environmentalists seem to think that represents waste. They point out that Sweden and Germany have high levels of consumption but they do not use as much energy as we do because they do not live mainly in a suburban setting. That is an American style of life that people happen to like.

I think the environmentalists are engaged in a self-fulfilling march to set into motion both the science and the politics to prove that we are using too much energy. They would prefer a different kind of life in order to cut back on energy use, but, surely, the American people would not.

The Morality of Capitalism

The question now is, are the capitalists moral? Are they "good guys"? Does our system provide the benefits that a moral system ought to provide? As I indicated, the role of capitalists in the intricate mechanism of our society is not to be moral. Just as our governmental system has checks and balances between the legislative, the judicial, and the executive branches, so, too, does the economic system. Business is checked frequently by big labor.

I am a particular fan of big business and big labor and big government. This is a big country, and it ought to have big central institutions to deal with our problems. In fact, it does. Big business is frequently checked by a very powerful pro-labor government in this country and properly so, because it would rip off all of us if it could get away with it. Everybody in business knows that. Many businesses that are not unionized give their workers a great many benefits simply because they know that if they are not good to the workers the unions will come in and get them.

My son, who is a nineteen-year-old college student, managed to get a union job on a freighter headed for Puerto Rico. He worked very hard seven days a week; he worked overtime and double time. And after twenty days at sea he came back with a thousand dollars. Just think—a thousand dollars in twenty days for a nineteen-year-old!

167

Without union protection, he would not have been paid nearly that much.

If unchecked, business would bid down labor in a descending spiral, playing one person against another. Unions represent a great check on corporate avarice, although they are not an all-perfect set of instrumentalities. The labor unions themselves are checked by business and by government. And government—though some of its regulatory rulings are annoying to many of us—is a great check on both business and on labor, frequently protecting Americans from the possibility of corporate avarice, for example, through the activities over the years of the Food and Drug Administration. One would not want a totally free market economy, given the acquisitiveness of capitalism. People might be tempted to do some things that would not be very constructive.

All that businessmen ask of a regulatory system is that government administrators stop changing the rules and tell them what they are allowed to do and what they are not allowed to do. Then, if left alone, the business community would be spurred by acquisitiveness or some other incentive to make economic mini-miracles.

We have created an economic system in this country that is moral in its effects because it is, if not greedy, at least self-fulfilling and incentive-oriented (there are several words, both good and bad, that can be used to express that idea). People work in a capitalist system because they can make something of themselves, more money, more fame, more of whatever it is they want. The system is moral in its effects because it has provided a remarkably high level of material well-being. And it has done that because it has managed to harness capital, and technology, and brain power to a very raw and basic human emotion—call it greed or incentive—the desire of people to move themselves forward. It must be checked by labor and government, surely, but only to a point. The system is, I think, sound. Checking it at various spots makes sense; overchecking can lead to its slow destruction.

We then have to ask ourselves perhaps a final question. On the one hand we have a system that is moral in its effects in that it provides a high level of goods and services, a high standard of living for people, a low level of disease, but that harnesses an inherent human power that is not necessarily regarded as moral. On the other hand we could choose a system that is moral in its precepts—each according to his needs, each according to his ability, all one big happy family—but that provides remarkably slow growth of prosperity compared with the other system. Which system is preferable? Is the amoral system more moral than the moral system?

My answer is yes, the amoral system is much more moral than

the moral system because little babies do not die, people live longer, and they live in nice houses, and they have a much higher quotient of human dignity. In addition, these amoral systems are, surprisingly, the systems in which political freedoms flourish. There are of course some examples of capitalist authoritarian repressive states, but there are no examples of states that are truly free that are not essentially capitalist. Systems that move toward massively high levels of public sector spending and approach total or near total state control produce neither prosperity nor freedom. Taiwan compared with mainland China and North Korea compared with South Korea are clear examples in recent history.

Therefore, I would vote for the amoral system that is moral in its effects. We have established a unique system in the United States. I don't know whether I would call it capitalist, or mixed, or social welfare, but it has worked pretty well. It has room for improvement, but I would be very wary of tinkering with it in a massive way, because when people start tinkering with things in a massive way they usually manage to mess it up.

Business as an Instrument of National Policy

We might now look briefly at the shady side of this remarkable, benevolent society that I have just described. On at least one specific issue this system does not operate very well.

At present, there is a struggle within the executive branch of government whether America ought to license a firm in the Southwest, Dresser Industries, to sell oil-drilling bits to the Soviet Union. This requires a special Department of Commerce license. That struggle, of course, is not a new one; it has been going on ever since the era of the Nixon-Kissinger détente. If we accept the notion that the Soviet Union is our adversary, in terms of cosmic issues such as the survival of human freedom, should we make its course easier or more difficult? The Kissinger-Nixon idea was that, by making it easier for the Russians, we would force them into a web of interdependence that would make it impossible for them to harm us without hurting themselves. That was one of the pillars of détente.

Since that remarkable dawning of international amity, the Soviet Union has supplied military equipment to North Vietnam and prompted us to go to a nuclear alert in the Middle East. Russia has gone through the fastest peacetime military build-up in the history of the world. And other great fruits of détente have ensued.

My argument, quite simply, is that we ought not to help the Russians, or if they need our technology or capital we ought to extract a price for it. The Jackson amendment is the classic example of this position. I regard it as one of the great moral pieces of legislation of our era. It said that we would not provide certain trade credits or tariff concessions to the Soviet Union or to any nonmarket economy unless we were assured that their emigration policies were in conformity with the United Nations Declaration of Human Rights.

Needless to say, that whole initiative has been systematically undermined by the business community in the United States. Although I earlier made the case that the business community is a splendid exemplar of all facets of Americanism, I would now suggest that it is, at the same time, remarkably self-destructive in the political realm. Businessmen may operate well in the economic realm, for the reasons already cited, but in the political realm, they do not.

In the economic realm, they fly in corporate jets to long-range planning seminars, at which they are able to determine, for example, the market share of cathode ray copper in the year 1998. In long-range planning for the survival of the system upon which they depend, however, their foresight is extremely limited. They encourage sales of technology through concessionary terms, helping the Soviet Union and its allies to grow and develop, without attempting, at the same time, to steer it into a more humanitarian mode. They do not sense that this failure severely undermines the chances for the survival of our free economic system, the foundation upon which they have built their corporate empire.

I have written a book in collaboration with Richard Whalen, *The Wealth Weapon*. The thesis of the book is that, in the last twenty years, the American foreign policy situation has changed dramatically. Whereas twenty years ago the United States was the preeminent and decisive military power in the world, that is no longer the case. At best, we are at parity with our primary adversary. Twenty years ago it was unquestioned that what we have come to call the American ideology was regnant; it was the ideology that people around the world were looking to as the shape of the future. That, too, has come under some question. In the forum of the United Nations, for example, the Western nations and America are attacked with stunning regularity.

If, in the course of furthering our own interests, particularly in relation to our adversaries, our military arrow has been blunted and our diplomatic and ideological arrows have become warped, we must look for alternative methods to encourage our interests around the world. When we look for available arrows, we find that one great advantage we have is the remarkable economic potency that has been built up in this country and in the nations that are our allies. Whatever might be said against the nations of the Western alliance, they have built up the most astonishing array of economic and technological power that the world has ever seen. In an era when our diplomacy, ideology, and military power are somewhat diminished, we have, then, instrumentalities to make our weight felt.

I mentioned one earlier, the multinational corporation. If it is as benevolent a device as I suggested, it is of enormous value in an era when our government is not as powerful as, perhaps, it once was. If nations all over the world seek the entry of our multinational corporations to provide them with all the goods and services they desire, should we not think about using them as an instrument of national policy? Should we not decide to export capital, for example, to an underdeveloped nation on the basis of whether that nation is in some way helpful, or at least not harmful, to the interests of the United States?

The same concerns should govern decisions regarding export licensing, technology transfer, and particularly agripower. Earl Butz, the former secretary of agriculture, used to say that the United States was feeding the world and that agripower was a tremendous instrument for the United States to wield at the appropriate moment. Because the secretary of agriculture was then, and probably always will be, a captive of the people who grow the goods, the time to use that power was never, because it would mean cutting back on some production and profits here in the United States.

Lenin said many years ago that the communists need not fear where they would get the rope to hang the capitalists—it would be sold to them by the capitalists. Lenin did not foresee that the capitalists would not only sell them the rope but would sell it on credit, at interest rates far lower than they charge other capitalists.

The business community, of course, vigorously rejects—for some sound economic reasons, I must admit—the idea of using our economic potency for any political end. But I am suggesting that there is power there that is almost entirely untapped by our government. And it would be useful if we attempted to direct the business community into channels where it could help attain the larger goals of the society.

This suggestion is not meant as a criticism of the multinational corporation. I am saying that the multinational corporation is a remarkable instrumentality. It moves capital and technology around the world toward ends that are basically benevolent, particularly for the people who receive that investment and technology. In fact, multinational corporations are so good that we ought to harness them to the sled to help pull a bit, instead of merely riding on it.

Interestingly enough, the business community regards this suggestion as an attack upon its honor and its substance at least as violent as the attack from the left, which regards multinationals as evil. In many ways, the idea that I am talking about is scarier to the business community than the attack from the left, because it could politicize the whole economic system. If overdone, that could be injurious to the whole nature of international trade.

Our economic power ought not to be harnessed in an extremist manner. The wealth weapon cannot and ought not be a battering ram. But the question is, Can it be a useful tool to further our national goals?

Discussion

QUESTION: You used several phrases which were new to me, such as "voting with dollars" and "dollar democracy." You also said "you can't be a good guy" and "we should all be good citizens," and you discussed what Americans want. Do you make a distinction between the definitions of, say, a first-rate human being, a first-rate consumer, and a first-rate American citizen? Do you use them as synonomous terms?

MR. WATTENBERG: No, I don't think so. When we talk about a consumer, we talk about an abstraction in an economic realm. When we talk about an American citizen, we would probably be speaking of a political realm. When we talk of a human being, it is in a spiritual realm, I suppose.

It is obvious that neither economics nor politics can be a substitute for religion or for spirituality. The only thing that economics or politics can offer is the absence of specific miseries: child labor, or pollution, or poverty. It cannot deal with the creation of human happiness, which is in the realm of the spirit.

One of the great confusions in American politics came about in the 1960s when people began feeling that politics and economics could substitute for spirituality. Some of the ideas introduced during the 1960s were beneficial to this country—parts of the women's movement, parts of the environmental movement, and much of the civil rights movement. The failure, however, of the new politics was its attempt to handle everything, the whole human experience. Government cannot deal with that; politics cannot deal with that. In my pessimistic moments, I am not sure religion can either.

Let me give an example. The environmental movement began with good ideas such as clean air and clean water. Now, however, power plants that we need are not being built because of the environmentalists, and in Alaska, they have just taken 100 million acres and said we can only go in there on foot. The movement we call environmentalism has become counterproductive toward the rank and file of American citizens.

QUESTION: You implied, in your presentation, that the rapid rise in spending for environmental purposes was diminishing the American standard of living by that much. Of course, one of the purposes of the environmental movement is to improve the standard of living, assuming that quality of life is part of that standard. Granting the possible excesses of that movement, would you agree that at least part of the money will, over a period of time, have a positive impact on the standard of living?

MR. WATTENBERG: Yes, I surely would. Much of the environmental legislation as originally passed made a great deal of sense. What troubles me about the whole movement is what I would call its mentality. The sense one gets from reading much of the environmental literature is that something has turned obscene, rotten, and ugly in the twentieth century—namely the things that most people in America desire. Environmentalists talk about "suburban sprawl" and "the cancer of suburbia," yet suburbia appears to be a desirable place to live. Proof of that is that so many people are prepared to spend so many of their hard-earned dollars to have a home there.

It comes down to this. Should consumers decide what they will get or should the government tell them what they will get? The first is what "dollar democracy" is all about. If a book is going to be published, somebody has to want to buy that book. If we want all of those local beers, people have to be willing to pay the extra nickel. The same is true for the mom and pop grocery store. It was in the neighborhood, we knew the owners, and they would give us credit. But the supermarket wiped them out, because we could get our groceries cheaper at a supermarket. If we want to keep the mom and pop store in business for some romantic notion, we have to pay for it.

The environmentalist, it appears, would have the government tell consumers what they can have, so he comes up with bizarre regulations. It stems from a basic philosophical difference as to what is good social engineering and what is bad social engineering.

QUESTION: In regard to our international policy, you stated that you did not really have a specific program or plan for implementing your insights, but I wonder if you have some idea of a very general nature. For example, would such an aim be better accomplished by an educational crusade, by business leaders, or by institutionalizing it in the public sector? I am particularly interested in our long-range policy toward the Soviet Union, especially in connection with the dissidents. Should we, for instance, exercise a different sort of economic policy with the satellite nations of the Soviet Union—Poland, Czechoslovakia, Yugoslavia, and others—than we do with Moscow?

MR. WATTENBERG: First, I do not think it can be a crusade by business. It has to be done governmentally, and astutely—as if with a scalpel rather than a battering ram. Concerning the dissidents, for instance, it probably has to be done case by case, with specific linkages to human rights and to emigration.

That method, however, should not lead us to regard the struggle as one to save the lives of a few dissidents, no matter how noble they may be. That should not be the aim of a policy of human rights, which I think really ought to be the hallmark and the keystone of American foreign policy. The real issue is not the survival of a few dissidents; it is the survival of the Western notion of human freedom. If the Soviets want economic advancement and development, they must understand that we will provide them with the necessary capital and technology only if there is a relaxation of repression.

I think we ought to deal with each nation individually, concerning its political circumstance. The only problem is when that is interpreted to mean that all trade with the Eastern European countries is, in and of itself, good because it sets up a web of interdependence. That is not the way I would execute it. I would still be looking for a specific performance, to use a legal term.

The Jackson amendment is an excellent example. It states that we will not provide most-favored-nation status to any country that does not allow people to emigrate. The Rumanians—and I think the Hungarians —have qualified under the Jackson amendment for most-favored-nation status, because they have relaxed emigration standards. Such a status is of enormous value to any country in the world. No nation has achieved economic progress without having access to the American market. That is really our basic economic potency: a country of 225 million people with enormous buying power. That is an enormous lure, and we ought to use it.

In 1970 the rate of Russian-Jewish emigres was about 2,000 a year. Through a combination of private and public pressure, that rate is now at a median of 15,000-18,000 a year, with some peaks and valleys in the middle. Without the Jackson amendment, without public pressure, all the private pressure in the world would never have succeeded. Public pressure is one weapon we have that they do not. When I was in the Soviet Union in 1975, dissidents told me that it is the only thing that keeps the heat on the Soviets, and the record bears them out.

A Social Democratic View

Penn Kemble

I hope that what I have to say will be a little more optimistic than some of the things we have heard. I think that there is much more ground for hope in our political and cultural situation than some have suggested. Perhaps my social democratic outlook accounts for this.

My sense is that what is valid in capitalism probably cannot be saved by capitalism alone. It will, in part, be saved by movements and ideas which have arisen from the general tendency in the industrial, democratic world which can be called social democratic.

Irving Kristol described our system as capitalistic. That is something of a misnomer. Ours, rather, is a system which incorporates two sectors—a capitalist sector, and a sector which can properly be described as social democratic. Our system is not wholly dominated by either of these sectors. To describe our system as capitalism, as he insisted we should, seems to me to concede a large and very valuable ground to the international opponents of the democratic way of life. It also gives capitalism more credit than it deserves for what is our reasonably successful form of society.

I also am uncomfortable with the prophecies of doom that recurrently appear in these discussions. There is a similarity between some of the prophecies that we have just heard and the tone that was set by the New Left in the mid-1960s. Then we were told, over and over, that our system was verging towards terrible catastrophe, and that, unless we rejected the status quo and accepted what was being preferred by the new radicals, disaster would surely befall us.

Norman Podhoretz once remarked that when we hear people preaching impending catastrophe, we have to be wary: they often are less concerned with having us save ourselves than with persuading us to give them more power so that they can save us.

Sources of Pessimism

I do not think we are necessarily headed for catastrophe, but we are indeed suffering from a failure of nerve, a sense of panic and paralysis that can lead to what Senator Pat Moynihan calls "identification with the aggressor." I suspect that many young people in the mid-1960s were moved to embrace ideas quite foreign to our democratic values because those ideas seemed to represent an inevitable wave of the future, and either one had to learn to ride with it, or one would be engulfed by it.

Prophecies of doom have a tendency to be self-fulfilling. They lead to despair, they lead to flights from reality, and they often contribute further to the difficulties we are in. Let me cite two sources of the current neoconservative pessimism that seem misconceived. The first is its conviction that the state is inherently an enemy of the moral and cultural values of liberty. The second is that there is a new class developing in the industrial world that is somehow inherently opposed to, or at the least indifferent to, the values of democratic culture.

Let me offer a personal observation about the new class. I am a child of the new class—a child of its social milieu and of its era. Many people here appear to share that background and experience. But was there not much that was really quite promising in the 1960s, at least in the early period? I identify very much with the temper of the country in the period, say, from 1958 to 1964—the period of the civil rights movement, the New Frontier, the experiments with the War on Poverty, even the explorations in cultural values and "life style."

But in about 1964-1965—some people date it from the time of President Kennedy's assassination, but for all the importance that event holds in our lives, it may not have been quite so central—a shift occurred in the prevailing culture, certainly the culture of the intellectual community. Most of what was attractive about the first years of the 1960s was lost to us. An important conflict rose up over the direction that liberalism should take, and those who share the values that appear to be prevalent in this conference were defeated. This conflict was very poorly perceived by many, but it was fairly well understood by the groups at its center.

One of the failings that led to the defeat of our kind of liberalism was its lack of emphasis on what might be called moral and ideological matters. That was partly the result of a misconception that arose in the late 1950s in a school of thought that encompassed many who today consider themselves to be neoconservatives. This school argued that America had entered a period in which ideology was no longer essential; in fact, from the standpoint of all sensible people, ideology was to be avoided. Ideology was seen as something standing in the way of the kind of consensus and incremental progress that had brought America to its pinnacle of well being and power in the world.

This was often described as the "end of ideology" school, and I am sure many of you are familiar with it. When rereading that debate over the end of ideology recently, I was struck by an exchange that took place in *Commentary* magazine about 1964 between Daniel Bell and Henry David Aiken, a professor of ethics, I believe, at the University of Chicago. Aiken argued that if one accepts the thesis that ideology—that is, political ideas that are infused with passion and that guide action—is an impediment and source of misfortune, we will put ourselves at a profound disadvantage in our debate with the totalitarian world.

Aiken was suggesting that Bell's thesis might have some value when applied to the old debate between socialists and capitalists in the western democratic world. But if the thesis were applied to all political encounters, it could rob us of the moral spirit, the commitment, the will to controversy and even struggle that we must have to defend our system against the ideas of the totalitarian and authoritarian world.

Aiken was hardly an enthusiast for all things American, and probably by today's standards would be thought quite dovish, but he was deeply antitotalitarian. In this debate he struck a very important truth, the neglect of which contributed a good deal to our defeat in the debate about liberalism in the mid-1960s.

Some of those who shared the view that ideology had become irrelevant now see the danger to democratic values principally in the growth of the state or in the growth of a new class—in vast, inexorable, mindless forces. They do not acknowledge the great default by our side in the debate in the mid-1960s. There actually *was* a great need for ideology. There *was* a great need for moral conviction, for understanding, for argument, for controversy. But too many of us were immobilized. The New Left won, and today, in response to their victory, we are retreating toward notions that have a very conservative basis. We are still abandoning ground to the left that it does not deserve to hold. And we are rationalizing our surrender with two sophistical theories: the theory that the constituency we lost was actually a new class irredeemably antidemocratic in outlook, and the theory that our enemy is really the state rather than the ideas, programs, and people who today are guiding so much of the activity of the state. So long as these theories hold sway, we will never regain the ground we lost.

The State

Would it not be more accurate to see the state as a mere mechanism, whose behavior is determined chiefly by politics, not by its own inherent characteristics? To talk about the growth of the state as though that inevitably entails a decline in individual liberty is nonsense. The state can be used for many purposes—civil rights, social security, TVA, and the like. There is a long list of impressive things the state has done in the democratic world that have unarguably expanded human freedom. On the other hand, the state can be put to very harmful uses. The imposition of racial quotas, the imposition of a kind of antigrowth regulation on business, the destruction of neighborhoods that is sometimes carried out in the name of urban planning—all of these things show the destructive capacities of the state. Totalitarianism shows this destructive capacity in its full fury.

But the state itself does not create these abominations—it merely executes them. The mere size of the state or the amount of GNP that is devoted to the public sector cannot be taken as a valid index of the degree of freedom or lack of freedom in a society.

To be sure, the American business community, out of its own peculiar experience, has often seen the state as a threat to freedom. It often perceives limitations on its own particular forms of freedom as limitations on freedom in a general sense. One of the reasons why businessmen, and the intellectuals who share their outlook, tend toward pessimism is that the traditional prerogatives of private business in America, and in much of the industrial world elsewhere, are declining or are gone. I do not think they will be restored. Those who identify freedom with the relatively unlimited freedom once enjoyed by free enterprise are bound to be disappointed. I do not much share in that disappointment.

On the other hand, one has to acknowledge that those of us who have sought an expansion of the democratic state have neglected to acknowledge some of the virtues of private business. Perhaps we should now help to restore some confidence to the business world by taking greater pains to explain that we do, indeed, regard private economic activity as having valid and virtuous aspects. Even though we favor the expansion of democratic government in some areas, we must be prepared to defend the private business sector when government unjustifiably saps its capacity to function in the areas where it is effective and fulfills legitimate social purposes. We have to make very clear that we are not merely attempting to slice away, slice by slice, every bit of private economic freedom. One cannot but be dismayed by the kind of know-nothing antibusiness sentiment one finds in the intellectual atmosphere these days, and one can appreciate why people who see an important role for private business are despairing. Those of us who speak from the social democratic tradition have an obligation to be more explicit in our defense of those aspects of capitalism we acknowledge to be valid.

The "New Class"

Is the term "new class" really a sound one for the group it seeks to describe? This group hardly has the weight and strength of a social class, properly so-called. A class is not just an assortment of people with a common point of view; it is a social group whose members share a particular and profound relationship to the fundamental processes of economic production and distribution. That is the sense in which I see class as a usefully descriptive concept.

Some argue that there is a "knowledge sector" distinct from the other sectors of economic activity, but to what extent is this knowledge sector really a separate, cohesive grouping? The business world employs its intellectuals and technicians, the government employs its intellectuals and technicians, and so do the unions, the civil rights groups, and the foundations. These people have no essentially common interest. Their interests are determined by the larger classes, in the true sense of the term, to which they have attached themselves.

As individuals, however, they may be more open to political persuasion and pressure than some other elements in this society. They make up a swing group. They are educated, relatively unfettered, and they like to believe that they are quite advanced. If many of them have gone against the values of what some of us held to be the true liberalism over the past decade, that in good part may be the result of the failure of our side to uphold its side in the debate. These people are not inherently and necessarily opposed to the things we value.

But if we are to carry this debate, it will be necessary to draw members of the business community into deeper and more serious discussion about democratic values and democratic culture. There is a tendency on their part to sulk back, to feel defeated, and to believe that their bona fides are not accepted when they try to participate in democratic controversy. This only strengthens the impression that they are corrupt. In order to bring them into the debate, those of us from the social democratic tradition must acknowledge many of the mistakes we have made. Let me mention a few.

The socialist tradition has not been clear enough in its understanding of and commitment to democracy. This flows from a deep flaw in the Marxian outlook, in which democracy is seen as an inevitable outgrowth of a certain set of economic arrangements. One reads vainly through the great classics of socialism to discover just how a socialist society would be organized and how the politics of the socialist society would enable individuals to impose their will on the administration of the state.

Second, socialism has inclined toward a welfare view of economic problems. We have tacitly acknowledged the importance of capitalism in our world by leaving it up to capitalism to deal with all the problems of production and of attaining a social morale that will sustain a vigorous economy. We have given ourselves the easier task of proposing ways in which the product will be distributed.

Problems of Capitalism

On the other hand, the procapitalists also must acknowledge some difficulties, which were somewhat neglected in this seminar program. It is not quite true that free enterprise flourishes in America. There is oligopoly, there is restriction of competition, there are attempts to engage government unfairly on behalf of one producer or another. This was evident, for instance, in the decision by the auto companies to increase the prices of automobiles in 1976. Sales had fallen off, and yet prices went up, and cars sat unsold on the lots. We do not have a pure, free enterprise economy, and, surely, those who would defend capitalism must acknowledge that reality.

There is also a tendency in capitalism—which has been described both by Joseph Schumpeter and Daniel Bell—to encourage escape from the rigors of entrepreneurial culture. One sees this in the solicitation of government subsidies by so many of the business lobbies in Washington. One also sees it in the shifting cultural values of business culture. Daniel Bell's book *The Cultural Contradictions of Capitalism* goes a long way towards relieving social democrats of responsibility for the tendency towards hedonism and indiscipline that took hold in much of the Western world in the late 1960s.

Capitalism made its own contribution to that cultural change, a very profound one. It cannot be wholly blamed on the social programs, the welfare state, or the anticapitalist mood that socialists have created; it grows out of capitalism itself. Capitalism has lost its vigor. On one hand it has become cautious and bureaucratic, and on the other it searches for instant gratifications. There are few would-be captains of industry waiting for a tax cut so that they can go to work rebuilding a business civilization. It will take more than throwing money at capitalists to restore vigor and productivity to the American economy. Nor will that be accomplished simply by freeing capitalists from some annoying regulations. It will require a change in the ethos that has come to prevail in the capitalist world itself.

181

Finally, as Ben Wattenberg pointed out, capitalism suffers gravely from its own vulnerability to the totalitarian temptation. This seems to contradict Irving Kristol's contention that the left is the source of the widespread sympathy with, or at least agnosticism toward, the totalitarian world. American and European capitalism have both shown an alarming tendency in the last decade to disregard the freedom of their own societies and to seek private and profitable collaboration with the totalitarian world. Many of the citizens of the totalitarian nations will pay a terrible price for this, and, in time, so will we ourselves. I am referring to our willingness to sell advanced technology to the Soviet Union and to the practice of American bankers of investing huge sums in the Eastern European and in the Soviet economy and of becoming political hostage to those investments. The Republican party has consistently criticized even the rather half-hearted human rights campaign mounted by the Carter administration, because the business supporters of the Republican party are anxious to exploit the markets, the raw materials, and, in some instances, even the captive work force of the totalitarian world. Capitalism is not immune from a tendency to collaboration or sympathy with the totalitarian world, and ought not to assume self-righteous airs towards those of us on the democratic left who have difficulties in combating that impulse in our own ranks.

A Message of Hope

Finally, back to the virtues of optimism. We have a great message to tell the world about how spectacularly our system has succeeded, and how well others who have adopted that system have succeeded. I fear the spirit of a return to "orthodoxy," as Irving Kristol put it, and the tendency to belittle new social or political visions of possibility taking hold among some "neoconservatives." That inclination towards pessimism could prevent us from carrying forward our message, a message which I think is quite valid.

It is a message of hope, and, if argued with spirit, it could have an enormous impact in the world. Our mixed political and economic system, part capitalist and part social democratic, is, despite its familiarity for us, still a revolutionary enterprise. Why should we act as if it is a system in which pessimism and restraint are the dominant mood? On the contrary, it is we—as Jean François Revel put it—who have begun to explore the future, and the true boundaries of liberty. I fear that the mood of some who consider themselves to be neoconservatives will make it harder for us to persuade the world of that truth.

Discussion

QUESTION: You talked about the positive and negative potentialities of the state and the new class. I would like to hear you comment about the labor movement. If social democratic movements have been able to give us some of the benefits of socialist vision without some of the perceived drawbacks, and if the labor movement has been at the forefront in giving us this, how do you now perceive the present discussion *within* the labor movement? Some people charge the labor movement has been co-opted. How do you see it functioning in the future as a vehicle for social democratic values, and as a useful check on the dangers that exist within capitalism?

MR. KEMBLE: Let me answer with something a little off the point. There is talk today about antagonism of the new class to liberal democratic values that reminds me of the talk about the labor movement thirty years ago. Much of the conservative world assumed that the labor movement was a natural carrier of a kind of centralized, undemocratic, authoritarian socialism, which they feared. One of the most remarkable occurrences of the last thirty years has been that the labor movement turned out not to be at all hostile towards democratic values. In fact, it became one of the main strengths in our political system for their defense. Today, the labor movement is undergoing a debate of its own about these very questions. They are put in the language of the labor movement and grow out of the experience of the labor movement. My sense is that those who upheld the tradition of the past generations of American labor leadership will prevail.

QUESTION: A lot of the discussion about social democracy uses the term in too broad a sense. It seems to me there is a comparable difficulty with the term "private business" or "private property." In comparison with, say, Ed Jones's Auto Repair Shop, which is more or less an extension of one man and his own tools, in what sense is Gulf and Western private? Do you think it is necessary to make this distinction in the word "private"? Would there be not only a quantitative difference between owning shares in AT&T and only owning the handtools necessary to make a living, but a qualitative difference as well?

MR. KEMBLE: What is called a public corporation must indeed be distinguished from a family-owned or individually owned business. But there is a valid distinction between those economic institutions that, in some way, are governed by government, and those that are governed by nongovernmental owners and processes. Gulf and Western and an individually owned repair shop do have one thing in common—they are businesses, and they are not run by the government. The difference between a concern that is government owned and operated and one that is privately owned and operated is certainly a valid one. There are degrees, of course. A utility, for example, is usually regulated very closely by a state utilities commission, which sets its rates and determines where it can build plants. That is why I said in the beginning that I don't think you can describe our system as capitalism. There is an enormous amount of public leverage over private economic decisions in this country, and I think much of it is good. We ought to be telling the world that, yes, we do have a social democratic sector in our country, in some respects. When we defend our system against the totalitarian system, we are not defending the rule of a clique of robber barons. We are defending a system which is much more progressive, civilized, and just than that.

QUESTION: Would you speak to the question of how your political view would be distinguished from Ben Wattenberg's and from those of the new conservatism?

MR. KEMBLE: That's a large question. Today in the countries of the industrial democratic world, the commanding heights of the economy are still very much in private hands. In my view, there are many areas in which there should be greater democratic, political influence exercised at the commanding heights of the economy. Eugen Loebl's book *The Responsible Society* suggests, through his profit-sharing approach, one way of bringing greater democratic influence to bear in the higher reaches of economic activity.

To take one example, I do not see how we can solve our energy problem if it is left entirely to private energy businesses to solve it. I think it will take too huge an investment, too wide a degree of coordination in our patterns of production and consumption. It is too important to be left to any private agency. Government needs to play a central role.

I think Ben Wattenberg would be more dubious of that, and, certainly, many others in the neoconservative group would share that doubt.

In the areas of antitrust and regulation of U.S. trade abroad, I would like to see the government play a larger role, perhaps more than Ben would approve. We have a need for some labor-intensive manufacturing in this country. And government has an obligation to restrain the outflow of capital and technology that is destroying such industries.

Neoconservatism is very much the creature of a moment in American politics. To think of it as a school built around a coherent philosophy that covers this whole range of questions, I think, is a great mistake. Its common basis is its commitment to democracy, democratic culture, and liberty, and beyond that, there are many differences among the so-called neoconservatives. I suspect those differences will become more and more sharply pronounced. If the threat to our democratic values from abroad subsides, I think neoconservatism will probably disappear.

QUESTION: I was somewhat gratified to see you publicly recognizing the link between the capitalist ideology and the kind of materialist, individualist, hedonist culture that we have today. Daniel Bell speaks of the so-called public household and the need for a consensus of commonly shared values other than greed and private individualism. Would you say something about creating a noncapitalist ethos, with greater attention to the communitarian ideal shared by Christianity and classical Marxism.

MR. KEMBLE: Let me respond very briefly. I have regained a great interest in questions of moral philosophy recently. I consider myself a humanist, and a rationalist, and I am not interested much in a theological approach to such questions. But I find that, more and more, our problems rest on matters that are often among the principal concerns of religion: courage, loyalty, civility, and the like. What some thought to be an impending nihilism really has begun to ebb, and an interest in questions of ethics seems to be taking hold.

QUESTION: I would like to go back for a minute to your comment about the new class. Did you dislike the label new class because "class" is defined by relation to the production and access to production? In my view, the power of the new class is that it is of a new type. It is based in the production and distribution of symbols. The new class has a peculiar kind of power to spread its own ideals and values.

MR. KEMBLE: Production of symbols? It sounds as if you are making a long leap from the old Marxian notion of the production of commodities to a similar view of the production of ideology. My point

185

about the new class is that the symbols that are produced by these people in the knowledge industry are quite various. There are many different points of view. Many of the groups and institutions to which they are attached have conflicting interests. I don't see the act of writing television news scripts, for example, as something that leads one to certain political views. I can see how producing machinery for the cotton industry can lead one to certain political views.

If someone proclaims an end to ideology, he can hardly expect his ideology to dominate in public discourse. In a way, I think that has happened—in the business community, in the trade union movement, in certain cultural sectors. People felt the values they held were widely accepted, but suddenly, to everyone's surprise, up sprung a new right and a new left, whose adherents were intensely ideological. And into the vacuum at the center flowed the worst, filled with passionate intensity. I think it was a moral and a spiritual default that produced this, rather than the increase in the number of people in America who are writing.

BIBLIOGRAPHY

I. A useful context for the seminar:

Bell, Daniel. *The Cultural Contradictions of Capitalism.* New York: Basic Books, 1976.

Berger, Peter. *Pyramids of Sacrifice.* Garden City, New York: Doubleday, 1976.

Chickering, A. Lawrence, ed. *The Politics of Planning.* San Francisco: Institute for Contemporary Studies, 1976.

Clečak, Peter. *Crooked Paths: Reflections on Socialism, Conservatism and the Welfare State.* New York: Harper & Row, 1977.

Friedman, Milton. *Capitalism and Freedom.* Chicago: University of Chicago Press, 1962.

Galbraith, John Kenneth. *The Affluent Society.* Third edition. Boston: Houghton Mifflin, 1976.

Harrington, Michael. *Socialism.* New York: Saturday Review Press, 1972.

Hayek, Friedrich. *The Road to Serfdom.* Chicago: University of Chicago Press, 1944.

Heilbroner, Robert. *Business Civilization In Decline.* New York: W. W. Norton, 1976.

Kristol, Irving. *Two Cheers for Capitalism.* New York: Basic Books, 1978.

Laslett, John M. and Lipset, Seymour Martin, eds. *Failure of a Dream.* Garden City, New York: Doubleday Anchor, 1974.

Loebl, Eugen and Roman, Stephen B. *The Responsible Society.* New York: Two Continents, 1977.

Schumpeter, Joseph. *Capitalism, Socialism, and Democracy.* Third edition. New York: Harper & Bros., 1950.

Tyrell, R. Emmett, Jr., ed. *The Future That Doesn't Work: Social Democracy's Failures in Britain.* Garden City, New York: Doubleday, 1977.

Vree, Dale. *On Synthesizing Marxism and Christianity.* New York: Wiley-Interscience, 1976.

Wogalman, Philip. *The Great Economic Debate.* Philadelphia: Westminster Press, 1977.

II. Important background and foundational works:

Arendt, Hannah. *The Origins of Totalitarianism.*

Aron, Raymond. *The Opium of the Intellectuals.*

Berger, Peter and Neuhaus, R. J. *To Empower People.*

Carr, E. H. *Studies in Revolution.*

Cassirer, Ernst. *The Myth of the State.*

Djilas, Milovan. *The Unperfect Society.*

Fanon, Frantz. *The Wretched of the Earth.*

Hook, Sidney. *Revolution, Reform, and Social Justice.*

Howe, Irving and Coser, Lewis, eds. *The New Conservatives: Critique from the Left.*

Johnson, Paul. *The Enemies of Society.*

Kolakowski, Leszek. *Marxism and Beyond.*

Lekachman, Robert. *The Permanent Problem of Boom and Bust.*

Lichtheim, George. *The Origins of Socialism.*

Lindblom, Charles. *Politics and Markets.*

Lipset, Seymour M. *Socialism: It's Conspicious Absence in American Politics.*

Lynd, Staughton and Alperovitz, Gar. *Strategy and Power: Two Essays toward a New American Socialism.*

Maritain, Jacques. *Integral Humanism.*

Milibrand, Ralph. *The State in Capitalist Society.*

Niebuhr, Reinhold and Sigmund, Paul. *The Democratic Experience.*

Nisbet, Robert. *Twilight of Authority.*

Novak, Michael. *The Rise of the Unmeltable Ethnics.*

Ortega y Gasset, José. *The Revolt of the Masses.*

Pieper, Josef. *Leisure: The Basis of Culture.*

Reisman, David. *Abundance for What and Other Essays.*

Revel, Jean-Jacques. *The Totalitarian Temptation.*

Sakharov, Andrei. *My Country and the World.*

Schumacher, E. F. *Small Is Beautiful.*

Tillich, Paul. *The Socialist Decision.*

Veblen, Thorstein. *The Theory of the Leisure Class.*

III. Selected further readings:

Avineri, Schlomo. *The Social and Political Thought of Karl Marx.*

Axelos, Kostas. *Alienation, Praxis, and Techné in the Thought of Karl Marx.*

Barnet, Richard J. and Miller, Ronald E. *Global Reach: The Power of the Multinational Corporations.*

Barth, Karl and Hamel, J. *How to Serve God in a Marxist Land.*

Beckerman, Wilfred. *Two Cheers for the Affluent Society.*

Bochenski, J. M. *Societ Russian Dialectical Materialism.*

Boorstin, Daniel. *The Decline of Radicalism.*

Brandel, F. *Afterthoughts on Material Civilization and Capitalism.*

Brittan, Samuel. *Capitalism and the Permissive Society.*

Caves, Richard. *American Industry.*

Center for Advanced International Studies. *The Convergence of Communism and Capitalism.*

Childs, M. W. and Cater, D. *Ethics in a Business Society.*

Club of Rome. *The Limits of Growth.*

Cole, G. D. H. *History of Socialist Thought.*

D'Arcy, Martin. *Communism and Christianity.*

Dean, Thomas. *Post-Theistic Thinking: The Marxist-Christian Dialogue in Radical Perspective.*

DeGeorge, Richard. *The New Marxism.*

Delfgaauw, Bernard. *The Young Marx.*

Dell, Edmund. *Political Responsibility and Industry.*

Demant, V. A. *Religion and the Decline of Capitalism.*

Drucker, Peter. *Technology, Management, and Society.*

Dumont, Rene. *Socialisms and Development.*

Egbert, D. and Persons, S., eds. *Socialism and American Life.*

Ewing, David. *The Human Side of Planning, Tool or Tyrant?*

Faber, E. L., ed. *The Social Structure of Eastern Europe.*

Fetscher, Irving. *Marx and Marxism.*

Feuer, Lewis. *Marx and the Intellectuals.*

Fried, Albert, ed. *Socialism in America.*

Friesen, Abraham. *Reformation and Utopia: The Marxist Interpretation of the Reformation and Its Antecedents.*

Fromm, Erich. *Marx's Concept of Man.*

Gilison, Jerome. *The Soviet Image of Utopia.*

Girardi, Giulio. *Marxism and Christianity.*

Goldthorpe, John H. et al. *The Affluent Worker.* Three volumes.

Gollwitzer, Helmut. *The Christian Faith and the Marxist Criticism of Religion.*

Gouldner, Alvin. *The Coming Crisis of Western Sociology.*

Gregor, A. James. *A Survey of Marxism.*

Habermas, Jürgen. *Legitimation Crisis.*

Hamilton, Richard. *Restraining Myths of American Social Science.*

Henry, John M., ed. *Free Enterprise an Imperative.*

Hordern, William. *Christianity, Communism, and History.*

Jay, Douglas. *Socialism in the New Society.*

Jewkes, John. *The New Ordeal by Planning.*

Johnpoll, Bernard K. *Pacifist's Progress: Norman Thomas and the Decline of American Socialism.*

Jordan, Z. A. *The Evolution of Dialectical Materialism.*

Kamenka, Eugene. *The Ethical Foundations of Marxism.*

Keynes, John Maynard. *The General Theory of Employment, Interest and Money.*

Klein, R. et al. *Constraints and Choices.*

Knight, F. H. *The Economic Order and Religion.*

Kolko, Gabriel. *The Triumph of Conservatism.*

Laclau, Ernesto. *Politics and Ideology in Marxist Theory.*

Lavigne, Marie. *The Socialist Economies of the Soviet Union and Europe.*

Leonard, Wolfgang. *Religion and Revolution.*

Lochman, Jan Milič. *Church in a Marxist Society.*

Lowe, Adolph. *On Economic Knowledge.*

Lukacs, George. *History and Class Consciousness.*

Marris, Robin. *The Economic Theory of "Managerial" Capitalism.*

Mason, Edward, ed. *The Corporation in Modern Society.*

McKennan, George. *Populism.*

Moltmann, Jürgen et al. *Religion and Political Society.*

Monsen, R. Joseph. *Modern American Capitalism.*

Munby, D. L. *God and the Rich Society.*

Myrdal, Gunnar. *The Challenge of World Poverty.*

Nelkin, Dorothy. *Democratizing Technical Decisions: European Experiments in Public Participation.*

Nelson, Ben. *Religious Traditions and the Spirit of Capitalism.*

O'Connor, James. *The Fiscal Crisis of the State.*

Ofari, Earl. *The Myth of Black Capitalism.*

Okun, Arthur. *The Political Economy of Prosperity.*

Ollman, Bertell. *Alienation: Marx's Concept of Man in Capitalist Society.*

Popper, K. R. *The High Tide of Prophecy: Hegel, Marx, and the Aftermath.*

Poulantzas, Nicos. *Classes in Contemporary Capitalism.*

Putnam, George F. *Russian Alternatives to Marxism.*

Samuelson, Kurt. *Religion and Economic Action.*

Shonfield, Andrew. *Modern Capitalism.*

Silk, Leonard. *Capitalism: The Moving Target.*

Soelle, Dorothee. *Political Theology.*

Solle, Thomas. *Race and Economics.*

Sternberg, Fritz. *Capitalism and Socialism on Trial.*

Stigler, George. *The Theory of Price.*

Stone, Christopher. *Where the Law Ends: The Social Control of Corporate Behavior.*

Strachey, John. *Contemporary Capitalism.*

Stretton, Hugh. *Capitalism, Socialism, and the Environment.*

Swartz, Harry. *An Introduction to the Soviet Economy.*

Sweezy, Paul. *The Theory of Capitalist Development.*

Thomas, Norman. *Socialism Re-Examined.*

Tucker, Robert. *Philosophy and Myth in Karl Marx.* Second edition.

Venable, Vernon. *Human Nature: The Marxian View.*

Voegelin, Eric. *The New Science of Politics.*

Von Mises, Ludwig. *The Anti-Capitalist Mentality.*

Von Weizsaeker, C. *Steady State Capital Theory.*

Weisskopf, Walter. *Alienation and Economics.*

West, Charles. *Communism and the Theologians.*

Wilcox, Clair. *Public Policies toward Business.*

Wilczynski, Josef. *The Economics of Socialism.*

Wolfe, Alan. *The Limits of Legitimacy: Political Contradictions of Contemporary Capitalism.*

Worsthorne, Peregrine. *The Socialist Myth.*

Yorburg, Betty. *Utopia and Reality.*

CONTRIBUTORS

PETER BERGER is professor of sociology at Rutgers University and an adjunct scholar in religion and social issues at the American Enterprise Institute. He has been a lecturer at the University of Georgia; research director of the Evangelical Academy at Bad Tolz, West Germany; associate professor, graduate faculty, New School for Social Research; and professor, Brooklyn College, City University of New York. Among his writings are *The Noise of Solemn Assemblies*, *A Rumor of Angels*, *Facing up to Modernity*, *The Sacred Canopy*, and *Pyramids of Sacrifice*.

PENN KEMBLE served as a personal aide to Daniel Patrick Moynihan in his 1976 senatorial campaign and, prior to that, served as executive director of the Coalition for a Democratic Majority, which he helped form in 1972. In 1967 he was among the founders of Frontlash, a nonpartisan voter registration campaign that accounted for the registration of nearly 1 million voters in more than twenty states during the 1976 election. Mr. Kemble has published articles in *Commentary*, *New Leader*, the *Wall Street Journal*, and the *New York Times*, among others. He is a member of the National Committee of Social Democrats, USA, and serves on the Board of Directors of the League for Industrial Democracy.

IRVING KRISTOL is the Henry R. Luce Professor of Urban Values at New York University and co-editor of *The Public Interest*. He is also a senior fellow at the American Enterprise Institute. He has been managing editor of *Commentary* magazine (1947 to 1952), co-founder and editor (with Stephen Spender) of *Encounter* magazine (1953 to 1958), editor of *The Reporter* magazine (1959 to 1960), (1961 to 1969) and executive vice-president of Basic Books, Inc. He is a fellow of the American Academy of Arts and Sciences and a member of the Council on Foreign Relations. He also served a six-year term, 1972 through 1977, on the National Council on the Humanities. As a member of its Board of Contributors, he writes a regular monthly article for the *Wall*

Street Journal. He is the author of *On the Democratic Idea in America* and co-author of *The American Commonwealth.* His latest book is *Two Cheers for Capitalism.*

SEYMOUR MARTIN LIPSET is professor of political science and sociology at Stanford University and a senior fellow of the Hoover Institution. He is also co-editor of *Public Opinion* and an adjunct scholar at the American Enterprise Institute. He is the president of the International Society of Political Psychology, past vice-president of the American Academy of Arts and Sciences, 1974–1978, and a member of the National Academy of Sciences. He is the author of *Agrarian Socialism, Union Democracy, Political Man, The First New Nation, Revolution and Counterrevolution, The Politics of Unreason, The Divided Academy,* and most recently *Dialogues on American Politics.*

MICHAEL NOVAK is a resident scholar at American Enterprise Institute, on leave from Syracuse University, where he is Ledden-Watson Distinguished Professor of Religion. He has also taught at Harvard, Stanford, and The State University of New York at Old Westbury. He has published many articles in *Commentary, Commonweal, Journal of Ecumenical Studies,* and *New Republic,* among others. His books include *The Guns of Lattimer, The Joy of Sports, The Rise of the Unmeltable Ethics,* and *Ascent of the Mountain, Flight of the Dove.* His *The American Vision, The Future of Democratic Capitalism* is another American Enterprise Institute publication in this series.

MUHAMMAD ABDUL-RAUF has been the director of the Islamic Center in Washington, D.C., since 1971. He has lived in the United States since 1965, when he became the director of the Islamic Cultural Center of New York. A graduate of the School of Theology at Al Azhar in Cairo, the world's foremost Islamic seminary, he also earned degrees from Cambridge University and the University of London. Dr. Rauf founded the Muslim College of Malaya in 1955 and the Department of Islamic Studies at the University of Malaysia in 1958. He is the author of books and articles on Islamic history and civilization.

BEN J. WATTENBERG is a Senior Fellow at the American Enterprise Institute and is co-editor of *Public Opinion* magazine. He has been host-essayist of the public television series "In Search of the Real America," based on his book *The Real America* (1974). He is co-author of *The Real Majority* (1970), which was used by both the major political parties in the 1970 and 1972 elections to plan their strategies. Mr. Wattenberg was an aide to President Johnson and assistant to former Vice-President Humphrey. He was a campaign advisor in 1972 and 1976 to Senator Henry Jackson's presidential campaigns, and he co-founded the Coalition for a Democratic Majority, of which he is now chairman.

SELECTED AEI PUBLICATIONS

Public Opinion, published bimonthly (one year, $12; two years, $22; single copy, $2.50)

The Past and Future of Presidential Debates, Austin Ranney, ed. (226 pp., $5.75)

The Islamic Doctrine of Economics and Contemporary Economic Thought, Muhammad Abdul-Rauf (23 pp., $2)

A Conversation with Secretary Ray Marshall: Inflation, Unemployment, and the Minimum Wage (27 pp., $2.25)

Referendums: A Comparative Study of Practice and Theory, David Butler and Austin Ranney, eds. (250 pp., $4.75)

The American Vision: An Essay on the Future of Democratic Capitalism, Michael Novak (60 pp., $2.75)

Unsafe at Any Margin: Interpreting Congressional Elections, Thomas E. Mann (116 pp., $3.25)

The New American Political System, Anthony King, ed. (407 pp., $6.75)

A Conversation with the Reverend Jesse Jackson: The Quest for Economic and Educational Parity (26 pp., $2.25)

The Federalization of Presidential Primaries, Austin Ranney (40 pp., $2.25)

Dismantling the Parties: Reflections on Party Reform and Party Decomposition, Jeane Jordan Kirkpatrick (31 pp., $2.25)

The Peace Corps: Myths and Prospects, Michael P. Balzano (21 pp., $2)

AEI ASSOCIATES PROGRAM

The American Enterprise Institute invites your participation in the competition of ideas through its AEI Associates Program. This program has two objectives:

The first is to broaden the distribution of AEI studies, conferences, forums, and reviews, and thereby to extend public familiarity with the issues. AEI Associates receive regular information on AEI research and programs, and they can order publications and cassettes at a savings.

The second objective is to increase the research activity of the American Enterprise Institute and the dissemination of its published materials to policy makers, the academic community, journalists, and others who help shape public attitudes. Your contribution, which in most cases is partly tax deductible, will help ensure that decision makers have the benefit of scholarly research on the practical options to be considered before programs are formulated. The issues studied by AEI include:

- Defense Policy
- Economic Policy
- Energy Policy
- Foreign Policy
- Government Regulation
- Health Policy
- Legal Policy
- Political and Social Processes
- Social Security and Retirement Policy
- Tax Policy

For more information, write to: AMERICAN ENTERPRISE INSTITUTE
1150 Seventeenth Street, N.W., Washington, D.C. 20036